Radicals, Revolutionaries, and Terrorists

Radicals, Revolutionaries, and Terrorists

Colin J. Beck

polity

First published in 2015 by Polity Press

Polity Press
65 Bridge Street
Cambridge CB2 1UR, UK

Polity Press
350 Main Street
Malden, MA 02148, USA

ISBN-13: 978-0-7456-6211-4
ISBN-13: 978-0-7456-6212-1(pb)

A catalogue record for this book is available from the British Library.

Library of Congress Cataloging-in-Publication Data

Beck, Colin J.
    Radicals, revolutionaries, and terrorists / Colin J. Beck.
       pages cm
    Includes bibliographical references and index.
    ISBN 978-0-7456-6211-4 (hardback : alk. paper) -- ISBN 978-0-7456-6212-1 (pbk. : alk. paper) 1. Radicalism. 2. Revolutions. 3. Terrorism. I. Title.
    HN49.R33B43 2015
    303.48'4--dc23
                                2014043389

Typeset in 11 on 13 pt Sabon by
Servis Filmsetting Ltd, Stockport, Cheshire
Printed and bound in Great Britain by Clays Ltd, St Ives plc

For further information on Polity, visit our website: politybooks.com

For Soc 121, past, present, and future

Contents

Figures and Tables

Figures

Tables

Acknowledgments

When Emma Longstaff of Polity first approached me about writing a book on radical social movements, I thought that a work focused on movement theory alone would be both boring to read and boring to write. So I suggested that I might model the manuscript after a course I had developed at Pomona College, Sociology 121: Radicals, Revolutionaries, and Terrorists. When Polity agreed to the scheme, I was delighted – here, the curriculum I dreamed up while getting a cup of coffee a few years previously would now also be a book. I am appreciative of all the good people at Polity, including Emma Longstaff, Elen Griffiths, and Jonathan Skerrett, for their help in bringing this to fruition and their patience with my delays during a particularly difficult time.

This book is dedicated to the students of my course on which it is modeled. They were the first audience for these ideas and shaped their presentation in many ways, both large and small. Robert Chew may recognize his influence on my definition of radicalism. In addition, the students of my social movements class in the spring of 2014 helped reinvigorate my interest in collective action and gave me the energy to finish the manuscript. And I am thankful for several talented research assistants over the years: Emily Miner, Eli Kaplan, Kuniko Madden, and Megan Pritchett.

Outside of the classroom, I owe special debts to Al Bergesen who was the first to suggest that I do something scholarly with my interest in political violence, Doug McAdam who has been my guide to understanding contention, and John Meyer who has

Acknowledgments

taught me more about being both a social scientist and a human than anyone. David Frank and Richard Lachmann both gave encouragement to pursue this project at crucial times. At Pomona, various friends and colleagues have been sources of support and necessary distraction. In particular, I thank Hillary Gravendyk, Benjamin Burrill, Kevin Dettmar, and Bob Herman.

I would be lost without the love and support of my partner, Robin Cooper. While writing this book was not always seamless, she has made everything else so. Soon we will be a triumvirate.

May 30, 2014
Claremont, California

Part I

The Known Knowns

1

What is Radicalism?

In the course of a couple of decades, the world was riven with conflict that occurred not between states but between states and organized movements, where individual citizens became both participants in and targets of contention. A loosely organized international movement placed bombs in crowded, public places, staged assassinations and made the overthrow of the global order their goal. At the same time, organized oppositions overthrew autocratic rulers and instituted new, democratic governments in their societies, and radical mass movements struggled against economic inequality and corporate systems of production.

The reader contemporary to the publication of this book might suppose that I am describing the wave of international Islamic terrorism of the last two decades, the Arab Spring revolutions of 2011, and global justice groups like the Black Bloc or animal rights activists. But in fact, I am describing the turn of the twentieth century, when anarchists used terrorism to create "propaganda of the deed," republican movements in Turkey, Persia, Russia, Portugal, and elsewhere sought constitutional monarchies, and labor activists formed new international unions that were sometimes suppressed violently by governments. As this book demonstrates, radicalism, revolution, and terrorism are a recurrent feature of world history.

The basic premise for this book is the interchangeability of mass movements. This idea, drawn from Eric Hoffer's (1951) philosophical reflections on Nazism and Stalinism in *The True Believer*, is that all movements share many features. Rather than consider the goals of social movement radicalism, the occurrence of revolution, and the use of terrorism and political violence separately, I consider them here conjointly. Each is a form of collective action, which can be defined as coordinated action by two or more people to change the conditions for a group. Imagine a Venn diagram with three circles. While each circle – radicalism, revolution, and terrorism – has some aspects that are uniquely its own, there is a space where the three overlap. Thus, to understand radicalism or revolutions or political violence, we must understand all three.

This is not an entirely new view. Besides Hoffer, scholars of social movements and revolution have long spoken to each other and found many commonalities. However, the study of social movements, which we can define as "collective challenges, based on common purposes and social solidarities, in sustained interaction with elites, opponents, and authorities" (Tarrow 1998: 4), tends to focus on a particular western and democratic form of politics in the model of well-known 1960s cases like the civil rights movement, women's movement, and anti-Vietnam War protest.[1] Revolution scholars, in contrast, have tended to focus on the environments in which governments fail to quash their challengers, particularly in famous cases like France in 1789, Russia in 1917, Cuba in 1959, and Nicaragua in 1979. And the study of terrorism tends to operate in isolation from theories of movements and revolution, focusing on contemporary examples like nationalist-separatist groups of the twentieth century or recent terrorism by Islamist extremists. The reason for these tendencies has much to do with how each field has developed over time. Before I more precisely define radicalism, revolution, and terrorism, it is helpful to briefly introduce the history of scholarly work on the subjects.

The study of movements, revolution, and terrorism

Revolution has been a central concern of social scientists ever since the discipline's origins in the nineteenth century. Famously, Karl Marx (1848) placed revolution as the ultimate endpoint

4

of his theories of economy and society, and other early social scientists and historians also wrote on the subject. Notably, Alexis de Tocqueville published what can be considered the first social scientific study of revolution in 1856, *The Old Regime and the Revolution*, in which he used comparative-historical analysis to examine the fall of the French monarchy in 1789 (Tocqueville 1856). This legacy was drawn upon by early twentieth-century social scientists of revolution. "Natural historians" of revolution, such as Crane Brinton (1938) and George Pettee (1938), primarily thought of revolution as a process that had distinct stages in which different groups, like elites, intellectuals, or the military, played crucial roles (see Goldstone 1982).

In contrast, in the nineteenth century and the early twentieth century, movements and terrorism received much less attention. The form of political action that we now recognize as a social movement had its origins in the mid-eighteenth century in Europe but had yet to be thought of as a rational form of political participation. Thus, collective action was thought to be the product of crowd behavior and mob psychology rather than a distinct feature of social life (see Le Bon 1896). And terrorism generally meant the repressive actions of states, like the Great Terror that occurred during the French Revolution, rather than the actions of groups and movements. This remained the case until the mid-twentieth century, when the "collective behavior" tradition of the study of social movements emerged. Drawing on their scholarly predecessors, collective behavior theorists still saw collective action and social movements as inherently irrational and risky rather than as a calculated political strategy. So scholars looked for the psychological strains that would lead to spontaneous contention and thought that participants must be isolated from larger society (Kornhauser 1959; Smelser 1962). Revolution studies at this time also drew on strain theory, arguing that contention occurred when social systems were disrupted by rapid change and came from groups that were relatively deprived of economic resources (Davies 1962; Gurr 1970; Johnson 1966). In short, protest and revolution were thought to emanate from the grievances of marginalized social groups.

This view of contention was challenged by the social movements of the 1960s and early 1970s. It quickly became clear that participants in the civil rights movement and the anti-war movement were not just isolated or psychologically strained individuals. Further, grievances no longer seemed to be a sufficient cause of contention and revolution – many activists and revolutionaries came from relatively privileged and educated social classes. Since everyone has some sort of complaint most of the time, grievance theory was unable to explain where and when movements would emerge (see McAdam 1982: ch. 2). Scholars thus emphasized the structural conditions in which movements and revolutions occur. "Structure" refers to larger social patterns and factors that persist over time and are outside of the thoughts and actions of individuals. For example, religion, forms of government, and economic systems are types of social structures. The first structural theory was resource mobilization, where the key idea was that some groups had access to the money, skills, and other resources that enable them to mobilize a group of participants in an organized fashion (see McCarthy and Zald 1977; Tilly 1978). Resource mobilization theorists thus focused on professional organizations that form the core leadership of movements. While resource mobilization did a good job of explaining the capability of movements, it was less able to identify the times in which protest or revolution would break out. So a second key idea was introduced – political opportunities. Political opportunities are moments in time when a social and political system relatively opens up to a movement's demands. For example, the civil rights movement was able to find success when it did because the Cold War made the American government want to lessen racial inequality as its enemy, the Soviet Union, claimed communist societies were more equal (McAdam 1982). Structural theories of revolution, in particular, also became popular in the 1970s. Most famously, Theda Skocpol (1979) introduced the state breakdown theory of revolution. Skocpol argues that revolutions occur not as the product of a revolutionary movement but because a government becomes relatively weak and begins to fall apart under competing demands. State-centered theory of revolution was very influential and remains so today.

What is Radicalism?

In the 1980s and 1990s, social science in general began to undergo the "cultural turn," where scholars moved away from solely structural theories to examine how culture, ideas, and individuals affect social processes. In the study of movements and revolution, these ideas penetrated deeply. David Snow and his colleagues (1986) introduced the idea of framing, which is how movements use rhetoric strategically to recruit participants and make successful claims by linking their goals to larger ideas about justice and politics. European scholars also emphasized what they called "new social movements" based on identity and solidarity rather than social and economic classes (Kriesi et al. 1992; Melucci 1980). In revolution studies, social scientists began to reconsider the role of leaders, ideology, and identity (Moghadam 1995; Parsa 2000; Selbin 1993), and how histories of resistance against government could be a resource for contention (Reed and Foran 2002). In contrast to objective structural conditions, scholars in both fields began to emphasize subjective experiences and perceptions of individuals and how these affect the mobilization process (Foran 2005; Kurzman 1996; Sewell 1996). Most recently, "relational" views of mobilization have become popular (see McAdam, Tarrow, and Tilly 2001). Here scholars emphasize that movements exist in relationship to other actors, like governments and counter-movements, and explanation rejects general theories that apply to all instances in favor of specific mechanisms that combine and operate differently in different social contexts.

The astute reader will have noticed that this brief history has left the study of terrorism mostly aside and said nothing at all about radicalism. This is because the study of terrorism developed on its own parallel track to the study of movements and revolution. Like social movement theory, terrorism studies also emerged as a reaction to the experience of the mid-twentieth century. The earliest social scientific studies explored campaigns of terrorism by national liberation groups, inspired by anti-colonial revolutions and groups like the Irish Republican Army, Basque Liberation Front, and Palestine Liberation Organization (e.g., Bell 1971; Crenshaw 1978). In the 1970s, highly visible instances of international terrorism occurred – for instance, the hostage taking of Israeli athletes at the Munich Olympic Games and multiple hijackings of airplanes for ransom and publicity – which focused attention on it as a distinct phenomenon. Yet terrorism had trouble establishing itself as a credible field of academic study, partially because of its practical nature – many terrorism experts were located inside of governments instead of universities (see Stampnitzky 2010). This changed substantially in the wake of the September 11th attacks on the World Trade Center and Pentagon by Al-Qaeda hijackers. Since that time, the number of studies of terrorism has grown tremendously and it has become a common focus, primarily in political science. Scholars now investigate the tactics, targets, claims, success, and environments of terrorist groups voluminously (e.g., Abrahms 2006; Brandt and Sandler 2010; Crenshaw 2011; Krueger and Maleckova 2003; Pape 2005; Piazza 2006). Methodologically, terrorism studies still uses case studies of terrorist groups, but the availability of large datasets of terrorist events like the Global Terrorism Database has allowed for quantitative and statistical studies, as well. This trend is evident in Figure 1.1, which shows the number of books and articles published by social scientists on terrorism, revolution, and radicalism every year since 1970.

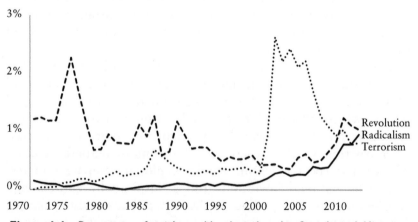

Figure 1.1 Percentage of articles and books indexed in Sociological Abstracts and Worldwide Political Science Abstracts by subject heading, 1970–2013

Terrorism studies did have a small increase in the 1980s as scholars investigated the "new" wave of religious terrorism and international terrorism (Rapoport 2004), but it did not surpass the popularity of revolution studies until after September 11th. Revolution has seen a revival in the past few years as attention has focused on the Arab Spring revolutions of 2011, but it has yet to reach the level of popularity it enjoyed in the 1970s, when it was perhaps inspired by the examples of Cuba and Vietnam. Radicalism, however, has usually been much less popular. Most investigations of radicalism come through case studies of single groups, hence its increase in the 2000s as religious fundamentalism and extremists' use of political violence got more attention. Interestingly, it appears that studies of radicals may even be surpassing those of terrorists in the last two years. Even so, studies of radicalism as a unique phenomenon are very rare, confined to just a few considerations of how radical flanks influence larger social movements (e.g., Haines 1984; Isaac, McDonald, and Lukasik 2006; Jenkins and Eckert 1986).[2] Filling this gap in social scientific knowledge is one of the goals of this book. But to do so successfully, we need to know what, exactly, it is that we are considering. For that we must provide conceptual definitions of terrorism, revolution, and radicalism.

Conceptualizing terrorism

Common wisdom is that terrorism is a label that individuals, movements, and governments use to stigmatize those they do not agree with or do not like. Yet governments struggle to define terrorism in a consistent fashion. The American government has at least 22 different legal definitions of terrorism (Perry 2003), and there is wide disagreement among governments about which groups and individuals should legally be considered terrorists (Beck and Miner 2013). "One person's freedom fighter is another person's terrorist," the old adage goes. While this common view might be wise – in that it recognizes the power of language – it is not enough for social science. Social scientists need to carefully define the phenomenon that they are interested in so that when faced with an example, they can know whether a given theory would be expected to apply to it.

As with many contested concepts, the use of the word "terrorism" has seen lots of conceptual "stretching," where some have adopted it to refer to the use of any organized violence outside of formally declared wars. In the 1980s, Alex Schmid and his co-author Albert Jongman (1988) surveyed 109 different academic definitions of terrorism and found 22 commonly used elements. However, only three of these appeared in a majority of the definitions: (1) violence or force (83.5% of definitions); (2) political (65% of definitions); and (3) fear or terror emphasized (51% of definitions). (The use of "threat" was a close runner-up appearing in 47% of the definitions considered.) More recently, Weinberg, Pedahzur, and Hirsch-Hoefler (2004) repeated the examination, looking at 73 definitions that appeared in social scientific journal articles through 2001. They found even less consensus – only "violence/force" and "political" appeared in a majority. It is no wonder that Brannan, Esler, and Strindberg (2001: 11) claimed the field is in the "perverse situation where a great number of scholars are studying a phenomenon, the essence of which they have (by now) simply agreed to disagree upon."

But we can make progress if we try to boil a definition of terrorism down to what it must address. Jack Gibbs (1989) suggests that any conception of terrorism needs to answer five questions:

1. Is terrorism necessarily illegal (a crime)?
2. Is terrorism necessarily undertaken to realize some particular type of goal and, if so, what is it?
3. How does terrorism necessarily differ from conventional military operation in a war, a civil war, or so-called guerrilla warfare?
4. Is it necessarily the case that only opponents of the government engage in terrorism?
5. Is terrorism necessarily a distinctive strategy in the use of violence and, if so, what is that strategy?

Answering all of these questions in one short, nicely worded definition is quite the challenge. To illustrate, let us consider two popular definitions. The first is a legal definition from the US State Department: terrorism is "premeditated, politically motivated violence perpetrated against noncombatant targets by subnational groups or clandestine agents, usually intended to influence an audience." In answer to Gibbs's questions, this definition does not explicitly tell us if terrorism is a crime (though, since it is a legal definition, we might suppose its illegality) or if it can be used during conventional warfare, but it does suggest that terrorism's goals are political, undertaken by opponents to or agents of a government, and is distinctive in that it targets noncombatants and seeks to influence a larger audience. A second definition comes from the terrorism expert Bruce Hoffman, who defines terrorism as "violence – or equally important, the threat of violence – used and directed in pursuit of, or in service of a political aim" (Hoffman 1998: 2–3). Hoffman's definition explicitly tells us terrorism has a political goal and that it includes threats as well as violence, but it does not tell us explicitly whether it is illegal, how it differs from war, who uses it, or if it is a distinctive strategy.

We thus might need to simplify the matter even further. Terrorism, as well as any contention, has three basic things that must occur: a perpetrator, an action, and a target of that action. Let us consider these in turn. First, how can we conceptualize the perpetrator? Omar Lizardo (2008) proposes that the legitimacy of the actor is key to defining terrorism. Lizardo argues, in part, that terrorism is violence initiated by any non-state actor who is not recognized as a legitimate wielder of violence. This draws on the classic Weberian conception of the state as having the monopoly on the legitimate use of violence. In the modern world, the international system sanctifies states and thus legitimates their actions, whether we approve of them or not. Crucially, however, the international system does not sanction violence by non-state actors which means that it will be inherently illegitimate and thus terrorism. This helpfully captures one dimension of the common adage about terrorists and freedom fighters – the illegitimacy of the perpetrator as seen from outside is a key element of what most would consider terrorism.

Terrorism also requires an action to come into being. We already have seen that many definitions include the use of violence or the threat of violence as a key characteristic (in fact, it is difficult to imagine nonviolent terrorism). Charles Tilly emphasizes that terrorism is a strategy of political contention that can be used by various actors. Tilly (2004: 5) defines the strategy as "asymmetrical deployment of threats and violence against enemies using means that fall outside the forms of political struggle routinely operating within some current regime." The key idea here is routine versus non-routine forms of political struggle. There are lots of violent actions that take place during war, but because we understand a war as a set of organized violent actions, we expect this and no terror results. On the other hand, detonating a bomb at the finish of a marathon can be considered terrorism because it is non-routine and outside the common forms of politics. Tilly's definition thus builds on the root of terrorism as being terror – unexpected violence and threats are more terrorizing. There is also another genius in this conceptualization. Tilly is intentionally agnostic about who the terrorist actor is as long as they act outside of common routines and act asymmetrically (in other words, not just responding in kind). This allows for terrorism to be an action that both state actors and non-state actors can use. While this book does not focus on state terrorism, we may not want our conceptualization to unnecessarily preclude it either.

Finally, all violent or threatening actions have a target – the person, persons, or actor that the action is directed towards. In most interpersonal violence, the victim of violence is the target of action. For example, a victim of premeditated murder is killed because the murderer wanted them dead. Terrorism may be distinctive in that it often separates the victim and the target. For instance, the terrorist kills civilians in order to influence the policies and actions of the civilians' government. Albert Bergesen (2007) calls this the "three-step model" of violence, as it chains together three different actors through the use of violence – step one is the terrorist perpetrator, step two is the victim of terrorism, and step three is the actor the terrorist wants to influence. Such victim–target differentiation is somewhat common in terrorism conceptions (Schmid and Jongman (1988) found it in 37.5% of definitions), but thinking of it as a logical chain brings two other key issues into play. First, there is the goal of terrorism, which must be larger than merely the death of the victim. While the actual content of the goal might vary substantially from case to case, we know it as terrorism because of the chain of logic present in the action – if Americans are killed, then the American people is terrorized and the American government is influenced. (Note that this presupposes a relationship between the victim and the target that is legible to the observer; a terrorist could not easily kill Americans to influence, say, Madagascar.) Second, the three-step model also suggests the role of claim-making, which is common in terrorist attacks – a bomb goes off and a group takes responsibility, issuing a communiqué explaining their action and demands. Here, the terrorist actor is making the logic behind the chain of violence explicit.

In short, I propose that we can usefully think of terrorism by considering the legitimacy of the perpetrator, whether their action is routine, and who the intended target of the action is. While this does not add up to a precise definition, conceptualizing terrorism along these dimensions is helpful for distinguishing it from other violent or threatening actions. For example, the attacks on September 11th were initiated by an illegitimate actor (Al-Qaeda), using a non-routine form of political struggle (skyjacking and crashing planes into buildings) with a target beyond the immediate victims present in the World Trade Center, the Pentagon, and airplanes (the American public or government). Thus, we can easily call September 11th terrorism. In contrast, consider two violent interactions that occurred as a consequence of this event. The American government caught, imprisoned, and tortured a number of Al-Qaeda members and affiliates, and the Taliban use suicide bombers to attack American military forces in Afghanistan. In the first case, the perpetrator is a legitimate state using a non-routine but legally sanctioned action for the purpose of extracting information rather than just deterring future Al-Qaeda members. It thus fails at least two of the criteria and can be ruled out as an instance of terrorism, whether or not we condone it. In the latter case, the Taliban are a less legitimate actor but use a common and symmetrical strategy of violence against their opponents in the ongoing war. While we might argue that the ultimate target of the violence is the American government, the death of American soldiers is a practical and proximate goal. Thus, we can rule out many of the Taliban's actions as terrorism, whether we like them or not. Even though social scientists struggle to come up with a consensus around a single definition, we do not need to conclude that terrorism is in the eye of the beholder. In the rest of this book when I refer to terrorism, this is the conceptualization I am using.

Conceptualizing revolution

Fortunately, there is much more agreement among scholars about what a revolution is. This is partially because of the nature of the field. In contrast to terrorism where, as we saw above, experts struggled to establish it as a distinct field of study, revolution has always been central to social science. In the past few decades, the study of revolution also benefited from the influence of one central author – Theda Skocpol. In 1979, Skocpol's book *States and Social Revolutions* reinvigorated the field through a comparative analysis of the French Revolution of 1789, the Russian Revolution of 1917, and the Chinese Revolution of 1911. Prior to her book, scholars of revolution constantly debated what the types of revolution were – national revolutions, western revolutions, great revolutions, peripheral revolutions, revolutions from above, and so on. But Skocpol unified these definitions with a new concept – the social revolution.

Social revolutions, according to Skocpol (1979: 4), are "rapid, basic transformations of a society's state and class structures . . . in part carried through by class-based revolts from below." The key idea here is transformation. Revolutions are social revolutions only when they change the basic features of a society as well as change who is in power. The transformation can occur along multiple dimensions – economic, social, or cultural. For example, the French and Russian Revolutions substantially altered social relations when they abolished the monarchy and the feudal privileges that aristocrats enjoyed. The Russian and Chinese Revolutions also substantially altered the economic systems of their societies, instituting a state-directed communist system. And the French and Chinese revolutionaries also tried to substantially change cultural practices, creating a new civic religion in France or suppressing traditional practices like foot-binding in China. The other key idea is that change is not a revolution unless there is substantial popular contention outside of the state that helps accomplish it. Later scholars have mostly dropped the view that this need be "class-based," as Skocpol was writing in response to Marxist views of revolution which are less popular now, but the idea of mass uprising remains a key feature of those events we consider revolutionary. This serves to distinguish revolution from other governmental and social changes that occur by the actions of elites, such as in coups d'état or reformative democratic transitions.

But this concept of social revolution does not include changes in regime accompanied by mass revolt from below that do not substantially alter a society's make-up. So it is helpful to specify another type of outcome, the political revolution. The political revolution, notes Jack Goldstone (1998: vii), has two characteristics: "irregular procedures aimed at forcing political change within a society . . . and lasting effects on the political system of the society in which they occurred." This is a broader definition that brings other types of conflict, such as civil wars and mass protest, into our conception of revolution.[3] But both of these definitions assume that we know when a revolutionary struggle is over so that we can assess its outcome. Unfortunately, here there is much less consensus. For example, if revolutions are over when challengers are no longer active then "the French Revolution ended in Thermidor in 1799 when Napoleon took power," or if it is when government takes on a stable form, then "the French revolution ended only with the start of the French Third Republic in 1871" (Goldstone 2001: 167). Or we might even extend the consistent turmoil of French politics through to the founding of the Fifth Republic in 1958 or de Gaulle's resignation in 1969. So when did the French Revolution end – 1799, 1871, 1958, or 1969? I do not pretend to have an exact answer, but a helpful place to start when thinking about this is Stinchcombe's (1999) view that revolutions involve substantial uncertainty about who will be in power in the future. When we become more certain that a particular regime will last for the foreseeable future, we might be able to safely say the revolution is over. Revolutionary regimes have two key problems to solve to reduce uncertainty, according to Eric Selbin (1993). First, revolutionaries must institutionalize their victory, that is, create new political institutions that will outlast the revolutionary leaders. Therefore, truly complete revolutions solve the succession issue and do not just rely on the personal power of the revolutionaries. This can happen in various timeframes. Becker and Goldstone (2005) found that major social revolutions lasted as little as less than a year (Iran in 1979) or as long as 38 years (China in 1911). Among the 47 revolutions they surveyed, half were over in less than eight years and the average time was just under 13 years. Second, Selbin argues that completed revolutions involve consolidation, that is, winning the hearts and minds of the population and ensuring their support for the new regime. As we shall see later, the ideology and actions of revolutionary leaders are key factors here. But determining consolidation in these terms is also very difficult.

Given these issues, we might want to separate the end of a revolution from its beginning. Thinking this way also gets around the problem that the two definitions considered so far have – there is no such thing as a failed revolution. To address this, Charles Tilly (1993b: 10) offers the term "revolutionary situation," which occurs when "two or more blocs make effective, incompatible claims to control the state, or to be the state." According to Tilly, we can know that a bloc's claims are effective when they command the support of a significant segment of the population. This definition draws on Leon Trotsky's idea of dual power, developed in his firsthand account of the Russian Revolution (see Trotsky 1932). Crucially, it does not suppose that power changes hands or that society changes – a revolutionary situation can fail to do either or continue to occur for many years, but we can still consider it as part of what we talk about when we discuss revolution.

These three concepts – social revolution, political revolution, and revolutionary situation – thus cover much of the needed terrain. We know that an event is revolutionary when there is mass contention against an existing state, when it overthrows a regime, or creates lasting social change and establishes new political structures. Recent work on revolution has continued to define subtypes, for instance Third World revolutions (Foran 2005), constitutional revolutions (Kurzman 2008; Sohrabi 2011), and nonviolent revolutions (Stephan and Chenoweth 2008; Zunes 1994), but these are less competing definitions than "scope conditions." Scope conditions are the limits a scholar sets as to what their theory is intended to apply. Notably, Skocpol's own theory of social revolution was intended to apply to only agrarian-bureaucratic states and not all governments, but scholars have adopted her concept more generally. In short, when I refer to revolution in this book, I am referring to accomplished political and social revolutions as well as failed or ongoing revolutionary situations.

Conceptualizing radicalism

Scholars often refer to radical movements to indicate ideas and actions that are outside of what a social movement commonly does or believes. But very rarely is a precise definition of radicalism given. "One person's radical is another's moderate," we might say. This is problematic for the same reasons that an ill-defined notion of terrorism is. What is radical at one time or in one place may not be radical later or elsewhere. Just as the researcher should know what constitutes terrorism, or a revolution, so that they can understand what explanations may apply to a particular example, we also must know what might constitute radicalism.

We see the common strategy in Kathleen Fitzgerald's and Diane Rodgers's (2000) attempt to distinguish radicalism from moderation in social movements by looking at organizational features. According to them, radical social movement organizations tend towards non-hierarchical forms, have a "radical agenda," are ignored or misrepresented by the media, and have limited resources. This certainly does seem like a decent description of contemporary radical movements in western democracies, but may have limited utility in other settings. Further, many activists complain about their representation in the media and many organizations struggle to find resources. Are all of these radical?

Of the few precise definitions of radicalism that have been offered, the idea of violence tends to be an integral part. Sophia Moskalenko and Clark McCauley (2009) try to distinguish radicalism from other forms of activism by measuring willingness to participate in legal and nonviolent political action versus illegal and violent action. Similarly, David Snow and Remy Cross (2011: 118) define a radical as "a social movement activist who embraces direct action and high-risk options, often including violence against others, to achieve a stated goal." These definitions both assume that violence is illegal or uncommon and thus high-risk for the activist. But imagine a society in which violence is commonplace, perhaps Syria during its ongoing civil war. Are there no Syrian radicals? Or are all participants in the war engaged in radicalism?

In short, we need a definition that deals with the issue of relativity. Since radical as an adjective can describe people, ideas, and actions, a conceptualization of radicalism should address three questions:

1. Which actors can potentially be defined as radical?
2. What are the features of radical strategies and actions?
3. How can ideas, claims, or goals be identified as radical?

In answer, I propose to define radicalism as *contention that is outside the common routines of politics present within a society, oriented towards substantial change in social, cultural, economic, and/or political structures, and undertaken by any actor using extra-institutional means.* This is quite the mouthful, so let us break it into its constituent parts.

First, the definition formalizes the relativity of radicalism with the idea of common routines. Note how this draws on Tilly's

(2004) conceptualization of terrorism. Radicalism is contention that does not look like politics, or even social movement activity, as usual. In this sense, it is often transgressive and innovative. Here, we can distinguish radical contention from "regular" contention, which can vary widely across time and place, without implying that radicalism necessarily entails violence, risk, or illegality. Second, the definition specifies that radical goals and ideas must involve changing society or social trends. This change can be progressive or reactionary; we can be agnostic about its specific political content. Thus, radicalism can be a feature of the political right as well as the political left. Similar to the definitions of revolution considered above, this change must be fundamental – change to structures and systems, not just the hearts, minds, or actions of individuals. Third, the definition specifies that radical action can be undertaken by anyone – individuals, organizations, movements, governments – as long as it does not use institutional means. This is an idea common to definitions of social movements generally as a form of "extra-institutional" politics. Institutional means of politics are things like voting, lobbying, legislating that take place within the institutions of politics. Extra-institutional means are those things that are not part of institutionalized governance, such as protest, boycotts, sit-ins, arson, violence, and so on. When institutional actors, like politicians, begin to use extra-institutional means, they approach radicalism.

Each of these three criteria must be met for us to view something as radical. For example, consider the Occupy Wall Street movement of 2011. Many Occupy activists expressed a desire for fundamental change to the capitalist economic system and American politics, and did so using a strategy that was not within political institutions. However, the contention was relatively routine in that it used tactics common to modern social movements – marches, sit-ins, speeches, and petitions. Per our definition, we would not consider this a radical movement, no matter its unexpected occurrence and surprising endurance. At the other end of the American political spectrum, the Tea Party of 2009 engaged in routine contention using the institutional means of running for office and voting with political goals that did not seek fundamental change. Again, not a radical movement. In contrast to both of these are the actions of environmental and animal rights groups like the Earth Liberation Front and the Animal Liberation Front. These groups seek fundamental change to social, cultural, and economic practices concerning nonhuman life and do so with uncommon and extra-institutional strategies – arson, vandalism, tree-spiking, and bombings. These are certainly radicals.

While it is difficult to think of non-routine contention that is not also extra-institutional, this criterion helps us determine whether or not the actions of governments can be considered radical. For example, mid-twentieth-century fascist parties, even though they won elections and held institutional office, used violence that was not sanctioned by law and was carried out by paramilitary party organizations to accomplish their agenda of change. This would count as radical. On the other hand, when a government uses the institutional means of the police or military to suppress opposition, as even many post-revolutionary states do, this by itself would not be considered radicalism.

In short, the proposed conceptualization helps distinguish radicalism from both social movements and governments, even in cases where we may not approve of their actions. In the rest of this book, I use the term radicalism in this manner. If we consider all three definitions of radicalism, revolution, and terrorism together, we might simply say that radicalism is an orientation, revolution is an event, and terrorism is a tactic. As such, they overlap (by design) substantially – many terrorists are radical, many revolutionaries use terrorism, and many radicals seek revolution. While we can imagine nonviolent radicalism, revolution without terror, and terrorism without radical goals, the rest of this book focuses on the places where they occur together, as illustrated in Figure 1.2.

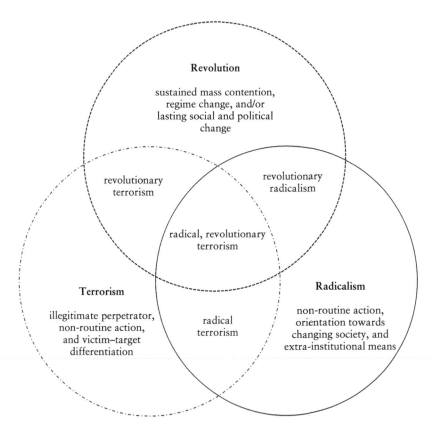

Figure 1.2 Conceptualizing radicalism, revolution, and terrorism

The chapters to come

This chapter has given some historical and conceptual context for thinking about radicalism, revolution, and terrorism. In the next part of the book, I focus on how these elements can be investigated on three different levels of analysis. Chapter 2 asks the question of who is radical, and examines the micro-level of individuals and small groups, including who participates in these movements, how they do so, and where sources of social support for them lie. Chapter 3 examines the meso-level of movements, asking how movements become radical by examining resources, frames, and organizational strategies. Chapter 4 considers when and where radicalism is likely to occur, investigating the macro-level context in which contention takes place. From Part I, the reader will gain a general understanding of research in these fields. Part II of the book examines three key problems in more detail. Chapter 5 takes up the issue of ideology, and explores how radical ideas emerge and inform action or not. Chapter 6 asks if there is a life cycle to radicalism, and details the common trajectories and dynamics of movements' beginnings and endings. Chapter 7 then considers the related issue of the diffusion of radicalism, exploring how and why waves of movements occur. Finally, chapter 8 contemplates the future of radicalism, as well as the issue of prediction of movements more generally, and draws broader conclusions.[4]

The book uses many social science terms and concepts. When I first use them, I provide a definition for the non-specialist reader. Consulting the index will be helpful if the reader wants to remind herself of this explanation. Throughout, I also use a number of examples to illustrate the research covered and key ideas introduced. These are intended to cover both contemporary and historical periods and domestic and international contexts. Some of the examples will reoccur frequently, and, where appropriate, I point the reader to key additional readings. Some examples may only be used once. I hope that those who particularly like these cases will not feel slighted, as there are many radicals, revolutionaries, and terrorists, and no one book can do them all complete justice.

2

Who is Radical?

After the Boston Marathon bombing of 2013, journalists and pundits quickly began asking why and how the Tsarnaev brothers became radicalized. Some pointed to Tamerlan's frustrated ambitions to become a boxer and his trips back to Chechnya where he became more religious. Others suggested that the younger brother, Dzokhar, admired his brother and tried to imitate him. Similarly, in the wake of September 11th, biographies of Osama bin Laden and top Al-Qaeda lieutenants like Ayman al-Zawahiri proliferated. Islamic militancy was portrayed as a consequence of misguided religious education, angry reactions to violence against Muslims, experiences in prison or of torture, and so on. While such psychological explanations may be useful for understanding a particular person's life course and decisions, they entirely miss the larger point – radicalism is first and foremost a product of social processes. This is the key wisdom of sociology – humans are more than the aggregate of their individual experiences; they are also embedded in larger social structures and affected by them. Examining this micro-level of analysis is the task of this chapter.

As described in the previous chapter, early accounts of collective action and social movements stressed the psychology of individuals. We see the approach in the political philosophy of Hoffer (1951). True believers in a radical movement, according to Hoffer, have experienced frustration and failure and are misfits, selfish, and generally the "undesirables" of society. There are two problems with trying to pin radicalism on psychology. First, radicals, revolutionaries, and terrorists do not tend to be available for psychological testing. Therefore, the data are very sparse and most psychological theories remain speculative (see Victoroff 2005 for a review). Second, what evidence does exist points to radicals being as normal as everyone else. This observation was made earlier by scholars of 1960s social movements – activists did not seem psychologically abnormal or irrational, and often came from the educated middle classes of society. Accordingly, radical groups often have to engage in methods to break socialization and allow individuals to use violence.

For example, members of the Weather Underground Organization had to desensitize themselves to violence. The Weather Underground was an offshoot of the 1960s student anti-war organization, Students for a Democratic Society (SDS). In response to the escalation of the Vietnam War, a faction of SDS argued for more radical action, adopting their name "Weathermen" from the lyrics of a popular Bob Dylan song. In 1969, this faction took control of SDS and planned a series of large demonstrations in Chicago, named the Days of Rage. The Chicago demonstrations were an abject failure in terms of number of participants and devolved into a riot, which was violently suppressed by the police. The Weathermen then decided to dissolve SDS in December 1969 and move their activities underground, focusing on violence against the government to gain attention to their cause by "bringing the war home." In response to an accident in which three members were killed in New York City by the premature detonation of a bomb, the group decided not to target people but buildings. The group planted bombs in government and corporate buildings for several years, struggling to maintain their profile and survive FBI investigations. By the late 1970s, with the end of the Vietnam War and increasing feelings of irrelevance, many members of the organization began to resurface. While some did time in prison, in many cases the most serious charges were dropped as the FBI had broken many laws in their pursuit of the activists through the COINTELPRO program. Weather Underground members tended to be white, middle-class college students with no experience of violence. To break the group's socialization into nonviolence, Mark Rudd describes the "gut check" in the 2004 documentary *The Weather Underground*. They would engage in a rhetorical game where each participant would propose more transgressive actions with the goal of psyching themselves up to commit violence.[1]

In more protracted conflicts, such processes are also needed – Palestinian suicide bombers often make "martyr's videos" before being dispatched on their mission. These videos serve not only as communiqués but more importantly as a way for their handlers to make it seem like their action is inevitable and encourage the bomber to follow through against their own doubts. Notably, part of military training around the world is to similarly re-socialize recruits to feel comfortable with killing. So if the answer to "who is radical?" does not lie in psychology, where is it? It is useful to take a classic sociological stance on the issue – attitudes and actions are formed in the context of an individual's position in the social structure and the social roles they occupy. Thus, it is useful first to consider the demographics of individual radicals and next look at which segments of society are more or less likely to support radicalism. But a bit of psychology can be saved as well if we consider the role of leaders in radical movements and social-psychological processes of a group's passion for and commitment to a radical cause. I explore each of these in turn below.

Individual participation in radicalism

Who participates in radical movements is a common concern of scholars. In the 1980s, social scientists tried to build profiles of participants of left-wing and nationalist groups. More recently, profiling has focused on Islamic militants, given the upsurge of interest in the phenomenon in the last decade. Much of the recent work on the radicalization of individuals is from European scholars (e.g., Cesari 2004; Gest 2010; Wiktorowicz 2005). This not only reflects Europe's experience with radicalization in immigrant and second-generation Muslim communities, but also perhaps Americans' discomfort with research that might stigmatize a minority community. In Table 2.1, I present the key findings of several studies, mostly adapted from summaries by Victoroff (2005), Kurzman and Naqvi (2010b), and Gambetta and Hertog (2009).

Even from this select sample of profile studies, there appear to be quite varied bases for radical, revolutionary, and terrorist movements. Men, particularly younger ones, certainly seem to dominate the ranks. As Wickham-Crowley (1992: 19) notes: "War has ever been the office of relatively young men (and occasionally young women), and this is true of contemporary guerrilla warfare as well." Yet this may be because the contributions of women to radical and revolutionary groups are often more hidden and unwritten by history (see Moghadam 1995; Viterna 2006). Radicals also have various levels and types of education, ranging from university to elementary, from religious to secular. And participants come from different social classes, from the elite to the peasant or the employed to the unemployed. We might thus come to the same conclusion that Kurzman and Naqvi (2010b) did in their more extensive study: the radicals can be anybody.

This suggests the problem with an individual-level psychological explanation of radicalism – activists reflect their societies in many ways. Thus, the most exhaustive studies (e.g., Krueger and Maleckova 2003; Kurzman and Naqvi 2010b) tend to find little or no correlation between social background and participation in a movement. To the extent that there is a trend, radicals seem to come from the middle and upper classes and have slightly higher levels of education. These are certainly not the misfits of Hoffer or the aberrant, socially isolated individuals of strain theorists. But let us dig into the slight tendencies a bit more deeply.

First, there is the issue of social class – radicals, especially leaders, seem to come from the upper classes and sometimes even the elite of society. We might take a Hofferian view and suggest that the upper classes are more likely to have their ambitions for the future frustrated and thus are more likely to engage in radicalism. James Davies (1962) proposed something similar in his "J-curve" theory of revolutions. He argued that revolutions occur not when economic or social conditions are at their worst, but

Table 2.1 Examples of studies on participants in radical movements

Study	Case and sample	Findings
Russell and Miller (1977)	350 members of 18 groups active 1966–1976	Age range 23–31 years old; two-thirds or more upper or middle class
Strentz (1988)	American leftist terrorists of 1960s and 1970s	Leaders range from 25 to 40 years old, followers in early twenties; generally middle class
Wickham-Crowley (1992)	111 twentieth-century Latin American guerrilla leaders	Tend to be young men, from elite and professional classes or students
Krueger and Maleckova (2003)	129 Hezbollah fighters, 1982–1994	Younger; compared to Lebanese population higher rates of secondary school and lower poverty
Pedahzur, Perliger, and Weinberg (2003)	819 Palestinian terrorists, 1993–2002	Average age 23 years old; 65% unmarried; almost all male; 55% secular education background; middle-range socioeconomic status
Pape (2005)	462 suicide terrorists, worldwide	Majority between 19 and 23 years old; 10% are females, tend to be over 24 years old; more educated than average; 76% working or middle class
Berrebi (2007)	335 Hamas and Islamic Jihad leaders and martyrs, 1980s–2003	57% have university education; 84% not poor; 90% employed
Kurzman and Naqvi (2010b)	42 Islamist leaders since 1970	Equal rates of secular and religious education; 43% sons of religious scholars; 25% middle class, 29% from poor families
Lee (2011)	740 early twentieth-century Bengali political activists	From privileged socioeconomic classes and castes

rather when they have begun to get better. If conditions improve, but not quickly, there becomes a mismatch between people's rising expectations and actual conditions (graphically this is the J-curve, while expectations would be a U-curve over time). Thus, people revolt. We also see this idea pop up in demographic theories of revolution and terrorism (e.g., Ehrlich and Liu 2002; Goldstone 1991b; Urdal 2006) – large cohorts of youth are less likely to be able to find employment and meaningful futures as the supply of labor outstrips the demands of markets and political instability results. From this view, economic conditions may only affect participation for a certain upper-class segment of society (see Kavanagh 2010).

But these theories obscure a more basic point about social class. Members of the middle and upper classes come from families with relatively more resources. Participating in any social movement, particularly a radical one, is a high-cost decision. Activists spend their time, forgo job opportunities, and in many cases face the very real possibility of prison and bodily injury. But if an individual has more economic resources to fall back upon, they are better able to weather these challenges. Activists of the Weather Underground reported that they knew that what enabled them to live a life on the run from the FBI was their background. For one thing, their families and friends sometimes provided them with money, enabling them to remain underground. For another, their background (and skin color) protected them from the worst reactions of the police. Poor black activists, like those of the Black Panthers, were not so lucky; they faced the possibility of being shot by the police as well as a sophisticated program of US government repression. In short, social class is a resource that permits participation in radical movements.

The second slight tendency seems to be a higher level of education among participants than in society at large. One interpretation of this is that education broadens the mind and allows more free thought. For instance, Halliday (1999) argues that revolution is primarily the work of intellectuals as they craft an alternative vision of the world. Another interpretation is that education might be a process of indoctrination – schools might encourage radicalism among their students through the curriculum. For example, Gambetta and Hertog (2009) examine the biographies of various members of violent Islamic groups and find that men with engineering degrees are common among their ranks. They argue that engineers (and, implicitly, the engineering curriculum) have a particular mindset that is amenable to becoming a terrorist. Similarly, a common account of the Taliban in Afghanistan is that their recruits come from Islamic schools, called madrassas. In fact, *talib* – the root of their name – means student in Pashtun, a language of Central Asia. Notably, however, systematic research has found that most religious education in Pakistan takes place in state-run schools (Andrabi et al. 2006).

So is education a radicalizing force? The answer appears to be "no." What appears to be more important is the social context of education (Kurzman and Naqvi 2010b). In some countries, more education might lead to a radicalization process; in others, less education might lead to fertile ground for recruitment. There is no correlation because the effects of education can cut both ways, leading to more or less radicalism. Education more likely matters for another reason. For decades, social movement scholars have recognized that students are a particularly important part of social activism (McCarthy and Zald 1973; Piven and Cloward 1977). Doug McAdam (1988) accounts for this by coining the term "biographical availability" in his book on college students' participation in the civil rights movement. Students, or recent students, not only have the resources that come with their higher social class, but also the time to participate in movements of all kinds. Students tend to be young and not yet constrained by the duties of marriage, parenthood, mortgages, or career advancement. Thus, they are available to participate, either as moderates or radicals; hence the tendency for guerrilla war to be a young person's game. Which particular academic degree is overrepresented in a movement is much more the product of social context than of a curriculum – the student radicals of 1960s America preferred sociology to engineering.

We see the processes of social class and education at play in the early life of a famous radical, Che Guevara.[2] Ernesto Guevara was born into a relatively affluent Argentine family that had leftist political leanings. In 1948, he enrolled at the University of Buenos Aires and studied medicine. Like many students, the flexibility of time in higher education allowed him to travel extensively through Latin America giving him firsthand experience of rural poverty. He eventually landed in Guatemala in 1953 where a democratically elected government was pursuing land reform and other leftist programs. There, Ernesto met a number of leftists and Cuban exiles and earned the nickname Che, derived from his habitual use of a common Argentine interjection, similar to "you know" in American English or "eh" in Canada. At this time, Guevara sought to reconcile his medical background with his political convictions. He drafted part of a book entitled *The Role of the Doctor in Latin America*, in which he posited that a "revolutionary doctor" could be a force for socialism as he fought all injustices that adversely affected the people. In 1954, a coup d'état took place against the Guatemalan government and Guevara fled to Mexico where he met Raul and Fidel Castro and joined their revolutionary movement. Here, we see that Che's social class, family background, and education all contributed to his biographical availability for recruitment to a radical movement. If we imagine the counterfactual (a term in logic for the opposite of what is observed) that could have been the case a few years later in his life course – an Ernesto encumbered by children and a medical practice – then it is unlikely we would be wearing t-shirts and hanging posters with his image in our dorm rooms today.

In short, the varied bases of radical movements call into question the psychological origins of radicalization as a sufficient explanation. It does appear to be the case that leaders of movements have certain characteristics. But these patterns are more likely due to an individual's biographical availability, rather than a tendency for particular social groups to be more or less radical. Exploring the sources of social support for radical movements is the task of the next section.

Social support for radicalism

Even if radicals can be drawn from all segments of society, we might guess that some segments are more likely to support radicalism and the use of violence. There have been many studies since September 11th on attitudes in Muslim countries that suggest an answer to this question. The previously mentioned study by Krueger and Maleckova (2003) also looks at opinion poll data of Palestinians' support for the use of violence against Israel. They find that there is no consistent effect of the level of a person's education and their support for violence, and no correlation with poverty either. More recently, Najeeb Shafiq and Sinno (2010) have studied support for suicide terrorism in six Muslim countries that have experienced suicide bombings. Their key finding is that the effect of education levels and income varies widely across countries, suggesting that the country-level context is more important than any particular demographic characteristic. Similarly, Fair and Shepherd (2006) find that opinions on terrorism varied widely among the 14 Muslim countries they studied, and de Mesquita (2009a) also concluded that education and economic factors had little effect on support for terrorism.

Studies of support for religious fundamentalism and Islamic political parties tell a similar story. Mansoor Moaddel and Stuart Karabenick (2008) examine survey data on attitudes among the youth in Egypt and Saudi Arabia, and find that, while fundamentalist youth rely on religious leaders for information about Islam's social and political role and watch less television, there are country-specific differences. For instance, women in Saudi Arabia are more fundamentalist than men, but the opposite is true in Egypt. Famously, Norris and Inglehart (2002) use data from a large-scale global survey, the World Values Survey, to explore differences in social and political attitudes between Muslim and western countries. They find that Muslims are just as likely to support democracy, and people in some western countries are just as likely to support a role for religion in politics as are those in Muslim nations. The crucial opinion divide seems to be about gender equality and sexual practices. Tellingly, these popular attitudes show up when Islamists try to run for office. Kurzman and Naqvi (2010a), in another study, show that Islamic political parties do not tend to do very well in elections, and the freer the election is the worse they do. Further, even when Islamic parties get into office, they tend to become more liberal and less fundamentalist over time. All these studies point to a particular issue of conflating religion with politics – there is substantial variation among Muslims and Muslim countries as it is a world religion. Many of the effects we presume to be religious may actually be regional (Stepan and Robertson 2004).

Even so, we might think that other radical ideologies would have a different basis than Islamic movements. Judging from Table 2.1, it appears that left-wing movements are more likely made up of elites and the educated, and others have argued that right-wing movements have a distinctively populist flavor (see Rydgren 2007). But the evidence does not support this either; the demographic basis of left and right is highly dependent on time and place. In earlier eras, the left was primarily a working-class movement and the extreme right wing was a product of the middle class. Seymour Martin Lipset wrote a series of articles in the 1950s that made this point clearly (see Lipset 1959a, 1959b). In Latin America, left-wing movements today draw their support from the poor, while in the United States leftist radicals like the "eco-terrorists" of the Earth Liberation Front and the Animal Liberation Front seem to generally come from more affluent backgrounds. Conversely, neo-fascism in Europe seems to be a more populist movement, while in Latin America and Asia right-wing radicals are often supported by the business classes. In short, neither side of the political spectrum has a monopoly on support from any particular social segment. Nor does radicalism know any particular political stance. Rather, the social support for radicalism is highly contingent (a term social scientists use to mean that the effect is random or outside of a particular theory), dependent on national and historical context. This points to the importance of environments in explaining radicalism, which is the focus of chapter 4.

Radical leaderships

Most profile studies are of leaders since they are easier to find information on, but those that include the broader base of participation in a movement find little consistent basis. From these, there does seem to be a divide between the characteristics of leaders and the radical masses of a movement. Kurzman and Naqvi (2010b) note this pattern in looking at Islamic movements, and Wickham-Crowley (1992), in his study of Latin American guerrilla movements, finds that the educated and elite came first, and peasants entered into them second. It thus should be no surprise that leaders might differ from the participants in general. As discussed above, some are more biographically available to participate for long periods of time in a high-risk activity and thus are more likely to become leaders. For example, early leaders of Al-Qaeda like bin Laden and al-Zawahiri were relatively more educated and from higher social classes than many of the foot soldiers in the movement. This pattern has long been noted as a feature of revolutionary movements – their leaderships tend to come from intellectual classes that are able to creatively imagine alternatives to the existing social and political order. Second, the most effective movements unite elites and masses together in coalitions. There will be more on this latter point in the next chapter. This bears a resemblance to the earliest social scientific work on revolution. Recall that Brinton (1938) argued that revolution occurred in stages and different social groups entered into the process at different times.

So are there unique characteristics that make for leaders? Most social scientists would say no, arguing that the times make the person rather than the other way around. Randall Collins (2007) makes this point in a wonderful essay that critiques notions of crucial turning points in history. But we might make some headway if we think of leadership, i.e., what leading entails, rather than specific leaders. For instance, Marshall Ganz (2000), in his study of farmworkers' movements, also finds that leaders who have access to local knowledge and are flexible create more "strategic capacity." Sharon Nepstad and Clifford Bob (2006) argue that effective leaders possess "leadership capital" which is as much a product of their context as their own unique abilities. Capital here is a social scientific term for resources; sociologists often distinguish financial capital, human capital (the skills one has), social capital (who one knows), and cultural capital (non-financial advantages like intellect, speaking ability, and style). According to Nepstad and Bob, leaders can take advantage of opportunities if they have general social esteem and prestige, knowledge of the local activist landscape, and extensive social ties. This leadership capital also helps attract support from outside the movement and can turn government repression into a motivating force for the movement. Similarly, Brinton (1938) thought that leadership was a crucial part of revolutionary success, and Selbin (1993) has argued that such skilled leadership is crucial in institutionalizing a new vision of society after a revolution.

Hoffer (1951) notes that many movements have their origins in a "man of words" who is able to effectively use rhetoric and ideas to discredit existing regimes and instill hope for a new future. People of words are succeeded in a mass movement by "fanatics" who prefer chaos and anarchy and put words into actions. Fanatics, Hoffer thought, were more likely to come from the disaffected segments of society than the more intellectual and educated person of words. But fanaticism can only take a movement so far, and successful movements need practical "men of action" who save the movement from fanatics and effect widespread change. Saul Alinsky (1971) modifies this latter idea into the role of the "organizer" who does not seek power for him- or herself but for others to use for their betterment. Alinsky's organizer is most effective when possessing curiosity, irreverence for tradition, imagination, humor, a strong personality and ego, and an open mind.

While these can be thought of as characteristics of individuals, it is more apt to think of them as social roles within a movement. A role, in sociological terms, is a construct of a particular social structure or institution that enables and expects certain types of action while constraining others. Crucially, roles function similarly, no matter which individual occupies them. From Hoffer and

Alinsky, we might conclude that effective leaderships will have the characteristics of each of these roles – the ability to creatively start a radical movement, the Machiavellian ruthlessness to see it through, and the pragmatism to know when to choose different strategies. Here, there is a research study on roles within leaderships just waiting to happen.

The key idea is that effective leadership, whether from a strategic role or leadership capital, is not merely the result of the qualities and talents of individuals. Rather, leadership exists in relation to a movement and its environment. Thus, many personally exceptional leaders are not always effective. For example, Che Guevara was a master tactician and helped accomplish the Cuban Revolution, but failed to imitate it later in the Congo and Bolivia. Effective radical movements do have effective leaders, but this is likely the product of the movement itself. This is even more important for radical movements – radicalism often entails an organizational structure able to withstand government repression and keep strategic secrecy, and leadership might be diffuse and more equally shared among all participants.

The preceding three sections all emphasize a single point. Radicalism is not the product of individuals, their characteristics, or their psychology. Yet it would be foolish to rule out the micro-level of radicalization entirely. We can save psychology if we unify it with the social. Such social-psychological processes in small groups are the focus of the last section of this chapter.

The social psychology of radicalism

While psychology is often used as a framework for understanding an individual's paths into radicalism, it appears that there is almost no consistent set of stages in a person's journey into activism (Borum 2011; King and Taylor 2011). For example, Muslims in Britain interact with radical movements just as activists have with more traditional movements (Wiktorowicz 2005). What makes these activists radical has little do with their own psychology and more to do with the goals of the groups they interact with

(Gest 2010). Radicalization is thus as much a social process as it is a personal one (Cesari 2004). This is because collective action, at its root, involves a group of individuals who act together for political purposes. As such, group dynamics are very important for understanding how movements work. There is a large social-psychological literature on collective action dynamics, and social movement scholars have integrated it into their studies and theories. Here, I highlight just a few aspects: emotion, spontaneity, identity, and culture.

Activism, and even more so radicalism, involves passionate commitment to a cause. Without emotional investment, it is hard to believe that anyone would undertake radical action. For instance, participants in the Weather Underground report that the Vietnam War "just made them crazy," and Earth Liberation Front activists often speak of their rage and sadness at environmental destruction. Since the late 1990s, social movement scholars have begun to pay attention to the role of emotions in social movements (for a helpful review, see Jasper 2011). Emotions come in many forms. Some emotions are relatively temporary, such as reactions to events or excitement that energizes. Revolution scholars have suggested that the confusion and sense of possibility in "revolutionary moments" might be a key dynamic for explaining why protest turns to revolt (see Sewell 1996). Charles Kurzman (1996, 2004b) emphasizes this in his account of the Iranian Revolution of 1979. Protestors faced what most at first thought was a strong state, able and willing to engage in violent repression of the opposition. But as protests continued, Iranians began to believe that revolution was practically inevitable. As their neighbors joined in the revolution, so did they. Such "bandwagon" effects are common in movements, and point to the social aspect of individual participation. In a more recent case, the Egyptian Revolution of 2011, the revolution came not only from an organized campaign of rebellion, but also from a dynamic set of protests and interactions where popular beliefs in the possibility of change drew on the energy present in Tahrir Square (Austin Holmes 2012).

But sustained campaigns require more than just temporary moments of emotional outpouring and spontaneity. Here, other emotions that are stable and persist, such as general moods or feelings of loyalty and commitment, come into play. Such feelings are crucial for underground organizations – the stress of constant participation requires a particularly high commitment. Della Porta (1995) memorably reports that as the Red Army Faction's campaign of terror continued in Germany, members began to fetishize their guns, making an emotional commitment to continued violence. Commitment to a cause is also helped by what della Porta calls "martyrs and myths." Myths are the symbolic resources that organizations have to justify their action, such as remembrances of previous actions or hopes for success in the future. For instance, Castro's guerrilla movement put large stock in the symbolism of their first failed uprising at Moncada, naming the movement after the date of its beginning, July 26. During the Arab Spring, rebels in Benghazi adopted the old flag of the monarchy as a symbol of a Libya without Qaddafi. It is also quite common for post-revolutionary governments to institutionalize commemoration to help legitimate their rule (Burns and Dietz 2001). American readers have probably celebrated the 4th of July, participating in a myth that still has emotional resonance.

Martyrs are quite powerful symbols in any movement, but especially so radical ones as they are often created by government or counter-movement violence. Islamists continue to draw inspiration from the writing of Sayid Qutb, an Egyptian Muslim Brotherhood member, who was executed in 1966 by Nasser's regime. When such symbols combine with personal experiences of oppression, recruitment for a movement may succeed, as in the case of Islamic radicals in Britain (Githens-Mazer 2008; Wiktorowicz 2005). Even today, the image of Che Guevara has symbolic meaning for radicals, persisting despite its commodification (see Larson and Lizardo 2007). It is for this reason that the American government chose to bury Osama bin Laden at sea in 2011 – so that his grave would not become a site of pilgrimage. Martyrs are also powerful for revolutionary movements. In the run-up to the Egyptian Revolution of 2011, a Facebook webpage called "We are all Khaled Said" brought attention to the death at the hands of police of a young Egyptian man in 2010. Early protests featured images of his corpse and banners with rhetorical statements of identification.

Even more potent for radical movements is the development of stable identities that are shared by their participants. Polletta (1998) charts how narratives, a form of myth making, helped create a new identity for civil rights activists engaged in sit-ins and sustained their collective action. Recent work by Lorenzo Bosi (2012) on members of the Provisional Irish Republican Army suggests that joining, for many, was a product of their nationalist identity and that militancy was seen as a primary way to defend their personal honor and dignity in response to ongoing violence. Radical groups spend much of their time cultivating these identities through indoctrination and ritualistic displays of commitment. Marxist guerrilla groups often engage in the practice of "self-criticism," where individuals recount their mistakes and are criticized by their fellows. This works like Catholic confession – admitting sins and receiving absolution in turn. Thus, the group identity is reaffirmed and individuals stitched more tightly into it. It is also common for militant groups to publicly display their commitment – think of a battalion of Hezbollah fighters in black with green headbands marching through the streets. This is a demonstration to the public, but also a ritual of solidarity for the participants. In the 1930s, fascists adopted the uniform of colored shirts to display their affiliation – brown shirts in Germany, black shirts in Italy, and even blue shirts in China among the nationalists. Activists can also acquire tactical preferences as a consequence of their identity, even to the point of irrationality (Jasper 1997; Tsintsadze-Maass and Maass 2014). Hence, the Weather Underground still carried out bombings, even when their effectiveness was clearly limited, and Al-Qaeda affiliates continued to target airplanes after the increase in security following September 11th, even though other public spaces are much easier targets, as the 2013 al-Shabab attack on the Westgate Mall in Nairobi demonstrates. Terrorism may thus be a way to cement identities and emotional ties among participants as much as a strategy for accomplishing goals (see Abrahms 2008).

Self-identification with radicalism also changes individual

actions and identities in spheres besides that of collective action. Nicole Shepherd (2002), a former activist herself, observed radical environmentalists in Australia and found that a key to their commitment is the cultivation of a "green identity" – trying to consume fewer things and eat ethically, work on their personal issues, and commit to activism as a vocation. We can probably all think of the environmentalist who proudly purchases carbon offsets for the plane ride home; it seems reasonable to wonder if environmentalist saboteurs do the same for the fires they set. But identities are also social, formed in relationship to what others think. For instance, white-power activists face another conundrum as their racism is generally less acceptable, and so they mostly conceal their "Aryan self" from others (Simi and Futrell 2009), and animal rights activists cast their identities in relationship to society's charges of the irrationality of their beliefs (Einwohner 2002).

Identities that are formed outside of movements can also be a resource. New social movement theorists stress that collective action in the contemporary world is based on social identity more than on social class (see Melucci 1980). Thus, movements will have non-material goals and cultivate the idea of action in defense of an identity. Transnational Islamic terrorism might be thought of in this way (see Sutton and Vertigans 2006). Ayman al-Zawahiri's famous, and videotaped, cry from an Egyptian prison in 1981, "Who are we? We are Muslims!," is one such identity statement. In an earlier era, the French uprisings of 1848 and 1870 owed their differing courses to changes in the identities of Parisians and the resulting relationships among neighbors (Gould 1995). Public and private identities also can become intertwined. The Weathermen changed their name to the Weather Underground as a response to feminist critiques among their female members, and radicals from marginalized groups, such as women, ethnic minorities, etc., will sometimes go further to prove their credibility than activists from dominant groups.

Collective identity is at its most powerful when it creates a long-lasting potential for mobilization. Reed and Foran (2002) argue that the Nicaraguan Revolution was enabled by a "political culture of opposition" where liberation theology and the memory of Augusto Cesar Sandino's rebellion against American military occupation combined to undermine the state. These two cultural idioms affected how people experienced the repressive state and provided a resource for building a collective identity of opposition. John Foran (2005) has expanded this concept more generally and sees it as a key cause of revolutions worldwide. It is easy to imagine its applications elsewhere – Afghanistan's 30-year civil war makes violence and resistance a common routine, legitimating groups like the Taliban, and the legacy of Bahraini democratic activism since the country's independence in 1974 could have played a role in that country's Arab Spring. The Zapatista rebellion in Mexico in 1994 also made use of a historical hero, Emiliano Zapata from the 1910 Mexican Revolution, to mobilize. The success of such appropriations of radical memories is highly dependent on historical context; many different parties have tried to claim the memory of Zapata (Jansen 2007). Historical legacies and identities can also cut in the other direction for radicals – belief in democracy undermines the use of violence in the United States, for instance, and Arab monarchies all survived the Arab Spring, in part because of traditional culture and identity (Goldstone 2013).

In short, we can begin to save the psychology of radicalism if we make it social. Radicals are motivated by emotional reactions and form collective identities that enable them to pursue radical action. This makes radical psychology the property of small groups and their dynamics, rather than the mental afflictions of abnormal individuals. While most research along these lines has been on "normal" social movements, it seems likely that radicalism might be a particularly fruitful area to consider, given the high risks and extreme actions involved.

Summary

This chapter has focused on the micro-level of radicalism, which is the property of individuals and small groups. By looking at who participates in it, who supports it, the roles of leaders, and social psychology, I have emphasized two key ideas. First, radicalism is not the product of abnormal psychology – radicals can come from any segment in society and whether or not a particular social group is supportive of radicalism is more dependent on social and historical context than on any general rules. In short, radicals are not crazy. If they were, they would be far less dangerous. Second, I have argued that what appear to be individual processes are actually the products of social relations – how groups form and the roles present within a movement. This is not a novel idea; rather it is the classic contribution of sociology to understanding humanity. Unfortunately, popular commentators and journalists have yet to pick up on a century's worth of research in this tradition. We will get much further if we always remember the individual is a social being.

An implicit theme of the chapter has been agency. Agency is the term social scientists use to refer to the ability of people to act with free will, independent of social structure. Individual actors clearly have agency and are able to act creatively. Without this, it would be difficult to conceive of radicalism, revolution, or terrorism – which as we saw in the last chapter entails the ability to imagine alternate arrangements of social and political relations and/or act in ways that are not commonly accepted. Anyone who denies agency is a fool. But that does not mean that we have to deny the power of social structure either. That would also be foolish. Action is guided by social relations, and structure can enable certain things or constrain them at different times and in different places. Hence, we see few patterns in the characteristics of individual radicals. In the next two chapters, I consider two different levels of structure, one at the level of movements and organizations and the other at the level of the larger social environment.

3

How Do Radical Movements Organize?

On February 23, 1998, the World Islamic Front for Combat Against the Jews and Crusaders released a communiqué in the form of Islamic law opinion called a *fatwa*, stating that it was the individual duty of every Muslim to kill Americans and their allies in an effort to force foreign militaries to leave Islamic countries and liberate Jerusalem. The fatwa had five signatories, including Osama bin Laden. At this time, the name Al-Qaeda, meaning "the base" in Arabic, was not well known; the earliest reference in western media seems to be in 1996 as another name for one of bin Laden's charities. The mujahedeen who had fought the Soviet Union in Afghanistan and founded the organization in 1988 did not even use its name publicly, as Lawrence Wright (2006) argues. It was not until the bombings of the American embassies in Kenya and Tanzania in August 1998 that the organization began to be well known. Subsequently, Al-Qaeda has been linked to or claimed a number of other pre-September 11th events, including the first World Trade Center bombing in 1993, resistance to American intervention in Somalia in 1993, and the bombing of the *USS Cole* in Yemen in 2000. In summer 2001, just before the attacks on the World Trade Center and the Pentagon, Al-Qaeda formally merged with Egyptian Islamic Jihad, an insurgent terrorist organization in Egypt headed by Ayman al-Zawahiri. After the American invasion of Afghanistan, years of counterterrorism efforts, and the death of bin Laden a decade later, Al-Qaeda's future seemed in doubt. The central organization appeared to be mostly gone but a network of affiliates in countries like Iraq, Syria, Mali, and Somalia remained. Like many radical groups, the exact organizational history and structure of Al-Qaeda are unclear and contested – is it best thought of as an organization with leaders and hierarchies or a loose network of radicals and sympathizers?[1]

In either case, radicalism is as much a product of organizational dynamics as the actions and beliefs of individuals (Oots 1989). Organizations are one of the largest areas of research on social movements more generally. As described in chapter 1, the first research tradition to take organizations seriously was resource mobilization theory. An effective way for movements to gain financial support and recruit members is by developing a formal organization with a dedicated staff (see McCarthy and Zald 1977). Formal organizations are crucial to sustaining activism over a long period of time, as individual activists enter and leave the movement (Gamson 1975; Jenkins and Perrow 1977; McAdam 1982; Staggenborg 1988). But formal organizations carry a risk for movements – they can become professionalized, interested in perpetuating themselves rather than working towards the original cause. Thus, some scholars have argued that organizations are a conservative force on social movements (e.g., McCarthy and Zald 1977; Piven and Cloward 1977).

This picture of organizational dynamics does not seem to fit well with radical, revolutionary, and terrorist groups. When these are more organized, they are popularly considered to be more danger- ous and more radical. Further, clandestine movements, as many radical groups are, face unique challenges of organization and often seem to form loose networks of affiliation rather than formal associations. Or, as in the case of Al-Qaeda described above, both organizational strategies might occur within one group. In the sec- tions that follow, I examine each of these organizational strategies in turn. I then discuss inter- and intra-movement processes, con- sidering the formation of coalitions between groups and the effects of radical flanks and the migration of activists from one movement to another. The focus of the chapter is thus on the meso-level of analysis, which exists between the micro-level of individuals and small groups and the macro-level of environments and social conditions.

Types of radical organizations

We saw in chapter 1 that some scholars think a feature of radical movements is their non-hierarchical organizational structure. Instead of leaders directing a rank and file of participants, a non-hierarchical organization has a much more voluntary and fluid structure, where decisions are made collectively and sometimes independently of a central leadership. The Earth Liberation Front (ELF) is one such organization. The ELF was initially composed of former members of the Earth First! activist group in early 1990s Britain, who split from the organization to pursue more radical tactics. Earth First! itself had been formed by members of Greenpeace who left that organization as it became more moderate. ELF activists used the tactic of "economic sabotage," also called "monkeywrenching" or "ecotage," first vandalizing machinery at a company accused of destroying peat bogs. This tactic and model of organization quickly spread throughout Europe and had arrived in the United States by 1996. The earliest attacks in the United States included arson attacks on a forest ranger station, a Bureau of Land Management horse corral, and a lab facility at the University of California, Davis. Each attack was followed with a communiqué, explaining the group's actions. These were often released by the Portland activist, Craig Rosebraugh, initially a member of an unrelated activist group. Rosebraugh and colleagues later set up a dedicated group to represent ELF claims, called the North American Earth Liberation Front Press Office. The ELF became nationally prominent in 1998 with the destruction by arson of buildings at a ski resort in Vail, Colorado where the "Elves," as activists called themselves, accused the company of endangering habitat for the lynx. Other attacks followed, moving beyond the initial base in Oregon and the West to the entire country – including arson at Michigan State University, arsons and vandalism in Bloomington, Indiana, destruction of housing developments on Long Island, and firebombing of sport utility vehicles at a car dealership in California. The ELF consciously stayed away from interpersonal violence, limiting their actions to property destruction. Yet, by 2002, the FBI had testified to Congress that the ELF was one of the most serious domestic terrorist threats in the United States. The years 2001–2003 were the height of clearly identifiable ELF action (Beck 2007; Chermak et al. 2013), and the group's activities slowly declined throughout the decade as it faced more arrests and successful prosecutions.[2]

In contrast to more clearly violent groups, some scholars have argued that we should not consider this as terrorism but rather as a stigmatizing label that governments have put on activism which they seek to control and vilify (see Loadenthal 2013, 2014; Smith 2008; Sorenson 2009). There is no doubt that governments use the label "terrorism" in such a fashion (Beck and Miner 2013; Jackson 2005; Oliverio 1998). But I have argued elsewhere (Beck 2007) that some of the direct actions of environmental activists conform to a minimal social scientific definition of terrorism and that our scholarly concepts should not be formed in reaction to popular labels. More to the point, the ELF certainly falls under the definition of radicalism that I use in this book.

Organizationally, the ELF had no formal structure. Any activist, or group of activists, could carry out an ecotage attack and release a statement under the moniker of the ELF. While the radicals might be connected by prior social ties or participation in other movements, there was no central leadership guiding their actions. The ELF is an example of "leaderless resistance," a term used for organizations that have no central command structure and are made up of cells capable of acting independently. Many radical groups, such as white supremacists, anti-abortion activists, and Islamic terrorists, also have this structure. Lone-wolf terrorists, like Anders Behring Breivik who bombed government buildings in Norway and then gunned down teenagers at a political party summer camp, are sometimes mistaken for leaderless resistance. But, first and foremost, true lone wolves act independently and with almost no organizational context. Thus, leaderless resistance and a lack of hierarchy should not be mistaken for a defining characteristic of radicalism. Rather, it is an effective response to government repression and allows a movement to persist and carry out illegal clandestine action. A lack of hierarchy is also often a feature of movements with egalitarian ideals rather than a product of radicalism itself.

In contrast, many other radical groups have a more stable and formal organizational structure, even when organized in cells. Classically, revolutionary guerrilla groups are organized like armies with centralized command and control and hierarchies of battalions and squads. For instance, Mao's pamphlet title is *On Guerrilla Warfare* (1937) devotes a lengthy appendix to outlining an effective organizational structure. Che Guevara rose to prominence in the Cuban Revolution in part because of his skills as a tactical leader of one such battalion. The mid-twentieth-century Algerian independence movement Front de Libération Nationale (FLN) also was a hierarchical organization that adopted a classic pyramidal cell-like structure for its military wing (see Crenshaw 1978). The central organizing committee selected a few members to be cell leaders, who in turn would recruit a member of their cell. Each member would then recruit another member, and so on. The result resembles a pyramid, in which each member only knows the person who recruited him and the person that he in turn recruited. Hierarchy, in these cases, allows for more coordination of action and achievement of a practical goal, such as revolution, than a more diffuse organizational structure might.

Another organizational strategy is the bifurcated organization. Bifurcated organizations have separate political wings and militant wings that are organized, and sometimes act, independently of one another. Sometimes, there is a central leadership that unites the two, for instance, the "spiritual leaders" common to religious movements worldwide, but this is not always the case. The political wing may form a participatory political party, engage in social welfare programs, and try to build popular support for a movement. The militant wing engages in defense of its popular base and carries out attacks against its opponents, whether a state or a competing organization. Such movements often begin as parties and turn to militancy later. For instance, Hamas began as the

Palestinian offshoot of the Muslim Brotherhood political party and was even tacitly permitted by Israel at first as a counterweight to Yasser Arafat's militant Palestine Liberation Organization. Its first activities were running charities, and it was only during the First Intifada in 1987 – the general Palestinian uprising against Israeli occupation – that it turned to supporting and carrying out militant actions. The decision of political parties to turn to terror is structured by both their internal workings and their interaction with the larger political system (see Danzell 2010; Weinberg 1991). There is a danger for a movement that adopts such a structure, however. They might be more likely to split into competing factions, especially in cases where the political wing turns towards more moderate and participatory strategies. Notably, this happened to the Irish Republican Army as Sinn Fein, the formal political party, sought a political solution to the conflict, leading to the formation of more militant factions like the Provisional IRA and the Real IRA. But factionalization, or its absence, does not seem to affect the amount of violence that a movement will employ (Siqueira 2005), contrary to common fears of increasing radicalization.

Revolutionary guerrilla movements and bifurcated organizations often seek to control territory. In essence, they become quasi-government actors building the infrastructure of a government and providing the services that a state does. This can occur when the organization has separatist goals or is rooted in a geographically bounded community, and often leads to civil war. For example, the Liberation Tigers of Tamil Eelam sought an independent homeland for ethnic Tamils in Sri Lanka and during the Sri Lankan Civil War from 1983 to 2009 controlled an extensive territory which they administered as a government (Mampilly 2011). Territorial control also indicates a particularly effective and large organization. Smaller and less effective separatist groups, like the Basque ETA, have never been able to set up an autonomous area, and the Kurdish PKK in Turkey mostly engages in cross-border attacks from its primary bases in Iraq and Syria and has never established effective control over Turkish territory.

We see the importance of territorial control in the example of the Islamic State. The Islamic State in Iraq was initially formed during the insurgency against American forces that occupied Iraq after deposing Saddam Hussein in 2003. With the development of civil war in Syria after the failed uprisings in 2011, the group found a new foothold and adopted a new name that included the Levant. The organization was originally affiliated with Al-Qaeda but disputes grew among the various Islamist factions of the Syrian rebels, and Ayman al-Zawahiri designated the rival al-Nusra Front Al-Qaeda's representative in Syria. With the support of foreign fighters and military material seized from Syrian and Iraqi forces as well as other rebel groups, the group built itself into a formidable fighting force. In 2014, the group renamed itself the Islamic State, and declared its leader Abu Bakr al-Baghdadi caliph over a new state. The Islamic State rapidly expanded its territory in Iraq in the summer of 2014 as Iraqi security forces melted away. Within the areas it controlled, the Islamic State began to impose Islamic law and take on some of the functions normally associated with governments. In response to its gains, the United States began an air campaign in support of Iraqi and Kurdish forces. In return, the Islamic State began beheading western hostages, including journalists, uploading the graphic videos to the internet. In this case, territorial control was not just a goal but also a resource. The Islamic State generated revenue from the sale of oil produced in areas it controlled, as well as from ransoms for hostages. When groups build their capability as a cause and consequence of territorial control, they are often the most deadly (Asal and Rethemeyer 2008).

Other radical groups have a more mixed structure, falling in between hierarchical and non-hierarchical organizations. Here aspects of both formal and informal organization exist in tandem. Peter Bergen (2001) and Jason Burke (2004) report that Al-Qaeda operated like a modern business firm. Bin Laden, Zawahiri, and other members of a quasi board of directors provided financial and logistical support to militants, sometimes organized, sometimes not, around the globe. So while Al-Qaeda central in Afghanistan resembled a formal organization, it also had informal structures and connections outside the country. In terrorism studies, as described at the beginning of this chapter, this mixed structure has led to debate over the exact organizational structure of transnational Islamic terrorism. Marc Sageman (2008) has argued that Al-Qaeda is a form of leaderless resistance, while terrorism expert Bruce Hoffman (2008) responds that bin Laden and central control still mattered. There is no reason they both cannot be right, particularly when we consider the strategic shifts that the "war on terror" forced on the group (see Mayntz 2004; Mishal and Rosenthal 2005).

The key point here is that there are many organizational strategies available to radical groups. While there may be a penchant for types of groups to organize along certain lines – leftists might prefer egalitarian structures, revolutionary armies might form hierarchies, separatist groups might control territory, and communal groups might act in the social and political as well as militant realms – there does not appear to be a central tendency towards the formality and professionalization that many social movement scholars would expect. Rather, it appears that organizational strategies are a response to the environment in which a group finds itself, which is discussed in more detail in the next chapter. Organizational form might then be considered a type of strategy as groups try to attract participants and acquire resources that allow them to carry out their actions, particularly when faced with government repression. In the next section, I discuss a particular form of organization and way of dealing with resource dilemmas – the network.

Networks and recruitment to movements

Considering radical organizations as a type of social network has received much attention in recent years. This is not because network forms of militancy are new, but rather because social network analysis has expanded in the last decade and is one of the most cutting-edge tools that social scientists currently have. A social network is formed from the ties that various "nodes" have. A node is often an individual but could be any actor, such as an organization, a terrorist cell, and so on. A tie is often as simple as two actors knowing each other, e.g., friendship, but again could be anything, such as financial support, shared membership, tactical borrowing, and so forth. Thinking this way allows the researcher to visualize the underlying structure of social relations among actors and reveal patterns that could not be seen before. In studies of radicals, revolutionaries, and terrorists, there are two different ways that networks are usually discussed. Terrorism experts, who tend to come from the background of political science, view networks as a form of organizational structure. Movement scholars, who tend to come from the tradition of sociology, see networks as the social ties outside of an organization that may explain pathways to participation. I discuss each of these approaches below.

Radical groups, in particular terrorist ones, often seem to organize themselves in a network fashion. As we saw above, this often is a hybrid structure – mixing some elements of hierarchy with local networks of activists. For instance, Pedahzur and Perliger (2006) collected data on Palestinian suicide bombers and their network ties. They find that the central organizing structure is a network of hubs, one central node to which many others are connected, that is horizontal across a geographic area rather than hierarchical within the movement. Radicals in the hub take the place of leaders, organizing suicide attacks but without direct orders from the central terrorist group. The suicide bombers themselves seem to be peripheral rather than important activists. This is quite the rational strategy – in suicide terrorism, the terrorist is meant to be killed if not captured and so it is not an effective action for the higher echelons of leaders, planners, bomb-makers, and so on to undertake themselves.

The hubs described by Pedahzur and Perliger are a classic case of network organization. It is important to note that this is quite different from a leaderless resistance model of organization. In leaderless resistance, individuals or small groups are independent of one another, unconnected, uncoordinated, and united only by commitment to a cause. For example, as far as we know, the Tsarnaev brothers, who carried out the Boston Marathon bombing, undertook their attack on their own initiative. While they made use of ideological and practical tools for terrorism disseminated by other radicals, they were not part of a network. Leaderless resistance and network forms of organization are sometimes confused, even by researchers (e.g., Sageman 2004, 2008).

A key point of debate about network organization is whether it is more or less effective. When a group organizes as a network, it creates potential "cut points" – places where an individual or a group of individuals is the only connection between different parts of the network. Some counterterrorism efforts focus on such cut points, seeking to capture or eliminate them and thus disrupt and break apart a terrorist network (see Carley 2006). Even so, a loosely organized network might be better able to withstand repression as each part of it can act independently. But loose networks seem to be less effective at carrying out terrorist attacks. Centralized leadership, even in a network form, is better able to coordinate activities, respond to government actions, and adapt to changing circumstances on the ground (Enders and Jindapon 2010).

The other way that network analysis is used by social scientists is to account for the personal ties that participants in a movement have (e.g., McAdam and Paulsen 1993). These ties extend outside of a group, including a person's family, friends, co-workers, and neighbors. Such social networks are often the basis of radical groups. For instance, Kathleen Collins (2007) researched Islamist groups in Uzbekistan, Tajikistan, and Azerbaijan. She finds that the movements are built out of informal local networks. In authoritarian settings, these social networks allowed the groups to circulate ideas, create sympathizers, and recruit participants. Social networks are particularly useful for mobilization if they are dense, with lots of interconnections between participants. For instance, the initial uprisings in Syria in 2011 seem to have been based on dense local relationships centered in towns and small cities (Leenders 2012). Roger Gould (1991, 1995), in his masterful network studies of nineteenth-century Parisian uprisings, finds that dense neighborhood ties allowed the participants to be more committed and sustain their mobilization against government repression. An individual's network position, how connected he or she is and to whom, thus often explains their participation or not in a radical movement (see Bearman 1993; Gould 1996). For example, Earth Liberation Front activists were often brought into radical action through their existing friendships.

When social networks are less dense, key individuals can become mobilizing agents. These "brokers," people who have social ties that bridge different social networks, help pass information and unite smaller groups. Brokers are similar to hubs and cut points that exist in network forms of organization. A wonderful example of this comes from the American Revolution. In 1775, the British began to mobilize their troops to seize arms from the local militia depots. On the night of April 18, a Boston revolutionary leader named Joseph Warren dispatched Paul Revere on horseback to warn the American activists that the British were moving towards Lexington and Concord. The battle that followed was the first engagement of the Revolutionary War. The episode became Paul Revere's famous Midnight Ride, commemorated in American popular imagination and Henry Wadsworth Longfellow's poem. Revere and Warren owed the effectiveness of their message to their position of brokerage within the Boston area revolutionary movement (Han 2009). The movement was split among various organizations and groups. Of the five main ones, Warren belonged to four and Revere to three. The notable Patriots Samuel Adams, of beer-label fame, and Benjamin Church also belonged to three each. These crosscutting social ties allowed them to be effective mobilizers of the emerging revolution. Similar dynamics have been found in other historical cases, like the seventeenth-century English Civil War (see Hillmann 2008). More contemporarily, youth activists from Serbia played a key brokerage role in transmitting nonviolent tactics which helped activists in Georgia and Ukraine mobilize their Color Revolutions (Kuzio 2006) and, in 2011, Tunisian and Egyptian activists as well.

But not all social networks need to exist prior to the beginnings of a movement (see Munson 2010). When activists come together in an organization, they form new ties, and these can be the basis of future organizational forms. For instance, participation in the SDS brought the future Weathermen together. The resulting interpersonal relationships became the basis for the collectives and pyramidal cells that marked the underground phase of the movement. At the time, the SDSers even tried to erase prior personal ties, avoiding monogamous romantic relationships to cement feelings of loyalty to the group and, later, in the underground phase, cutting off contact from family and friends. Della Porta (1995) reports a similar dynamic among the Red Army Faction in Germany and the Red Brigades in Italy. Such intra-organizational ties allowed the groups to maintain their radical stance in the face of increasing evidence of their own ineffectiveness. Network ties between radical organizations also are a source of resources, training, and operational capability. Many mid-twentieth-century nationalist and leftist groups worked together. In my favorite instance, members of the communist Japanese Red Army helped the nationalist Popular Front for the Liberation of Palestine carry out an attack at Tel Aviv's international airport in 1972, killing 26 and wounding 80. The Palestinian terrorist Abu Nidal was also famous for his crosscutting alliances among terrorist groups, even working with the Libyan government to carry out attacks. In fact, the greater the number of alliances that a terrorist organization has tends to make them more deadly (Asal and Rethemeyer 2008).

So networks can mean two things for the study of radicals, revolutionaries, and terrorists – either a form of organization, often employed by terrorist groups, or a set of social ties, often used to mobilize a movement. While network forms of organization can be an effective response to the challenges that a radical group faces, it appears that dense social ties or individuals who can connect fragmentary networks together are important bases for radical movements. This general trend of findings accords well with one of the most consistent features of successful revolutions – the formation of broad coalitions that oppose a state.

Revolutionary coalitions

Beginning with Dix's (1984) observation that successful social revolutions tended to have a "negative coalition" of various social actors, scholars have focused on how coalition building is an integral part of the revolutionary process. A revolutionary coalition, unlike alliances among terrorist organizations or coalitions of social movement actors, unites more than just organized groups. It provides a way for whole social segments to participate in a revolution, bringing together actors from different socioeconomic classes, ethnic groups, and genders (Foran, Klouzal, and Rivera 1997). The key is that it bridges these social cleavages and creates mass identification with the revolutionary cause. For instance, in the popular imagination, the Cuban Revolution was the product of successful guerrilla tactics organized by a charismatic Castro and Che. In reality, the Cuban Revolution involved recruitment of the peasants to the revolutionary cause, support from urban movement activists, and alliances with other resistance groups (see Foran 2005; Goodwin 2001). Similarly, the Iranian Islamic Revolution involved strikes by workers and protests by communists, nationalists, and other non-religious groups. As the protests continued in the face of confused responses from the Shah's government, the urban business classes began to withdraw their support from the regime. It was not until after the Shah was deposed that the clerics led by Khomeini were able to consolidate their power and suppress secular and moderate alternatives within the coalition (see Abrahamian 1982; Kurzman 2004b). Broad coalitions bring people into the streets for various reasons, and this sustains mobilization, no matter what concessions a regime tries to make (Beissinger 2011).

So if effective coalitions are broad, what helps them form and what makes them successful? We can certainly point to the role of brokers and organizational strategies by key revolutionary groups. But, more importantly, coalitions are the product of political exclusion – a regime that relies on a narrow subset of the population for its rule makes many enemies (Goodwin and Skocpol 1989). I discuss political exclusion in more detail in the next chapter. But coalitions are successful for other reasons besides their mass appeal and involvement. First, coalitions among groups make it harder for the state to suppress them entirely. When a revolutionary group is faced with repression, it can literally seek safe haven within another organization. For example, the collapse of communism in Poland in 1989 was preceded by the mobilization of the trade union Solidarity a decade before. In 1981, the Polish government declared martial law and tried to suppress the movement. Yet activists were able to use their ties to other groups, foremost the Catholic Church, to continue to organize in safer venues and keep the movement alive (Osa 2003). Similarly, pro-democracy activists in 1980s Korea were able to withstand government repression by forging ties with other civil society organizations. Repression in this case helped form the coalition that would bring democracy to South Korea (Chang 2008). Shifting alliances in the Iranian reform movement of the early 2000s also sustained mobilization in the face of government and counter-movement reactions (Kadivar 2013). We might thus say that coalitions are a form of what Verta Taylor (1989) terms "abeyance structures" – those things that allow a movement to continue even when active protest subsides.

Second, broad coalitions encourage the participation of key, powerful social groups. The first among these is socioeconomic elites. Business classes and landowners control significant economic resources, and their participation makes these available to a growing movement in a very real way. Mobilization, radical or not, requires financial and material resources, and elites help solve this resource mobilization problem. Jack Goldstone's (1991b) account of the English Civil War shows well that elite disenfranchisement and subsequent participation were key factors in the fall of the monarchy and the rise of Oliver Cromwell's Roundhead army. In twentieth-century Third World revolutions, participation by economic elites was also a central element (Walton 1984). Elite participation also helps a radical group withstand and avoid severe government repression, as Slater's (2010) study of communist movements in post-World War II Southeast Asia demonstrates. A second key group is the intellectual classes. Scholars like to focus on the role of intellectuals in revolution not only because they are important but also because some scholars like to believe they are revolutionary intellectuals themselves. Revolution, like any radicalism, is fundamentally about ideas – without an alternate vision of social and political order, regime change is just a power grab or coup d'état. Intellectuals, like Hoffer's (1951) men of words, can help author the ideas of revolution and frame them in such a way as to gain mass support. Perhaps most famously, the era that included the American and French Revolutions was also the era of Enlightenment philosophy. Enlightenment intellectuals and their ideals of egalitarian governance played a key role in mobilizing revolutionaries and forming revolutionary coalitions (Markoff 1988, 1996). In the early twentieth-century constitutional revolutions in Russia, Turkey, Persia, and elsewhere, intellectuals also played a key role in implementing the idea of republics and constitutional monarchies (Kurzman 2008; Sohrabi 1995). The third powerful actor for a revolutionary coalition comes from members of the state's coercive forces such as the police and military. Regimes, particularly autocratic ones, often rely on coercion to deal with challenges to their rule. This occurs even in democracies, as the activities of the FBI while hunting the Weather Underground attest. When the military or police refuse to follow orders, or, even worse, join the revolution, then the regime is not likely to last long. In Ukraine's 2004 Orange Revolution, the security services refused to disband the protests occurring in Kiev's central square and this helped lead to a peaceful transfer of power (McFaul 2005). A similar dynamic lies behind other negotiated revolutions like South Africa in 1993, Chile in 1991, and Czechoslovakia in 1989 (Lawson 2005).

The importance of elites, intellectuals, and security services, and broad coalitions is well illustrated by the 2011 Arab Spring revolutions, particularly in Egypt. In late December 2010, a Tunisian street vendor, Mohammed Bouazizi, set himself on fire to protest police harassment. Popular protests against the regime began to mount in response, building throughout the month. By the middle of January, the police and security services had been unsuccessful in their attempts to suppress the protests, and the dictator, Ben Ali, called on the army to act. The head of the army refused, and Ben Ali fled into exile on January 14, 2011. Inspired by this example, Egyptian democracy activists and opposition parties organized a countrywide protest for January 25. While these protests began with long-time activists, drawing on the networks and organizational capability from prior demonstrations (see Clarke 2011), they increased substantially when the long-term opposition group the Muslim Brotherhood joined the protests on January 28. Protestors occupied central places in Cairo and other cities, most notably Tahrir Square, attacked government buildings, and organized to fight against attempts at police repression. The next day the Egyptian army was ordered into cities, but military leaders publicly stated their neutrality and desire to restore order by protecting protestors from police. By February 11, Egyptian dictator Hosni Mubarak's position had become untenable and he resigned, leaving power in the hands of the armed forces. Protests in Yemen played out similarly, with activists occupying public places and military commanders offering their support. In Bahrain, activists, primarily Shiite activists, drew on a legacy of opposition to the Sunni monarchy to stage wide-scale protests until their suppression by police forces assisted by forces from Saudi Arabia. In Libya, protest was intensely repressed by Muammar Qaddafi's security services and military until NATO-led intervention allowed locally organized militias to secure their cities and overthrow the regime. Syrian protests, faced with increasing state repression and a lack of success, devolved into civil war as defectors from the armed forces and local groups took up arms.[3]

The most significant of these revolutions was in Egypt. And it was accomplished by what was truly a revolutionary coalition that brought together democracy activists, intellectuals, Islamists, and opposition political parties (Austin Holmes 2012). The coalition saw success when the Egyptian army tacitly joined it. The countries where such coalition building did not occur had much less successful mobilizations, as in Jordan and Morocco. And a lack of elite, particularly military, participation seems to have influenced the course of conflict in Bahrain and Syria. While there were certainly other factors at play, coalition building and the participation of key social groups was one important condition for success during the Arab Spring, and revolution more generally (see Beck 2014). In fact, the difference between what we consider radicalism and revolution may only lie in the ability of a movement to organize diverse groups in sustained mobilization.

Radical flanks, spillover, and spill-out

Coalition building is one way that organizations within a movement and multiple movements relate to one another. But there are other forms of interrelation, not all of which are as positive for reaching a particular goal. It is an easy observation to make that what seems radical today may not be tomorrow. For instance, a century ago ideas of racial equality may have been radical, but today they are protected by law and normatively encouraged by society's views of appropriate language, thoughts, and action. "Social norm" is a term that sociologists use to describe the unwritten rules that guide our actions. These can often be identified by intentionally breaking them – if a behavior has the force of a norm, then others will not know how to respond or will try to influence the actor to behave appropriately. For movements, a radical flank might exert either a pull effect on a larger movement, which changes its direction, or a push effect, which makes it more moderate.

Herbert Haines (1984, 1995), in his study of the civil rights movement, conceptualizes these dynamics as negative and positive radical flank effects. Positive effects include making the moderates seem more reasonable, enhancing their bargaining power, and making elites or governments more likely to make some concessions as a way of undermining more radical goals. Haines finds that the activities of radical black organizations and urban riots actually increased the amount of giving to moderate civil rights groups by white supporters. Patrons of movements often prefer the moderates, and may help professionalize organizations through their resource allocation (see Jenkins and Eckert 1986). Today, the activities of the ELF and similar groups make the mainstream environmental movement seem more reasonable. In fact, the previously radical group Greenpeace is now often considered in the same breath as moderates like the Sierra Club and the Audubon Society. Negative effects include discrediting a movement and reducing the amount of resources given by third parties to more moderate organizations. In the ongoing Syrian civil war, much of the concern from foreign parties about arming the rebels centers on the presence of radical Islamist groups. Rebel ally Turkey even bombed Islamist rebel-held positions in October 2013 to demonstrate its intolerance of radicalism.

Radical flank effects are not confined to one movement. Often, activism in one movement revitalizes another. This can occur through a process of general inspiration. For instance, Isaac, McDonald, and Lukasik (2006) studied the effects of militancy among 1960s leftists on trade unions. They find that these movements, including the student anti-war movement, the women's movement, and the civil rights movement, helped stimulate union organizing through the development of new tactics and passion for leftist causes. As we will see in later chapters, tactical innovation is often effective because elites and states have not yet developed ways of countering it (McAdam 1983). This is why nonviolent revolutions have been so successful in the last few decades, including in the collapse of the Soviet Union, the Color Revolutions, and the Arab Spring – states did not know how to suppress a new tactical form (see Beissinger 2007; Bunce and Wolchik 2006; Stephan and Chenoweth 2008). More broadly, Doug McAdam (1995) suggests that initiator movements, if successful, generate spin-offs in various other realms. The initiating organization tends to have strategic advantages over later ones, including the newness of their tactics, and so the later in the cycle a movement comes, the less successful it might be. We see this in the Arab Spring, where the timing of mass mobilization correlates well with the success of the revolution – Tunisia and Egypt first, more contestation in Yemen, Bahrain, and Libya, and unending struggle in Syria (Beck 2014).

Radical flanks also influence other organizations and movements through a process called "spillover" (see Meyer and Whittier 1994). As a consequence of participation, activists can acquire a particular identity. This identity suggests ways of thinking, tactics, and models of organization that an activist can carry with him or her to another movement or organization which they might get involved in. Some leaders of the 1960s student movement that became the SDS and led later to the Weather Underground had their first taste of activism through participation in the 1964 Freedom Summer campaign to register black voters in Mississippi. One consequence of that bloody summer was increasing radicalization among the white youth participants and the civil rights movement in general, leading to the Black Power movement (McAdam 1988). In a similar process, extant movements can become the target of radical flanks. Here, the radicals try to recruit organizations or take them over to reorient them to a new political goal. Todd Gitlin, for example, described the Weathermen takeover of SDS as "organizational piracy." Similarly, early Chinese communists took over existing activist groups to form their revolutionary vanguard. The groups most susceptible to takeover already had an identity that was compatible with Bolshevism even if it was not yet communist (Xu 2013). Just as groups of radicals can develop an identity, so do organizations. And these identities suggest certain actions and organizational strategies, even to the point of irrational decisions (Jasper 1997), as noted in the last chapter. There is, in fact, a large sociological research tradition on these identity processes, called new institutionalism in the organizations literature (see Powell and DiMaggio 1991).

In other cases, spillover effects leave existing movement bereft of participants and resources as activists and sponsors move on to other causes. Hadden and Tarrow (2007) use the term "spill-out" to describe such a process in the global justice movement. Prior to September 11th, this seemed to be the largest and most dynamic social movement in the United States. While it continues to persist in Europe and other places, the movement has declined substantially in the last decade as activists became focused on anti-Iraq War and anti-Bush administration mobilization. In fact, the large-scale demonstrations that accompany national party conventions in presidential election years now are a clear tactical borrowing from the 1999 World Trade Organization protests in Seattle. This had a direct effect on radicalism – it seems little coincidence that the Earth Liberation Front dissipated at the same time as these new causes emerged. ELF, ALF, and anarchist Black Bloc members refocused their attention on the political, rather than the economic, realm.

These inter- and intra-movement processes are all cases of diffusion, which is the term for the spread of contention, tactics, or models of organization from one site to another. This issue is discussed at length in chapter 7. But radical, revolutionary, and terrorist organizations often have the state, not other movements, as their primary interaction partner. Thus, dynamics of repression, concession, and mobilization are a primary shaping force on the cycle of radical politics (see Danzell 2010; Della Porta 1995), which is the focus of chapter 6. For the time being, we can conclude that radical flanks, spillover, and spill-out – all processes found in mainstream social movements – apply to radical ones, as well.

Summary

This chapter has discussed organizational structure and cross-organizational dynamics which lie at the meso-level of analysis. The main conclusions that can be drawn are that there are many organizational forms available to radical, revolutionary, and terrorist movements and that these are adopted through an interplay of strategy, adjustment to the environment, learning from other groups, and, occasionally, culturally driven taste. Further, organizational form is not static or trending in a particular direction over time. Thus, the key question to ask may not be "Which form is more dangerous or prevalent?" but "How do forms solve different resource mobilization dilemmas?" We might then seek to understand if there are contexts and dynamics that seem to yield one type of organization more often than another. Table 3.1 summarizes the organizational structures discussed in this chapter, possible common contexts of their emergence, and key examples given.

In the last two chapters, we have seen that individual decisions, social support, roles, organizational strategies, and movement relationships occur not just at their specific level of analysis but in interaction with each other. Most broadly, there is a large interaction effect of the social, historical, and political context in which radical groups emerge and operate. This macro-level of analysis is the focus of the next chapter.

Table 3.1 Basic organizational structures, common contexts, and examples of radical, revolutionary, and terrorist groups

Type	Common context	Exemplar
Leaderless resistance	Illegal, unpopular movements	Earth Liberation Front
Hierarchical, central	Guerrilla warfare, insurgency, and civil war	Mao's Chinese Communist Party
Hierarchical, pyramid	Clandestine group, urban embedded insurgency, terror campaign	Algerian FLN
Bifurcated	Socially embedded group/ political party that uses terror	Hezbollah
Quasi-state	Territorial control	Tamil Tigers, Islamic State
Network, with hierarchy	Popular, locally based movements	Second intifada suicide bombers
Network, little hierarchy	Socially embedded opposition	Anti-Assad Syrian rebellion
Network, with brokers	Loosely affiliated members and organizations	Eighteenth-century American Patriots
Coalition	Revolutionary movements	1979 Iranian Revolution
Radical flank	Social movements, especially in democracies	Weather Underground

4

When and Where Does Radicalism Occur?

In 1914, World War I broke out across Europe, bringing the great and lesser powers of the continent into conflict with each other. By the end of the war in 1918, almost 10 million soldiers had died, millions of others had been wounded or gone missing, and governments on both sides of the conflict had fallen – the Russian Empire to Bolshevik revolutionaries, the German Empire to a democratic republic, and Austria-Hungary to resurgent ethnic nationalism and a redrawn map of Europe. From the ashes of Europe, one of history's most notorious radical movements emerged – fascism. In the debates over Italian participation in the war, a leader of the Italian Socialist Party, Benito Mussolini, was expelled for his interventionist views. Mussolini formed a new *fasci*, an Italian word meaning bundle or sheath used to refer to political factions. With the threat of communism as a pretext, Mussolini and his Italian fascists formed alliances with the business classes of Italy and used paramilitary tactics to fight their socialist rivals. In 1922, as a consequence of the disorder and threat of a Black Shirt coup, the king of Italy appointed Mussolini prime minister, creating the first fascist state. This model was later replicated by Adolf Hitler's National Socialist Party to seize power in Germany in 1933 using the emergency laws of the Weimar Republic's constitution. In an unfortunate coincidence of history, this provision – Article 48 – had been defended by the German sociologist Max Weber, who helped draft the constitution and its anti-bureaucratic measures. In 1936, an attempted coup by fascists in Spain against a young leftist republic resulted in the Spanish Civil War, leading to foreign intervention by Nazi Germany and the Soviet Union on opposing sides. The history of fascism after seizing power through means both legal and illegal is well known, ending with the horrors of World War II. Yet even today, neo-fascist and white supremacist groups in Europe draw on this legacy for their own radical mobilizations. While fascist movements had organizational strength and the ability to attract supporters and participants, it is difficult to imagine their meteoric rise without the crises brought on by World War I – economic recessions, weak states, political crises of socialist movements, and growing nationalism among them. The timing and location of fascism, and any radical movement, is explained in large part by these broader environmental factors.[1]

The environmental context of political movements has been a feature of social science since its beginnings – Marx's communism was dependent on economic structures and Tocqueville's associational account of American life was a function of state structure. Even many of the mid-twentieth-century scholars who thought collective action was irrational saw social context as an ultimate cause of protest. But environmental conditions got a major boost in the 1970s with the turn towards structural theories of movements and revolution. A unifying concept emerged at this time – political opportunities. Political opportunity structure, defined in the first chapter, was first coined by Peter Eisinger (1973) as a way to conceptualize why some cities experienced protest in the 1960s and others did not. Protest seemed to occur in communities with a political system that was relatively open to contentious claims from below. The concept was then extended by Charles Tilly (1978) to explain when mobilization might turn into revolution and Doug McAdam (1982) to account for why the civil rights movement had success when it did. An important development in its use has been to account for threat – closing opportunity structures could yield mobilization when a movement fears it might miss its chance (McAdam et al. 2001). But the use of political opportunities as a concept has expanded greatly beyond its origins as a feature of a political system's responsiveness to include economic conditions, contingent triggering events, global power arrangements, and much more. As a consequence, the concept has picked up a lot of critics along the way, both for its structural bias and general theoretical muddiness (e.g., Goodwin and Jasper 1999; Kurzman 1996). If political opportunities can be anything, then what use is there in thinking this way?

One solution is to be more exact in our theory development, carefully defining the factors we consider under the rubric of political opportunity (see Meyer and Minkoff 2004; Meyer 2004). And another might be to try to account for the conjunction of multiple political opportunities. Rather than just focusing on a single cause, a favorable political opportunity structure, at its most general, brings together many conditions at one time that lend themselves to mobilization. This is particularly important for rare events like revolution – successful revolutions depend on the conjunction of multiple conditions which is not a frequent occurrence (Foran 1993; Goldstone 2001, 2011). Similarly, the environmental context of terrorism is multifaceted and no single factor explanation is adequate (Crenshaw 1981).

Outlining what these various favorable conditions are is the task of this chapter. Chapter 2 has the theme of agency in looking at the micro-level of analysis. Here, the theme is mostly structure as we consider the macro-level of analysis. I first detail common structural causes of focusing on economic conditions, social structure, and demographic factors. I then focus on one consistent finding in the study of revolution – how the nature of political systems and regime type affects mobilization. But regimes are socially embedded as well, and so I next consider the broader system of civil society that surrounds them. Finally, I discuss the most macro of macro-levels – the global and temporal context of radicalism, revolution, and terrorism.

Structural causes of radicalism

The most influential structural account of revolution is Theda Skocpol's (1979) *States and Social Revolutions*. As discussed in chapter 1, her definition of social revolution cut through the various ones present in the field at the time, and so did her theory of the causes of revolution. In contrast to a Marxist account of class struggle and the participatory voluntarism of strain theories, Skocpol proposed that the primary cause of revolution is a challenge to a state's bureaucratic and administrative capacities. When failing or weak state structures are faced with contention, they tend to fall apart and become an arena for competition over who will control state power in the future. She specifically argues that the French Revolution of 1789, the Chinese Revolution of 1911, and the Russian Revolution of 1917 occurred because the old regimes had engaged in external, geopolitical competitions with other states and this created fiscal strain on the regimes. Economic pressures also made peasant rebellions more likely and these culminated in a revolutionary crisis as the fiscally weakened states could not suppress them. In short, state breakdown causes social revolution.

While this is a simplistic account of the detailed theory of revolution that Skocpol provides, it sets the stage for later structural theories of revolution. It also provides a framework for thinking about structural causes of radicalism and terrorism. How are they connected to war, economic conditions, and other structural strains? I look at each of these in turn. First, war as one pathway to radicalism is well substantiated by the historical record as well as subsequent research. Recently, Michael Mann (2013) has tried to synthesize theories of revolution by making international war the primary cause. Not only does military competition strain a state, war can actually destroy state capability. As Mann describes, the Russian Empire saw revolution as a consequence of its exhaustion in World War I, and the Japanese invasions of China destroyed nationalist and republican governance setting the stage for the communist takeover. Here no subsidiary mechanisms are needed – international war by itself creates the potential for revolution. A mechanism is a social scientific term for the process by which a condition has a causal effect on a particular outcome. Imagine a scenario in which an earthquake makes bricks fall from a building and strike a passerby, fracturing her skull. What is the cause of death? The immediate cause is a fractured skull. But death occurred under the condition of an earthquake, and the mechanism of a falling brick turned condition into cause. Even many scholars have trouble understanding this difference between condition, mechanism, and cause.

War also has effects on other forms of radicalism. As we saw at the beginning of the chapter, World War I set the stage for the rise of fascism. Al-Qaeda began as part of the Afghan war against Soviet occupation and then later shifted to American targets as a consequence of the US troops stationed in Saudi Arabia during and after the first Persian Gulf War. In the second American invasion of Iraq, a crucial mistake was made – the United States destroyed the Iraqi state, rather than using the Baathist bureaucracy and military as instruments for maintaining social order. This helped create an opportunity for the insurgency, with its campaigns of terrorism and growth of radical Islamic groups. A similar process can occur during civil wars, where general disorder and continued conflict encourages the formation and participation of radical groups, as the case of Syria's ongoing civil war illustrates. The Islamic State took advantage of the Syrian civil war to revitalize its group, and used the opportunity of the weak Iraqi state to seize territory. War and conflict may also have the perverse effect of isolating potential radical movements from mainstream public opinion. During times of war, there is a well-documented "rally around the leader" effect and an increase in social solidarity (see Feinstein 2012). This shift in opinion can make those with radical beliefs feel isolated and more willing to engage in extreme measures to advance their cause. This process seems to have occurred for the Weather Underground, where frustration with the ongoing Vietnam War and routine mobilization's lack of effect on policy and public opinion drove the group to a campaign of bombings.

The experience of terrorism could have effects similar to war under certain conditions. While general social solidarity increases after terror attacks (see Collins 2004), it can undermine confidence in a government's ability to protect its citizens. After the Madrid train bombings in 2004, the Spanish public punished the ruling People's Party by voting for the opposition socialists in surprising numbers. Research on the voting effects of Kurdish terrorism in

Turkey has also found that the government is blamed after terror attacks and this creates a preference for right-wing parties that are less willing to negotiate (Kibris 2010). In an autocratic system, such disaffection might become the basis for more radical expressions of discontent. Similarly, states who engage in war against their own populations, as in state terrorism, create political opportunities for oppositions. Political violence from below can thus be sparked by the state itself (Della Porta 1995; Goodwin 2006; Shor et al. 2014).

It is also worth noting that revolution can create international war as well as civil war. What are many civil wars if not failed revolutions (see Tilly 1993b)? Not only does revolution create domestic and potentially regional instability, it can increase other states' perceptions of threat that must be dealt with militarily (Walt 1996). Revolution also tends to invite intervention by other powers (Kowalewski 1991), whether in favor or against. This dynamic was part and parcel of the Spanish Civil War, as well as recently in Libya, Bahrain, and Syria. Similarly, terrorism can increase international conflict when other powers use it as an excuse for intervention, as the American invasion of Afghanistan in 2001 and Kenyan and Ethiopian incursions in Somalia over the last decade demonstrate.

Skocpol's other cause of revolution is fiscal and economic strain that affects both state capacity and the propensity for local rebellion. This, too, has been borne out by multiple research studies, reaching as far back as the first generation of revolution theory (e.g., Merriman 1938). Economic strain need not only be caused by war – economic downturns and depressions seem to affect the onset of revolution (Walton 1984). States that have a primarily export-based economy are particularly susceptible – their primary source of revenue is dependent on the world economy and market factors outside of a regime's control (Foran 2005). Autocratic regimes may also become *rentier* states, where the profit from the sale of a particular export is funneled into elite luxury and regime control rather than into more general economic development. Such states, like 1970s Iran dependent on natural energy wealth, are even more vulnerable (Farhi 1990; Skocpol 1982). These economic strain accounts tend to have a class-based perspective on revolutionary conflicts, sometimes explicitly Marxist (e.g., Wolf 1969) and sometimes not (e.g., Foran 2005). For instance, Jeffrey Paige's (1975) classic work *Agrarian Revolution* charts how the relationship of cultivating and non-cultivating classes to agricultural production leads to differing types of revolt. When the agricultural production system ties peasants and their class superiors to the land in a classic Latin American *hacienda* system, a peasant-based revolt will take place but not necessarily lead to national revolution. On the other hand, when peasants are dependent on wages paid for their labor on land owned by the elite, then social revolution is more likely. When the elites tend to receive their income from economic capital, rather than from land, reform is the most likely outcome. Here, we see the classic ideas of Marxist class struggle and the relationship of people to the economic means of production updated to the peasant agricultural systems of the twentieth century.

As discussed in chapter 2, there is little linking economic deprivation and the occurrence of terrorism (see Krueger and Maleckova 2003; Piazza 2006), and recent research has cast doubt that resource dependency breeds armed conflict in general (Magnus Theisen 2008). Similarly, social movement scholars have shown repeatedly that there is no relationship between economic grievances and protest. But movement radicalism may have a relationship to economic conditions. For example, it seems little coincidence that fascism arose in a period of economic crisis in Europe. William Brustein in a series of studies (e.g., Brustein 1988, 1991, 1996) has argued that fascist parties owed their popular support to different groups' calculations of their material interests, particularly when socialism was perceived as an economic threat. Tellingly, the Belgian fascist party received more votes in regions dependent on subsistence agriculture and medium-sized farms, and it was less popular where workers were engaged in the market economy (Brustein 1988). This suggests fascism is a mirror image of Paige's argument about when peasants support social revolution. For neo-fascism, the relationship also seems to hold – the Great Recession of 2008 has given new life to right-wing parties across Europe, including the Right Sector that helped accomplish the 2014 revolution in Ukraine. In another example, Greece's nationalist Golden Dawn party uses extra-institutional tactics of intimidation and violence to further its cause. A wonderful study by Nella van Dyke and Sarah Soule (2002) finds a similar relationship between economic conditions and right-wing Patriot militias in the United States. Patriot militias are a diffuse movement of militant, libertarian resistance to government. Timothy McVeigh, who bombed the Oklahoma City Federal Building in 1995, had connections to this movement. The movement remains active. After Obama's election in 2008, the US government noted the increase in threats of violence from the right wing. Van Dyke and Soule find that the variation in the number of militia organizations in an area is related to economic restructuring: they are most popular where manufacturing jobs and family farms have declined. It is an open question if American left-wing movements are similarly affected, whether positively or negatively, by economic conditions and modes of economic production. While all protest may not be based in economic conditions, it appears that at least some radicalism is.

In addition to the pressures of war and economic fortunes, it is possible to imagine other pressures that can generate state breakdown. States with weak administrative capacities, for instance, may have trouble controlling their hinterlands, particularly when these are relatively inaccessible mountains or jungles (see Fearon and Laitin 2003; Kittikhoun 2009; Li 2002). Or failed states with almost no bureaucratic structures may become safe harbors for militant organizations, like Afghanistan did for Al-Qaeda, and Somalia has for al-Shabab (see Coggins forthcoming). Another prominent argument about the roots of both revolution and terrorism is demographic pressure. As mentioned in chapter 2, youth bulges, where a large proportion of the population is young, can challenge states' ability to provide gainful economic opportunities or a share in the spoils of a regime's autocratic rule. In response, state breakdown may result (Goldstone 1991b) or groups may turn to terrorism (Ehrlich and Liu 2002). While recent work has cast doubt on a demographic theory of instability and conflict

(Fearon and Laitin 2003; Goldstone et al. 2010), Henrik Urdal (2006) argues that this is because of improper measurement. Rather than there being a threshold for the size of a dangerous youth bulge, for instance 20 percent, it is an effect that increases with the size of the bulge. The truth of this line of argument, or if it is capturing something else like the biographical availability of the young, remains to be established. But in any case the logic remains similar to Skocpol's state-centered theory of revolution – radicalism can be the result of strains on states rather than of the actions of movements.

But not all states may be equally affected by war, changing economic structures, geography, or demographic pressures. Some types of regimes are more susceptible to radicalism, revolution, or terrorism, no matter what other structural conditions there are. I discuss this in detail in the next section.

Regime type and radicalism

Prior to Theda Skocpol's advancement of state breakdown theory, regime type was often considered as a consequence of revolution rather than a cause. Most famously, Barrington Moore (1969) posited three revolutionary paths for states into the modern era – bourgeois revolution leading to democracy, revolutions from above leading to fascism, and peasant revolutions leading to communism. While economic systems and peasantry's revolutionary potential are key factors, Moore rests his argument on the strength of the bourgeoisie class (Skocpol 1973). A strong bourgeoisie – in Marxist terms, a wealthy, capitalist, market-oriented ownership class – sets the tone for political formation. In short, "No bourgeoisie, no democracy" (Moore 1969: 418). Skocpol's argument that revolution's occurrence was due to the combination of economic production and political structure in agrarian bureaucracies also focused attention on regime type as a causal condition of revolution. Since Skocpol, social scientists of revolution have also focused on other regime types and their susceptibility to revolution. This has created one of the most robust findings in the field:

autocratic, personalist regimes that exclude large segments of society from the political system are more likely to fall apart when faced with oppositional challenges.

There are two key factors in this finding. First, an exclusionary regime, by the very nature of exclusion, means that the government does not allow all constituencies to participate in politics. Not only does this potentially politicize grievances (Goodwin 2001), it creates a potential resource and participant base for a revolutionary movement. Further, under conditions of exclusion, it is also more likely that there are marginal elites who do not share in the benefits of power, whether landowners, business classes, intellectuals, or others (Goodwin and Skocpol 1989). When contention erupts, this increases the possibility of revolutionary coalition formation (Foran 2005; Goldstone 1991b). As we saw in the last chapter, successful revolutions are often made by broad coalitions that bring together different segments of society. Second, personalist regimes have a relatively narrow base for their power. Social scientists refer to this as a neo-patrimonial structure. Patrimonialism is rule based not on law or institutions, but on the flow of power from a central ruler, like in a feudal system. While this can be based on traditional sources of legitimacy, e.g., religion, patrimonial regimes often secure their power through the distribution of resources to the loyal (Skocpol 1982). Thus, support for the regime is based on what the regime provides. As we saw above, such a state is especially susceptible to external strains, for instance falling revenue. Further, a narrow power base is often reinforced by coercion. Thus, when defection occurs, particularly by members of security services, repression's force is more easily diminished. This also creates the possibility of territorial fragmentation, as local elites seek autonomy from a central state (see Derluguian 2005).

Such regimes are especially brittle and more likely to fall in revolutionary crises. We see this pattern in quite a few modern and historical cases: the old monarchies of feudal Europe and Asia collapsed under revolutionary demands; personalist dictators like Batista in Cuba, Pahlavi in Iran, Marcos in the Philippines, and Qaddafi in Libya were unable to maintain loyalty when faced with insurrection; and exclusionary political systems like the Eastern European communist states and the Arab autocracies proved susceptible to elite defection. Further, attempts at reform by brittle regimes can also lead to their collapse. A plausible interpretation of the collapse of communism is that it was a product of a failed revolution from above – Gorbachev's *perestroika*. This suggests two key parts of a minimal formula of revolution; protest is more likely to turn into revolution when a personalist, exclusionary regime is faced with sustained mobilization by a broad coalition.

Other regime types may lead to different outcomes. A notable pattern in the Arab Spring was the successful persistence of the Arab monarchies. Saudi Arabia, Bahrain, Kuwait, Jordan, Oman, and Morocco each saw some protest but only in Bahrain did this become sharp enough to be considered a revolutionary situation. One possible reason might be that the oil wealth of the Gulf monarchies allowed them to make economic concessions and buy off potential protestors (Goldstone 2013). But this would not explain why Jordan and Morocco were able to withstand mobilization. Some have pointed to their foreign sponsors in the United States and France respectively (e.g., Lynch 2013), but the limited amount of material aid these provide makes this conclusion less probable. Rather, it seems that monarchy, in the modern world, might provide a source of legitimation. While this may be due to the religious system that legitimates their rule, political scientists have posited that Arab monarchies are durable because of the role of ruling families (Herb 1999) or their ability to form modern states (Anderson 1991). From the perspective of this book, we need not go down these paths to explain resilience. Arab monarchies are basically tribal structures, where the ruling class is not based on personalist connection as much as on a traditional social segment. This means that a regime's power base is relatively broad, and thus does not have the brittleness associated with other exclusionary regimes. Even more important was the strategy that the Arab monarchies used to face protest in 2011 – each relied primarily on concession rather than repression alone (except for Bahrain which almost did have a revolution), in contrast to Ben Ali in Tunisia, Mubarak in Egypt, Qaddafi in Libya, and Assad in Syria (Beck

2014). As I discuss in chapter 6, repression can actually motivate contention and radicalism rather than suppress it. In short, we might conclude that exclusion is not enough; it must be combined with personalism to make an authoritarian state especially brittle.

Regime-type arguments also occur in the study of terrorism. Robert Pape (2003, 2005; Pape and Feldman 2010), especially, in his series of studies of the prevalence of suicide terrorism, argues that democracies who engage in foreign military ventures are more susceptible to terrorism. First, military occupation, such as Israel in the Palestinian territories or the United States in Iraq, encourages the use of terrorism against the occupier. Second, democracies are more likely to be influenced by civilian casualties, which makes terrorism a rational strategy to pursue. But other studies have cast doubt on a link between international terrorism and democracy, arguing that the correlation is actually due to institutional configurations and state actions rather than regime type (Findley and Young 2011; Li 2005; Savun and Phillips 2009). Also, most terrorism is actually domestic in nature, carried out by citizens of one country against their fellows (Enders, Sandler, and Gaibulloev 2011), and suicide terrorism is less likely to occur in separatist conflicts (Collard-Wexler, Pischedda, and Smith 2014). Crucially, a different pattern emerges when regime type is specified more narrowly than as just being democratic or not. Erica Chenoweth (2013) shows that partial democracies are, in fact, more likely to experience terrorism while full democracies and autocracies are not. While there are many possible explanations for this (see Chenoweth 2013), including the possibility of underreporting of terrorism by autocracies (Drakos and Gofas 2006), we can also link it to a sociological observation about the nature of terrorism. Jeff Goodwin (2006) argues that conflict can involve categorization of civilians as complicit with the state, and thus fair game for terrorism, or not. He argues that such categorical terrorism is more likely when an organization sees the state as a perpetrator of extensive violence, and less likely when the population is seen as a potential source of support. This suggests that the terrorism and regime-type link may be caused by dynamics of popular support (Stanton 2013), state reactions to radicalism, or prior social cleavages in society (see also Piazza 2006). In any case, it remains an open question as to what exactly is the link between terrorism and democracy and the mechanisms that explain any correlation.

On the other hand, a link between democracy and radicalism might be drawn in a more straightforward manner. As conceived in this book, radicalism often occurs as part of social movements, and social movements are a common feature of modern democracies (Goldstone 2004). We might thus see radicalism as a consequence of movement-level processes that are more likely to occur where movements occurs – in democracies. Alternatively, we might expect radicalism to be the product of a lack of openness to a movement's claims: a negative political opportunity structure. But this need not be limited to a particular sort of regime. Della Porta (1995) argues that the reason German and Italian leftists turned towards radicalism was because democratic governments did not accommodate their claims. A similar process seemed to have operated for SDS and the Weather Underground in the United States. From this view, radicalism is one aspect of the cacophony of political contention encouraged by democratic political structures. We might also observe that democracies are less likely to experience large-scale revolutionary movements, due to their inclusive nature. Thus, movement radicalism, which might become revolution under other political structures, remains unable to garner enough support to transform into another type of movement. This is one aspect of Lipset's argument for why socialism never succeeded in the United States (see Lipset and Marks 2001). Given the lack of research on radicalism, these observations are speculative rather than definitive.

Overall, it does appear that there are correlations between regime types and types of political contention. Drawing on the robust insights from the revolutions literature, we might characterize regimes along two dimensions: the relative political openness of their political structures (political opportunities) and the relative breadth of their power base (exclusion). This is represented graphically in Figure 4.1 (with apologies to Charles Tilly), where regime types are arrayed on the two axes. We can

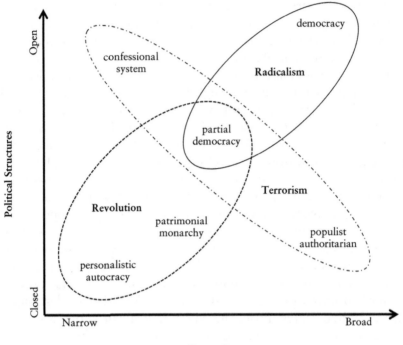

Figure 4.1 Regimes and propensity for contention type

then place radicalism, revolution, and terrorism on the axes, represented by the oval areas. From prior research, we would expect revolutions to be most likely when political structures are relatively closed and regimes have narrower bases of power and legitimacy. Terrorism should be most common where structures are relatively more open to influence but the regime does not incorporate all social segments, or its mirror image – wider power bases but few avenues for political expression. Finally, movement radicalism might be most frequent when a larger social movement sector exists, and thus be a by-product of democratic civil society. While this sketch is stylized and ideal-typical, it does suggest a way of organizing the findings about how regime type matters for contention.

The role of civil society and media

Regimes and states are not the only actors that radical movements interact with. Even in authoritarian societies, there are professional associations, trade unions, religious organizations, news media and other non-state actors that take on political roles. This constellation is what social scientists refer to as "civil society." Drawing on Alexis de Tocqueville's (1835) observation that early American political life worked in the absence of a strong central government because of associations, scholars have seen civil society as an intrinsic part of a functioning democracy (see Putnam 2001). But there is a darker side to civil society as well. As we saw in the previous chapter when discussing revolutionary coalitions, civil society can be a resource for creating oppositional challenges to the state (Chang 2008; Harris 2012; Kadivar 2013; Osa 2003). Tellingly, in the Egyptian Revolution of 2011, initial protests came out of civil society organizations like the April 6th Youth Movement and religious organizations like the Muslim Brothers provided much of the participant and resource base that helped make the revolution successful.

Civil society also provides a place for non-democratic movements to organize. Sheri Berman (1997) argues that the Nazi party in Germany used its associational membership to attract supporters and begin its rise to power. Similarly, the strong associational infrastructure of northern Italy seemed to provide a basis for Mussolini's fascists (Riley 2010). In these cases, a relatively strong civil society was combined with weak political institutions. This created the space for radical groups to mobilize and seize the political opportunity that the fragility of the state presented. Similarly, bifurcated terrorist organizations thrive due to their work as civil society actors – here, they replace the functions of the state and build up a separate power base. Radicals can also spring out of civil society. The radicalization of traditional social movements, like the anti-war or environmental movements into the Weather Underground and the ELF, shows that the dark side of associations can occur even in robust political systems.

One civil society actor deserves special attention – the news media. Terrorism experts have long noted that terrorism and media are intertwined (Hoffman 1998). If one aspect of terrorism is its performative nature (Juergensmeyer 2001), drawing an audience's attention to an act and demonstrating a group's commitment to a cause, then the media plays a key role in transmitting this performance. Radical groups seek this attention purposely by claiming their attacks. For instance, every significant ELF action was accompanied by a communiqué explaining the logic. The Weather Underground used the news media to draw the connection between their target and a diffuse set of leftist goals – retaliation for prison killings, government and private-sector involvement in Vietnam, and repression of workers and nationalist causes around the world. More recently, the Islamic State has used the spectacle of beheading hostages to demonstrate its resolve. Media attention to violence, by itself, can also help create further violence. Ruud Koopmans and Susan Olzak (2004) examine right-wing, often anti-immigrant, violence in modern Germany. They find that the visibility of an episode of violence makes further violence more likely, particularly when the media feature public reactions by a third actor, whether in support or condemnation. They suggest that media coverage thus presents a different type of political opportunity, termed "discursive opportunities," that allows radical groups to mobilize.

But media coverage does more than just publicize a group and its cause. It also creates an image of the radical, revolutionary, or terrorist in the popular mind. In an influential study of this process, Annamarie Oliverio (1998) analyzes two incidents of terrorism, the hijacking of the cruise ship *Achille Lauro* by the PFLP in 1985 and the hijacking of TWA flight 847 by Hezbollah and Islamic Jihad. She argues that in both cases the United States government successfully influenced the media to portray the hijackers as evil and delegitimate their cause. These events are thus remembered as terrorism rather than as part of national liberation struggles. Similarly, in the wake of September 11th, American media were influenced by civil society groups that sought to portray Islam as a fanatical religion and all Muslims as potential radicals (Bail 2012).

Conversely, media images can be a boon for radicals. Todd Gitlin (1980) charts how the media constructed an image of Weather Underground activists as romantic outlaws, like the popular movie *Bonnie and Clyde*, and helped create support among the left for their actions. He argues that the media destroyed the promise of the New Left movements by indirectly encouraging their radicalization. In some ways, we thus might say that all media coverage of terrorism is about constructing or supporting moral boundaries (Ben-Yehuda 2005). Terrorists seek to justify their actions as legitimate and appropriate, while their opponents seek to paint them in a negative light and delegitimate their broader goals. In short, not all publicity is good publicity – it depends heavily on the image being transmitted.

Recently, a different type of media has received much attention – social media. The Arab Spring was not the first episode of contention where internet, text messaging, and new media played a significant role. A series of protests in Moldova following a disputed 2009 election has been called the Twitter Revolution. But the Tunisian and Egyptian revolutions brought more attention to the potential of social media as a mobilizing resource. Activists used Facebook, Twitter, and text messaging to organize their protests, direct resources and participants, and broadcast their solidarity. Traditional media also played a significant role, with images of revolution being broadcast by Al-Jazeera and TV news organizations. Regimes and opponents across the region jostled to construct their images and outmaneuver each other discursively – for instance, Mubarak using state television, and protestors using the internet and foreign news services (see Alexander 2011).

In a repressive setting, the relative lack of controls on internet communication can be a powerful tool for radicals, creating a virtual space to organize similar to the actual spaces provided by civil society groups and religious institutions. Yet we should not overstate the internet's potential or effect. First, social media also provide a place for governments to monitor challengers; authorities in Belarus, for example, have used Facebook groups to identify, harass, and imprison their opponents. Second, internet ways of organizing provide only a complement to traditional methods of mobilization. The largest day of protests in the Egyptian Revolution, January 28, occurred after the Mubarak regime shut down internet and mobile phone services in the country. Here, the support of organizations like the Muslim Brothers, as well as local neighborhood networks, proved crucial. Third, there is nothing new about the effect of social media. In earlier eras, innovation in media and communication has always provided a mobilizing resource for radicals. Martin Luther used the printing press to distribute his grievances against the Catholic Church, Thomas Paine and other writers used pamphlets to create popular support for the American Revolution, and the Zapatistas in Chiapas, Mexico were known for their use of the fax machine and satellite phone to distribute their message. Rather than the specific media platform, the effect on mobilization might come from its relative novelty. Innovative tools are more effective because regimes do not yet know how to counter them, an issue discussed in more detail in chapter 6.

In short, civil society can provide a mobilizing resource for radicals. This can be actual organizing space and group alliances or it can be the virtual space created by communication technologies and media images. There is not a neat line of cause and effect here – civil society can support regimes or radicals and media images can help governments or revolutionaries. But the role of civil society does suggest a possible modification to regime-type arguments – it may be the combination of political structures and civil society that influences radicalism, just as they did in the case of the fascists' rise to power.

Global and historical contexts of radicalism

State-centered theories of revolution are attractive for their simplicity – all that matters for understanding radical mobilization is knowing the strains placed on regimes. Jeff Goodwin (2001) passionately defends state-centered theory for this reason, even if his loosely constructed and thinly detailed case comparisons are not quite convincing. But few states govern islands. Rather, states and societies exist in a web of international relationships and a specific historical context. Thus, the most macro-level environment – the global-temporal – is also crucial for understanding why and when revolutions, radicalism, and terrorism occur.

We saw this dimension in the previous discussion of strains on states. Skocpol's (1979) original state breakdown account placed emphasis on the cause of fiscal strain from international geopolitical competition and Michael Mann (2013) points to the destruction of states in war as a cause of revolution. Both are clearly international relationships. National economies, too, are set within international economic relationships of trade and investment. Thus, declining revenues are affected by the international price for exports (Skocpol 1982) and global economic downturns are a source of structural strain (Foran 2005). The general economic development of a country and its effects on revolution is also a result of global factors. Countries can have a dependent economy, in which the resources and wealth of an undeveloped country flow to developed states (Paige 1975; Walton 1984). Terry Boswell and Marc Dixon (1990, 1993) examine development and dependency in a Marxist fashion and find that internationally linked class exploitation increases the chances of political rebellion.

Much of the work on global economic factors is set in world systems theory. World systems analysis, originally proposed by Immanuel Wallerstein (1974), posits that the international community is structured by its economic relationships. Like Marx's concept of class struggle, countries either have an industrialized, manufacturing-based economy (core nations) or an agricultural, resource-based economy (peripheral nations). Core nations thus exploit the periphery as peripheral countries produce the raw materials needed for manufacturing and then provide markets for manufactured goods at a substantial markup. Over time, a certain core country will accumulate enough economic and military power to impose its hegemony on other nations, determining international relationships of war and peace. But economy and hegemony are both cyclical, and can rise and fall (Hopkins and Wallerstein 1979). Thus, some scholars have posited that revolution is more likely at times of hegemonic decline; declining military and economic power reduces support for peripheral, client states and creates a political opportunity for revolt (Foran 2005). As I discuss in more detail in chapter 7, waves of radical movements may also be more likely at different points in this cycle (see Arrighi, Hopkins, and Wallerstein 1989). International terrorism, too, might occur as part of hegemonic cycles, being the "canary in the coal mine" that encourages a hegemonic state to rely on military force, overextend itself financially, and thus decline (Bergesen and Lizardo 2004). This metaphor seems particularly apt when we consider the American response to September 11th – intervention and occupation in Iraq and Afghanistan that has led to unsustainable spending in the face of global economic recession (see Johnson 2001; Mann 2005; Wallerstein 2003).

But hegemony and economy are not the only set of international relationships. Culture is a flip side to political-economic structure, and scholars have seen it as a promising key to understanding revolution for more than two decades (see Foran 1993; Goldstone 2001; Sewell 1985). Most cultural accounts of revolution are micro or meso, focusing on the construction of meaning during revolutionary events (Moaddel 1992; Sewell 1996) or on how movements strategically employ cultural meanings to mobilize (Snow et al. 1986). These perspectives are covered in more detail in the next chapter. At the macro-level of analysis, states exist in a larger cultural environment that affects what form they take, their policies, and actions. In sociology, the research tradition called world society theory, or world polity theory, stresses this dynamic the most. World society scholars argue that a global civil society exists and contains ideas about the proper form of politics (see Meyer 2010; Meyer, Boli, et al. 1997; Schofer et al. 2012). These ideas legitimate some forms of governance rather than others. Thus, states mimic each other and adopt similar institutional structures, for instance, setting up mass education systems and environmental ministries whether or not they actually educate children or protect the environment (Boli, Ramirez, and Meyer 1985; Meyer, Frank, et al. 1997), signing human rights treaties even when they consistently violate the rights of their own citizens (Cole 2005; Hafner-Burton and Tsutsui 2005), and amending their constitutions to reflect one another, no matter their actual practice of government (Beck, Drori, and Meyer 2012). The effect of regime types on radicalism, revolution, and terrorism may thus be dependent on global constructs. In the contemporary period, democracy is considered the most legitimate form and so non-democratic states, particularly personalistic ones, face more challenges. Other instances of radicalism may also draw on large cultural constructs; Nazism found a home in Germany because of its cultural resonance (Sewell 1985; Skocpol 1985).

World society also determines who is a legitimate political actor. In the modern era, cultural legitimacy is given to individuals and they are encouraged to act in the social and political realm (Meyer and Jepperson 2000). We thus see more social movements as a consequence of the growth in world society and a country's membership of it (Tsutsui and Wotipka 2004). In my own research, I thus find that world culture is a primary cause of revolutionary waves (Beck 2011), described in more detail in chapter 7. We can also see world cultural effects on terrorism and radicalism. The members of the ELF took it upon themselves to act in defense of the whole planet. This should not be dismissed as narcissism but seen as a belief in their own individual role and agency as activists. Scholars of Islamic radicalism have often noted that the term fundamentalist seems misplaced (Hellmich 2005, 2014; Roy 2004) – there is nothing fundamental about their religious philosophy. Rather, Islamists engage in modern reinterpretations of religious practices and cobble together their ideology, even though they do not have the traditional qualifications to do so. Recall that Osama bin Laden issued a fatwa against the United States even though he was not a religious authority. Modern beliefs in the capabilities and legitimacy of individual action can have radical effects.

But cultural ideas, like economic relationships and hegemonic power, change. We should thus expect to see "era effects" – certain types of collective action will predominate at different times. Historical studies of revolution have borne this out. Charles Tilly (1993b) in his survey of 500 years of European revolutions discovered such a trend – revolts moved from localized, often religious conflicts and civil wars into large-scale social revolutions. Here, revolution was dependent on state form, which shifted from territorial empires and monarchies to modern nation-states. Ho-Fung Hung (2011) charts a similar dynamic in early modern China. Protest would be directed against either the state or local officials, depending on the legitimacy of the imperial Chinese center. Such effects can go both ways. The wave of early twentieth-century constitutional revolutions precipitated a change in the cultural model of revolution (Sohrabi 1995). Formerly, the model of the French Revolution, a constitutional republic of citizens, loomed large in these reformers' consciousness but the model's general failure helped create the space for a new template of revolution created by the socialist, class-based Russian Revolution of 1917 (see also Mann 2012). The forms of terrorism also change over time. In the mid-twentieth century, most international terrorism was leftist in nature, and in more recent decades most was Islamic (Robison, Crenshaw, and Jenkins 2006). The essential change was the end of the Cold War – leftist violence became less relevant and more religious. We can see a similar dynamic in movement radicalism. The radicals of the 1960s seemed to emanate from the political left – Weather Underground, Black Panthers, and Italian Red Brigades – while the most active radicals of today seem to be from the political right – Patriot militias and neo-fascists in Europe. Such clustering in time suggests effects on revolution, terrorism, and radicalism that are larger than the dynamics of any one society.

In short, the global environment affects the national context of radicalism. This can occur through material economic relationships, political and military power dynamics, or cultural constructions of politics and collective action. Unless we understand how these conditions structure political opportunities, our explanations of radicalism are ahistorical.

Summary

This chapter has focused on the macro-level of analysis, charting how environments might affect radicals, revolutionaries, and terrorists. Here, much of the dynamics are structural: war, economic cycles, regime type, civil society, the international system, and era each have important effects on conflict. While some of these can be considered under the rubric of political opportunity, radical movements are affected by larger structures before their formation, during their mobilization, and in their aftermath. This complements the dynamics of individual agency and movement organization that were charted in the previous two chapters.

In the first part of this book, I have drawn a general overview of what is known about radicalism. The careful reader will have no doubt noticed that each of the last three chapters primarily draws on research from one of the fields under consideration. This is because much of the research in each field has focused on a particular level of analysis. Terrorism studies has often been micro in focus, considering why individuals turn to terrorism, how groups radicalize, and from where they draw their social support. Social movements research has placed more primacy on the meso-level of organizations, focusing on mobilization dynamics, resource dilemmas, and cross-movement relationships. The study of revolution has preferred macro-structural accounts of its causes, considering political economy, regimes and states, and historical processes. Of course, this is stylized; as we have seen, terrorism research has also considered organizations and environments, revolution scholars have provided movement and micro-process theories, and social movements studies relate contention to individual participation and larger political opportunities. But it is a useful way to think about the Venn diagram proposed in chapter 1 – each of these fields has a part of the story and provides different ways of thinking about and analyzing what is really a conjoint phenomenon.

The second part of this book takes on three specific issues that are often in the backdrop of research on radicalism. The goal here is to help make the implicit explicit and show how research from all of the traditions can be synthesized to provide a fuller understanding of key dynamics of the known unknowns. The next chapter takes on the issue of ideology, exploring to what extent beliefs and ideas factor into radical movements. Chapter 6 then explores the life cycles of radical groups and the interplay of tactics and state responses. Last, chapter 7 considers how radicalism spreads, as well as the repeated occurrence of waves of contention in the contemporary and historic world. In some ways, these can be thought of as a series of essays on radicalism that draw on the overview provided by the first four chapters.

Part II

The Known Unknowns

5

Is Radicalism about Ideas and Ideology?

In 1847, a small political party, the Communist League, assigned a scion of a wealthy English-German business family, Friedrich Engels, to draw up a statement of the party's political platform. Engels originally drafted a catechism – answers to twenty-five questions ranging from "What is communism?" to "What will be the course of this revolution?" Engels found the first draft lacking and so enlisted a friend and fellow party member who had been working as a political journalist to rewrite the statement. Karl Marx used the opportunity to summarize his new theory of history, where society was split into competing classes, differentiated by their ownership of economic production and control of material resources. The resulting pamphlet is one of the most famous in history – *The Manifesto of the Communist Party* (1848). The Manifesto might have remained in obscurity except its publication in February 1848 occurred in the same month that a general uprising in France deposed the July monarchy and inspired a wave of revolutions across Europe. In the wake of 1848, European governments blamed the revolutions on communists and Karl Marx fled into exile in London. Communism subsequently became a basis for revolutionary parties throughout Europe. Fifty years later, a group headed by Vladimir Lenin sought to limit membership in the Russian Communist Party to those most committed to revolution. Lenin had adapted Marx's theory of proletariat revolution caused by industrialization to the non-industrial Russian context by arguing for a revolutionary vanguard to lead the way. The party split into Bolshevik and Menshevik factions. The Bolsheviks would ultimately help overthrow the Tsarist monarchy of Russia in 1917 and win the resulting civil war, establishing the world's first communist state. Beginning in the 1920s, Chinese communists further adapted Marxist ideology to their situation, arguing that in the absence of industrial workers the peasants could be a revolutionary class. The resulting doctrine, Maoism, was in direct contradiction to Marx's own theories of class struggle but proved its worth when the communists seized state power in the wake of World War II. Marxism and Maoism were powerful tools for insurgent groups, particularly nationalists fighting for independence in the colonies of European empires, such as Algeria and Mozambique. With the establishment of new communist states and splits between others, new variants of Marxism proliferated – Trotskyism, named for the exiled Russian revolutionary Leon Trotsky, Hoxhaism, named for Albania's Enver Hoxha, and so on. Even today, insurgent and terrorist groups, such as the Kurdistan Worker's Party (PKK) in Turkey, base their ideology on Marxism.

The history of Marxism shows us that there is rarely a straight line between ideology and action. According to Engels, Marx himself famously claimed not to identify as a Marxist, though it is unclear what exactly he meant. Even though formally laid out, Marxism was continually re-theorized by its believers and shaped by the circumstances in which movements found themselves. If it were not, unindustrialized Russia or peasant China could never have experienced a Marxist revolution. Thus, most social scientists reject a view of ideology as programmatic. Ideologies are not adopted wholesale by blind believers, nor do they provide authoritative commands for action. Rather, ideology is incoherent, adopted piecemeal, adapted to the larger social context, and continually recreated. Social scientists have thus struggled to agree upon a definition of ideology. For instance, Hamilton (1987) identifies twenty-seven different common conceptions of the term.

Yet the spread of Marxism also suggests the power of ideology. Radical movements need to have beliefs, for without them they could hardly be named radical. Ideology may even be the very root of all collective action (Oliver and Johnston 2000; Zald 2000). Its incoherence thus creates a problem to be studied rather than a rejection of its causal power. There are two primary ways that scholars approach the problem of ideology. The first emphasizes the process of ideology – as a way in which meaning is made, identities are created, and beliefs are performed. Here, ideology connects beliefs to collective action. The second approach emphasizes how ideology can be a bridge between cultural and structural perspectives on movements, focusing on rhetorical strategies, frames, and the broad cultural contexts of mobilization. Each of these approaches recommends different ways of studying the problem. Further, we see conceptions of ideology in two ongoing scholarly debates – the continued exploration of religious terrorism and work on the aftermaths of revolution and the building of new states. In this chapter, I detail each of these in turn.

Culture and action in radicalism

Sociologists make a distinction between beliefs and ideology that is often overlooked in debates over the power of ideas. Beliefs are ideas that individuals hold, which need not be connected to one another. For example, I could believe that central government is bad. And I could also believe that I have a right to own guns. Without a bridge between them, these are just ideas that I have alongside a number of others, for instance, the idea to paint my house this weekend or the belief that football is the quintessential American sport. Beliefs become ideologies when I begin to connect them. So I might take my beliefs about governments and guns, and bridge them with the idea that I need to stockpile guns in case I need to resist the central government. This bridging makes for the basis of an ideology. The systematic connection of beliefs in an ideology does an important thing. It creates a greater potential for my ideas to be shared by others. Because of its system, an ideology has the potential to incorporate many beliefs, relating them to its core content. Thus, an ideology of armed libertarianism could suggest that I paint my house in a camouflage pattern to avoid detection by the government and that any attempts to regulate football and prevent injuries is government meddling in the American way of life. With the bridge, ideology has become portable and adoptable by others who have different ideas.

The bridging of beliefs to create ideologies by itself does not answer two crucial questions. First, what is the relationship of culture to ideology? And how are these translated from the world of ideas to practical action? The most influential statement on the relation between culture and ideology comes from Ann Swidler (1986). A century of anthropology and sociology basically views culture as sets of beliefs, symbols, meanings, and practices that are transmissible across generations. Swidler argues that culture is relatively incoherent and inconsistent, lacking the systematization found in ideology. As such, it has only a weak effect on action. Culture thus provides a "tool kit" of habits and skills that individuals use to construct their strategies of action by using tradition and common sense. On the other hand, ideology is relatively coherent, consistent, and has a strong influence on action as it provides a whole system bundled with ways of acting. Swidler proposes that, most of the time, society is relatively settled and thus actors primarily use the tool kit of culture. But in unsettled times, when societies change rapidly or there is greater uncertainty, actors rely on ideology with its new strategies of action.

This has obvious implications for radicalism. As we saw in chapter 4, radicalism often occurs during periods of social change. Here, following Swidler, we could argue that tradition breaks down and common sense is less effective. So actors rely on ideology as a guide. For example, the ideology of Marxism provided a way for people to make sense of industrialization and of changes in social structure and pointed the way towards radical class-based mobilization. The ideology of fascism helped make sense of the economic and political chaos caused by World War I, and charted a path towards stability and geopolitical power through nationalism and racism. The potential appeal of radical ideologies thus might be due to how well they seem to address unsettled times. Their longer-term survival, according to Swidler, is a product of how well they compete with alternate ideologies and the structural opportunities they have for persistence, for instance, finding an organizational home in radical parties that are able to take state power, as in 1917 Russia or in 1922 Italy. Movements, from this perspective, might be nothing more than "ideologically structured action" (Zald 2000).

Another approach to dealing with the link between culture and action discounts ideology. As described earlier, new social movements scholars argue that modern movements are primarily about the creation and maintenance of identities. Here, ideology and beliefs are less important, and social solidarity among participants is more important. Action itself is thus meaning making and the basis of culture. While explicit new social movements research has faded, this view of culture has become quite popular in studies of collective action (e.g., Jasper 1997; Johnston 2014; Polletta 1998). Even early structuralists like Charles Tilly have written about contention as a type of performance (see Tilly 2008). For radicalism, this view suggests that we should look less at ideological platforms and more at how identity relates to mobilization (see the discussion in chapter 2). Abrahms (2008) argues that terrorism in general is actually more about identity than ideology, noting that most of the rank and file of terrorist groups do not fully understand the leadership's political claims. And, we could consider Al-Qaeda a new social movement that tries to establish an Islamic identity and engage in action to promote it (Sutton and Vertigans 2006).

If action is meaning making, then we should expect a variety of meanings to be made by participants in a radical movement. This has been argued to be a central dynamic of revolutions (see Selbin 2010). Revolution provides a liminal space, which means that participants are in between cultural models, and thus meaning is created by the event itself. William Sewell (1996) argues that such a process occurred during the storming of the Bastille during the French Revolution. What began as a mob action intended to free prisoners and seize gunpowder ended up being a revolutionary event when participants understood their actions as such. Similarly, the Cultural Revolution in China provided a liminal space for young members of the Red Guards and shaped their identity and Chinese politics throughout the course of the participants' lives

(Yang 2000). Some sociologists thus point to the concept of discourse, which is a process by which ideas are transformed into ideologies through meaning making (often revealed by language), as the place where culture and action meet (see Wuthnow 1989). Hank Johnston (2008) has argued that contention has a "deep grammar" rooted in cultural practices that strongly guides action. Actors have a collective identity (a subject), engage in collective action (a verb), and target others (an object) (Johnston and Alimi 2013). How this grammar is articulated then constrains or enables different types of actions and ideologies at different times. Note that this has a similar logic to Bergesen's (2007) three-step model of terrorism. Also, discourse and language may create revolutionary ideology that challenges a regime in its current form. Mansoor Moaddel (1992) argues that this was a primary dynamic of the Iranian Revolution of 1979. Shiite Islam became the predominant ideology of the opposition through a discursive process and led to the outcome of an Islamic state, rather than some other form. But revolutions can include multiple meanings, as suggested by the liminal view, and potentially multiple ideologies. Thus, the primary ideological battle might not be with the state but within the revolutionary coalition itself. Ideology is formed as one faction triumphs over another (Burns 1996; Goldstone 1991a).

If we wanted to apply this to the study of militant Islam, we might consider how Islamists tried to create meaning during a period of rapid social change in the Middle East. This ideology was only one of several competing systems, such as Pan-Arabism, Baathism, Marxism, or nationalism. Their solution was not the adoption of a western philosophy but the revitalization of their cultural traditions. Our analysis would thus focus on how religious discourse was used and the factors that allowed Islamist groups to succeed over others in particular conflicts.

These different views on ideology and mobilization all hinge on the linkage between culture and action. For some, ideology provides this link by informing the strategies and course of action. For others, action affects culture through identity and meaning making, and thus ideology is only a by-product. But there is another way to approach the problem. Instead of trying to understand how culture is linked to action, we can try to understand how culture is linked to social structure.

Culture and structure in radicalism

The other primary approach to understanding ideology is to try to consider it as a link between cultural and structural causes of movements. This has taken two forms. The first rejects the notion of ideology and argues that meaning in movements is all about strategy. The second regards ideology as a form of structure itself.

The framing perspective on mobilization, introduced briefly in chapter 1, argues that ideology is irrelevant to movements. Rather, what we perceive as ideology is in fact the deployment of rhetorical strategy. First introduced by David Snow and his collaborators, framing theory draws on the work of Erving Goffman (1974) about how individuals interpret daily life. Snow proposes that social movements engage in "frame alignment processes" where the interpretations of individuals and organizations are linked (Snow et al. 1986). In the original formulation, there are four key frame alignment processes. First, frame bridging occurs when two interpretations are linked to one another. For example, a peace organization can draw attention to itself by reaching out to groups focused on liberal causes. Here, the bridge is made between liberalism in general and peace in particular. Second, frame amplification occurs when interpretations are clarified and invigorated by using values and beliefs. For example, neighborhood activism against a homeless shelter clarifies its position as protecting families, a value, against dangerous transients, a belief. Next, frame extension occurs when things that are important to potential supporters but not part of the original movement's claims are incorporated. For instance, peace movement organizations have broadened their appeal by extending their goals beyond disarmament and anti-war activities, incorporating anti-racism, sexism, and other social justice goals. Finally, frame transformations are wholesale re-creations of an interpretation. For instance, historic preservation activists may begin with anti-development ideas and transform these into the value of architecture and history itself and, more recently, into sustainability in building practices. When transformation is particularly successful, the frame can transcend its original domain and become a "master frame" that many movements can use (Snow and Benford 1988).

It is easy to imagine applying framing to a particular movement. Take, for example, militant Islamism, as Snow and Byrd (2007) have done. Rather than focusing on its incoherent ideology, we could analyze how the interpretations of the movement identify and propose to solve problems, such as American forces being stationed in Saudi Arabia. Bin Laden and Al-Qaeda amplified their frame by claiming this as a breach of Islamic values. They thus tried to bridge their cause to the beliefs of Muslims everywhere. Al-Qaeda further extended this frame to include western influence in any Muslim country as a violation – gaining adherents among Islamic movements in Afghanistan, Somalia, and Egypt. As the interpretation became established, Islamism became a powerful frame for all sorts of militant organizations to adopt, leading to the appearance of a global Al-Qaeda with numerous affiliates around the world. This analysis would sidestep the problem of ideology and action, and focus on the effects of strategy – when effective, it creates powerful rhetorical resources for radicals to use. Frame analysis is thus one of the core tools that social movements scholars have that link the structural forms of organizations to their rhetoric and goals (see Benford and Snow 2000; Gamson 1992).

The second approach to the ideology–structure problem is to focus on culture itself as a type of social structure. Meaning making here plays little part. Rather, actors might perform cultural and ideological meanings without remaking them. Jeffrey Alexander proposes a "strong" cultural paradigm, arguing that collective action is governed by dynamics of performance and counter-performance. Embedded in cultural discourse, Alexander argues, are dialectical oppositions of beliefs, e.g., justice vs injustice or law vs power. These are cultural codes for larger systems, e.g., democracy vs non-democracy, and persist across different contexts (Alexander and Smith 1993). Actors are merely performing, and counter-performing, the different sides of these belief systems. Thus, ideology is embedded in our social structure. Alexander (2011) applies this framework to the Egyptian Revolution of 2011, showing how the Facebook posts and text messages of the activists and the speeches of Mubarak are oppositional performances of different ideological systems.

More broadly, we might point to power as being dependent on cultural systems. Classically, neo-Marxists like Antonio Gramsci (1971) and Louis Althusser (1971) argued that states exercise cultural power in addition to repressive power. Through education systems and constructions of what is considered legitimate political expression, regimes limit what the public thinks is acceptable. Thus, revolutionary movements can have trouble gaining support due to hegemony – myths that support the state. Gramsci believes that the only way a movement can overcome this is to create its own intellectuals who will author a counter-hegemony. From this perspective, we would expect the ideological basis of movements to differ substantially based on their class position. Recall that Seymour Martin Lipset (1983) argued that we see this in the radicalism or conservatism of movements. In another example, early modern revolutions have been considered not to be socially transformative because their ideological goals were authored by social elites rather than by the masses, a pattern that would stay in place until the Enlightenment (Allardt 1971).

But we need not be Marxists to think that culture might have structural features. Theda Skocpol and William Sewell had a famous interchange, where Sewell (1985) argues that Skocpol ignores the ideological frailty of the French monarchy in the lead-up to revolution in 1789. Ideology here was part of social order itself and should be considered a cause of the revolutionary crisis (see also Beck 2011; Sewell 1992; Sharman 2003). Skocpol (1985) responds that Sewell has broadened the concept of ideology too far, but allows that certain cultural idioms might provide a resource for revolutionaries, e.g., Nazism's deep resonance with Germanic culture. As I describe in the last chapter, such cultural systems should be considered part of the larger environment in which movements find themselves. Thus, nonviolent revolutions, like the Arab Spring and Color Revolutions, become more likely when cultural ideas of human rights are well established. From this perspective, we would analyze militant Islamism in a very different way. We could take Alexander's approach and argue that September 11th and the American military responses were performances of a long-standing divide between the West and Islam (Alexander 2004). Or we could focus on how Islamists like Sayid Qutb became the leading intellectuals of a counter-hegemonic movement opposed to secular, authoritarian states. These states are ideologically frail, caught between the traditions of their society and the ideologies of the world system. Alternatively, we could pin Islamism's appeal not on framing activities but on the cultural resonance that religious symbols have among Muslims. In short, treating ideology as part of social structure moves analysis away from both meaning making and strategy and to a more macro-level of investigation.

The last two sections have outlined the different ways in which social scientists have tried to solve the problem of ideology. We can consider it as linkage between culture and action or see it as an expression of the meaning and identities that action creates. Alternatively, we can reject it and prefer to think of ideology as a rhetorical strategy or treat it as a form of structure, persistent across time and space, which action is dependent on. As seen in the examples of Al-Qaeda and militant Islam, each suggests a different way of conducting research. This is summarized in Table 5.1. I do not propose to know which approach is best. However, it does provide the conceptual backdrop for understanding the role of ideas in radicalism. We thus can learn more from two common areas of research on the power of ideology, starting with religious terrorism.

Religion and terrorism

Of all the places where ideology and radicalism seem inextricably linked, religious terrorism has received the most attention. Even before September 11th, scholars of terrorism noted that interna-

Table 5.1 Different approaches to understanding ideology and militant Islam

Approach	Exemplars	Implications
Culture as "tool kit"	Swidler 1986 Zald 2000	Islamism arose as activated form of religious culture during rapid twentieth-century social change
Ideology as identity	Sutton and Vertigans 2006 Abrahms 2008	Al-Qaeda expresses and defends religious identity, enhancing social solidarity
Meaning making and discourse	Moaddel 1992 Sewell 1996 Selbin 2010	Islamism emerged during political struggles as a way of making sense of events and articulating this understanding
Framing	Snow et al. 1986 Snow and Byrd 2007	Political Islam is a rhetorical strategy, adopted to attract participants and public support
Performance/ counter-performance	Alexander and Smith 1993 Alexander 2004	Militant Islam is part of a "deep" cultural dualism between the West and the Muslim world
Hegemony/ counter-hegemony	Althusser 1971 Gramsci 1971	Political Islam counters western dominance, created by native intellectuals
Ideology as structure	Sewell 1985, 1992 Sharman 2003 Beck 2009b, 2011	Islamism emerged due to social structural and historical patterns that favored religious ideology over secular alternatives

tional terrorism was becoming based more on religion than on ethnic or class identities (Juergensmeyer 1994; Rapoport 1984). In 1993, the political scientist Samuel Huntington wrote an article for *Foreign Affairs* entitled "The Clash of Civilizations?" (Huntington 1993). Huntington argued in this famous piece, later expanded into a book (Huntington 1996), that in the post-Cold War world conflicts would increasingly take place along civilizational fault lines. Though his civilization boundaries were laughable at face value, lumping all of Latin America and Africa together, yet separating Japan from China, Huntington's article became very influential. Many readers seized on the underlying narrative of unavoidable war to take place between "western" civilization, by which Huntington meant European and North American countries, and "Islamic" civilization, covering all Muslim-majority nations. After September 11th, Huntington's argument seemed prescient. What was this horrible event if not the opening salvo in a new world war between religions?

Huntington was not the only one to locate conflict and terrorism in religious tradition. In reaction to September 11th, Bernard Lewis, a historian of the Middle East, published a book with the provocative title *What Went Wrong?* (2002), the answer to which formed the subtitle of the paperback edition: *The Clash between Islam and Modernity in the Middle East*. In 2003, Lewis followed this up with another book entitled *The Crisis of Islam* (2003). In both of these works, Lewis argues that the West is under attack from a misguided fundamentalism that believes that the Islamic world has fallen behind due to western influence and exploitation. Thus, many Muslims see a return to a sacred and pure past as the only solution. In fact, Lewis argues, the Islamic world has lagged in social, political, and economic development due to its own shortcomings and rejection of the modern world. Huntington's and Lewis's arguments seem to explain a lot. There is, however, only one problem. Islamism has almost nothing to do with fundamentalism or a civilizational tradition.

This point, made repeatedly by academics, is probably best stated by Olivier Roy. Roy, a French anthropologist, spent the early part of his career tramping around the mountains of Afghanistan studying the mujahedeen who would later become the Taliban, Al-Qaeda, and other Islamists. Jihad, Roy argues, is a modern invention and there is nothing fundamental or traditional about it. The militants "do not follow their natural communities, but join an imagined one. There has almost never been an example in Muslim history to parallel today's terrorist acts" (Roy 2004: 42). Fundamentalism looks more like Marxist revolutionary rhetoric than Islamic religion, Roy concludes. In another excellent exploration of the issue, Charles Kurzman (2011) flips the question of Islamic terrorism on its head: why are there so few Muslim terrorists, he asks? If militancy and jihad are as popular among Muslims as Huntington and Lewis might presume, then why do Islamic terrorist organizations struggle to recruit members? Further, why do they have trouble pulling off further terrorist attacks in the United States? The answer is not counter-terrorism, but the very unpopularity of Islamism and terrorism themselves in the Muslim world. Kurzman follows Roy in clarifying the modern nature of fundamentalism (even Mohammed Atta, the lead hijacker on September 11th, failed to invoke Allah's name correctly), but goes further and charts the divisions within the Islamic world itself. There is little Islamic terrorism, he argues; rather there are groups composed of Muslims who use terrorism for different goals. For instance, Hamas is primarily a Palestinian nationalist organization which tries to suppress pro-Al-Qaeda groups like Islamic Jihad. Similarly, Hezbollah is a product of the Lebanese Shiite community rather than a transnationally oriented terrorist organization. Even the Taliban in Afghanistan were primarily concerned with their own struggle for state power, and viewed bin Laden and Al-Qaeda with suspicion and mistrust. We see this play out in the case of the Islamic State as well. Syrian Islamists have clashed with the originally Iraqi group as they competed for the jihadist banner in the region.

Even so, the connection between religion and terrorism remains a popular area of research. Two studies deserve special mention. The first, by Bruce Lincoln (2003), is a brilliant analysis of the discourse surrounding September 11th. Lincoln examines the statements of various people to show how religious symbolism was embedded and used in the rhetoric of the event. This meaning making, whether intentional or not, is one reason that the event got cast in terms of religion and a good vs evil struggle, rather than some other narrative. In the best chapter, Lincoln considers the "symmetric dualism" of George Bush's address to the nation on October 7, 2001 announcing a military response to the attack and bin Laden's videotaped response released shortly thereafter. Bin Laden's statement was full of religious symbols – God, faith, infidels, paradise. According to Lincoln, 17 percent of the 584 words in bin Laden's speech were religious. But so, too, was Bush's speech. While Bush avoided outright religious language, he cast

September 11th as a conflict between good and evil and invoked biblical allusions. "The terrorist may burrow deeper into caves and other entrenched hiding places," Bush proclaimed, which Lincoln argues is a reference to the Book of Revelation in the Christian Bible. Further, use of phrases like "killers of innocents" and "there can be no peace" could be heard by the biblically aware as references to the Gospel of Matthew and the Books of Exodus, Jeremiah, and Ezekiel in the Old Testament. In Lincoln's analysis, religious ideology provided a resource for action and a justification for the ensuing conflict. Culture is thus linked to action.

The second study of note is Mark Juergensmeyer's (2001) comparative examination of religious terrorism. Juergensmeyer explores violence in different religious traditions: American Christian violence like that of Timothy McVeigh and abortion clinic bombers, and Catholicism in Northern Ireland; Jewish extremists in Israel, and the assassination of prime minister Yitzhak Rabin; militant Islamists and suicide terrorism; Sikh separatists in India; and the Buddhist group Aum Shinrikyo's attack on Tokyo's subways. Juergensmeyer concludes that religious violence has its own logic, similar to a type of performance theater. Here, Juergensmeyer connects religion and audience effects – religious violence demonstrates a particular symbolic meaning to fellow believers. Specifically, the conflict involves the idea of a cosmic war between good and evil that cannot be won on the material plane alone, and so radicals adopt a symbolic logic using terrorism where symbolism is created by victim–target differentiation. This recalls the three-step model detailed in chapter 1 (Bergesen 2007). Second, religion provides a way to construct targets as demonic enemies and the participating individuals as heavenly martyrs for the cause. This is similar to Della Porta's (1995) argument that radicalization requires "martyrs and myths," which she believes is caused by state repression rather than religious meaning. Thus, religion promotes violence by sanctifying individual action to make the world right and justifies killing, even if there is little hope of real success. Juergensmeyer here, seemingly without knowing, follows Swidler's model of how culture translates into action. Cultural traditions provide a resource for action in times of social stress, thus the religious view that the world has gone awry becomes a systematic ideology that directs collective action.

As should be clear from Juergensmeyer's comparisons, a seeming link between religion and radical action is not unique to Islam. In early modern Europe, the strict moral discipline of Calvinism provided a cultural framework for revolutionary transformations of states (Gorski 2003), and we might even consider the Calvinists the terrorists of the international system at the time (see Bergesen and Lizardo 2004). In the contemporary period, religious beliefs in the coming apocalypse have been argued to provide an ideological basis for right-wing and racist violence against the state (White 2001). Yet these dynamics are not unique to religion. As Roy (2004) reminds us, bin Laden is as much like Marx as he is Muhammad. Even secular radicals have a quasi-religious fervor; as Hoffer (1951) had it – fanaticism born of frustration and hope. For instance, radical environmentalists base their justification for violence on a philosophy of deep ecology that provides a quasi-religious belief system (Bergesen 1995; Taylor 1998).

Research on religious terrorism thus has a central problem. It tends to take the link between culture and action too seriously, without problematizing the nature of ideology. It is obvious that religious symbols and meaning making can justify violence (see Hall 2003). What is less obvious is under what conditions religion will be used to do so. Juergensmeyer (2001) attempts to answer this by arguing it is most potent for unwinnable conflicts, while others, like Jessica Stern (2003), argue that religious terrorism is actually about material grievances and social alienation. Yet these conditions do not tell us why religion is the ideological basis rather than nationalism, socialism, fascism, and so on. Each of these belief systems also provides an imagined community to defend, an identity to promote, and a set of symbols and meanings to adopt. In my own work, I have tried to address this puzzle (see Beck 2009b). From an analysis of the religiosity of Middle Eastern political organizations, I conclude that Islamism depends on the state legitimating religion's use in the public sphere by basing their own authority on it.

In short, the most interesting approach to religion and violence involves moving away from ideology in terms of the culture–action link to ideology as a culture–structure bridge. Here, research on ideology in another area related to radicalism – the course of revolution – may provide a guide.

Ideology and the course of revolution

We have seen above that the role of ideology in revolution has been a popular topic for study. One line of work suggests that the causes of revolution might be found in how cultural tool kits promote resistance against the state (Beck 2011; Foran 2005; Sewell 1985; Sharman 2003; Wuthnow 1989). A second stresses how symbols are deployed within a revolutionary situation for participants to make sense of the ambiguity that the competition for power creates (Moaddel 1992; Selbin 2010; Sewell 1996). A third line of work has explicitly focused on how ideology can be the bridge between a cultural account and a structural account of revolution. Many sociologists of revolution have viewed ideology as a crucial "shaping" mechanism on the course of a revolutionary situation. Much of this draws, sometimes explicitly, sometimes not, on Swidler's model of ideology and culture. For example, one of the first to take ideology's role in an account of revolution seriously was Farideh Farhi. Farhi (1988, 1990) argues that the worldview of a society acts as a shaping force for the revolutionaries' goals and actions. So the Iranian Revolution became an Islamic one as Shiite Islam provided a particular framework for the post-Shah government, and liberation theology created the basis for a socialist revolution in Nicaragua. Here, ideology bridges both popular support and structural causes of revolution.

In contrast, Misagh Parsa (2000) examines the role of ideology in the Nicaraguan Revolution, the Iranian Islamic Revolution, and the Philippines' "People Power" Revolution of 1986. Parsa's conclusion is somewhat cynical – most participants in revolution are only slightly aware of the different revolutionary ideologies that are in use. In fact, class-based ideologies may make revolution even more difficult as they factionalize, rather than unite, possible supporters. An exception to this rule is students, according to Parsa. Students are more likely to adopt the ideas and beliefs promoted by dissident intellectuals and become an ideological force within a revolutionary coalition. But even if ideology is not a primary cause of revolution in Parsa's model, he does conclude that the ideologies present within a revolutionary coalition will affect the possible range of outcomes. Here, he is in good company. John Foran and Jeff Goodwin (1993) examine the same cases as Farhi – Iran and Nicaragua – but in a different manner. In contrast to a worldview argument, ideology is defined as the set of beliefs and commitments that successful revolutionaries have. In their view, the political pluralism and later transition to popular elections of the Nicaraguan Revolution are not due to a worldview of liberation theology or a socialist program but rather to a product of political competition. The Sandinistas, unlike Khomeini's faction in Iran, were more evenly matched with their opponents and thus unable to impose their ideological vision on society more generally. Thus, while ideology can shape the outcome of a revolution, it does so through the capacities of revolutionary leaders.

Eric Selbin (1993) has noted the same process in the institutionalization and consolidation of revolutions. As mentioned in chapter 1, a true social revolution requires more than state building, according to Selbin. Revolutionaries must also win the hearts and minds of the public and consolidate their gains. This requires a visionary leadership that sees the ultimate goal of revolution as the transformation of society rather than just the seizure of state power. Only in Nicaragua and Cuba, among the Latin American cases that Selbin explored, was this present. And only in Nicaragua did revolutionaries solve the problem of institutionalization and the line of succession, although, arguably, the Cubans have finally done this as well with the devolution of power away from Fidel Castro in the last decade.

The reader may have noted that these four perspectives all made use of the same example as part of their investigation – Nicaragua. Depending whose side we take, we might conclude that the Nicaraguan Revolution was shaped by religion, or was little motivated by ideology, or failed in competition with other ideological factions, or was consolidated by its visionary leaders. This is a common pattern in the study of revolution more broadly – scholars tend to interpret the same event differently, and so theories of the causes and process of revolution proliferate in great numbers.

We can solve some of this disagreement if we follow Jack Goldstone in thinking that the role of ideology is different at different stages of the revolutionary process. Goldstone (1991a), in a paper predating all but Farhi, argues that ideology has the most causal force in the second and third stages of revolution – revolutionary struggle and state stabilization. In the pre-revolution phase, ideology and culture provide a basis for complaints against the state and moral critiques of its power, but they do not cause a state to break down. Rather, Goldstone argues, this is due to various structural causes. However, once the state has fallen, various groups of contenders fight over who will take control and each carries an ideology with them into battle. A successful revolutionary organization will be able to impose its ideological vision on its opponents and, in particular, on the army of the new state as its instrument. But ideologies are not set in stone; they tend to evolve as a consequence of this factional competition. Hence, revolutionary ideology often seems to radicalize. Not because radicals get more radical once they have free rein but because the struggle for power pushes them to more extreme opinions. As the revolutionaries try to reconstruct stable authority, the extent to which the cultural frameworks of society promote either reform or transformation will determine whether a true social revolution takes place. In short, the content of a revolutionary ideology does not matter; rather, its relationship to competing ideologies and the underlying culture of a society govern its content and effect.

If we apply Goldstone's stage model to the Nicaraguan Revolution, we can synthesize some of the disagreements. In Nicaragua, it was not that the revolution was caused by popular support for the Sandinistas' activation of liberation theology symbols and meanings, but rather that the Sandinistas became the dominant coalition partner of the revolution. Thus, the revolution took on a distinctly socialist character. Yet the post-revolutionary state was created in a culture that valued pluralism more than socialism, so the Sandinista leadership avoided creating a single-party state. This is not failure, nor does it refute the role of ideology; rather, it just expects different dynamics depending on how the researcher approaches the problem.

Work on ideology and the course of revolution thus has implications for research on religion and terrorism, and indeed for all work on ideology and radicalism. There are two primary lessons. First, rather than focusing on a link between mass belief in a religion or ideology and thus the use of violence or radical strategies, researchers should focus on the capacity of radical organizations and terrorist leaderships to assert their vision. The beliefs of the masses and the content of the belief system matter less. The goals of leaders and the capability of their organizations matter more. Second, researchers should pay attention to the competition between different religious or ideological factions. The winners of factional competition are also those most likely to be able to impose their ideological vision. Competition can radicalize ideologies, but it can also lead to stalemates that moderate politics overall. These lessons confirm the approach of Charles Kurzman (2011), Christina Hellmich (2014), and others to Islamic terrorism – its ideological content is incoherent, has little popular support, and the primary battle is between the moderate Islamists and the revolutionary ones.

Summary

This chapter has reviewed the many approaches to understanding ideology and radicalism. There are two key ideas to take away. First, many people, even scholars, are not always clear about what exactly they consider ideology to be. It can mean many things: a set of beliefs and skills that influence action; an identity that participants hold or create; a way of making meaning out of events; rhetorical frames that are used strategically; a performance of cultural discourses; the system of power surrounding the state; or a cultural framework in which society is embedded. Since each of these suggests a different strategy for analysis, it is thus helpful to think of two distinctions. First, following Swidler, we should distinguish ideology, which is a system of beliefs, from culture, which is a set of symbols, habits, and meanings. Second, we should acknowledge whether we are considering ideology as a link between culture and the action of individuals, or ideology as a link between culture and social structure. Each suggests a different line of thought, even for the same events, as we saw in the discussion of Nicaragua above.

The second key idea is that ideology should not be thought of in programmatic terms. One reason that scholarly approaches to the subject are so varied is because ideologies are so varied themselves. And they are rarely logically consistent. Rather, incoherence and change are the norm. Thus, saying that a radical group is socialist or Islamist tells us only a little about what the group may or may not do or what it may or may not want. This is a particular problem in the study of religion and terrorism, where the link between belief and action is taken for granted rather than made the object of study. Thus, any scholar or student of radicalism should reject an ideological or cultural account if the author is unable to explain how they define ideology and why doing so is useful for their purposes. This is even truer when reading popular accounts that try to draw a direct line between radical ideologies and radical actions.

6

Is There a Life Cycle of Radicalism?

As the Soviet Union broke apart in 1991, nationalist leaders in the Caucasus declared independence from Moscow and formed the Chechen Republic of Ichkeria. As the new Russian Federation consolidated, Boris Yeltsin ordered Russian forces into Chechnya in 1994. In a two-year war, Chechen insurgents fought the Russian government to a standstill. After the temporary victory, Chechnya remained de facto independent and a place for radicals to organize. In August 1999, a Chechen guerrilla leader, Shamil Basayev, led a column of Islamist guerrillas into the neighboring province of Dagestan, and the Russian government responded with air assaults to wipe out the insurgents. The Second Chechen War brought a series of terrorist bombings and a reinvasion of Chechnya by the Russian military. Fighting lasted for a year until the end of 2000, when Russian president Vladimir Putin established direct rule over Chechnya as the last pockets of organized resistance were crushed. Even so, guerrilla warfare continued in Chechnya and neighboring parts of the Caucasus, and the insurgency entered a new phase of recurrent terrorist attacks locally and elsewhere in Russia. In 2002, Islamist separatists seized a theater in Moscow and took 850 theatergoers hostage. The resulting siege, and use of chemical gas in the ventilation system, killed all 40 of the attackers and 130 of the hostages. In 2004, insurgents from Basayev's organization took more than 1,000 children and adults hostage at a school in the town of Beslan; more than 300 were killed as Russian forces retook the school. Basayev was killed in an explosion in 2006, most likely from mishandling explosives, but terrorist attacks continued, in recent years targeting the Moscow Metro in 2010, Moscow's airport in 2011, and the mass transportation system in Volgograd in December 2013 in the lead-up to the Sochi Winter Olympics. Notably, the Tsarnaev brothers who carried out the Boston Marathon bombings in 2013 were the sons of Chechen immigrants and possibly inspired by the ongoing conflict in Russia. In short, political violence seemed to radicalize over the course of the conflict – beginning with organized war between separatists and a central government and devolving into attacks on civilians, children, and even citizens of other countries.[1]

Examples like the Chechen insurgency suggest that there might be a life cycle to radicalism where violence and terrorism emerge later in a contentious episode and become increasingly indiscriminate and nihilistic in their targets, moving away from rational strategies (Bergesen and Han 2005). Donatella della Porta (1995), in her study of 1960s European leftist militant groups, concludes that terrorism was a product of the stages of a movement – violence helps sustain an organization when faced with short-term failure, and as groups move underground and become more isolated, radicalization results. Within group processes like group-think, a social-psychological process in which members of a small group prioritize loyalty and conformity over rationality, may encourage more use of violence (Tsintsadze-Maass and Maass 2014). Yet as competition among violent organizations increases, each group may be less likely to survive in the long term (Young and Dugan 2014). Terrorism might thus be part of a protest cycle as it clusters in time and space (see LaFree, Morris, and Dugan 2010). Protest cycles, originally formulated by Sidney Tarrow (1989) in his study of Italian politics, occur when conflict is heightened across a society leading to a variety of types of collective action. This can allow movements to overcome resource weaknesses and see more success than they otherwise would (see also Tarrow 1998). Interestingly, Enders and Sandler (2005) find two-year peaks in international terrorism in the latter half of the twentieth century, suggesting a cyclical logic, as well as increasing lethality over time (Enders and Sandler 2000).

A life cycle of radicalism could also involve a series of stages through which different movements pass. Eric Hoffer (1951: 147) posits such a stage theory in his exploration of radicalism: "A movement is pioneered by men of words, materialized by fanatics, and consolidated by men of action." The early twentieth-century natural historians of revolution also saw common stages in revolutions (Brinton 1938; Pettee 1938), often from the pro-totypical French Revolution (see Goldstone 1982). According to them, revolutions begin with the defection of intellectuals from the regime (the Enlightenment in eighteenth-century France) and failed attempts at reform (tax reform initiated under Louis XVI). Moderate reformers seize power first (like the National Constituent Assembly formed out of the Third Estate), but radical groups supplant the moderates as they fail to reconstruct effective rule (enter the Jacobins). The resulting chaos invites coercive rule in response (the Terror and widespread use of the guillotine), often from the military (and here comes Napoleon), and pragmatism emerges in the new status quo. Recently, Nadir Sohrabi (1995) revives this logic by examining how different models of revolu-tion, like the French or early twentieth-century constitutionalism, suggest different actions in each stage to the participating actors.

Yet protest cycles end much more variously than either a radicalizing life cycle or a stage model would suggest (Tarrow 1998). For instance, in the study of social movements more broadly, the resource mobilization tradition predicts an alternate outcome – organizational age will lead to increasing formaliza-tion and accompanying moderation in goals (McCarthy and Zald 1977; Piven and Cloward 1977). Recall that Kurzman and Naqvi (2010a) find that Islamist political parties tend to get less radical over time as they engage in the political process. Some radical groups are also self-moderating; for example, the Weather Underground turned away from violence as described in chapter 2 and contemporary ecoterrorists eschewed further radicalization (Beck 2007). Radical groups may also burn themselves out when action is constrained by policing or a public backlash (Ross and Gurr 1989). In fact, self-defeating terrorism is only one of many types of endings for terrorist organizations (Cronin 2009). An influential study by the RAND Corporation (Jones and Libicki 2008) of 648 militant groups concludes that 43 percent transition to engagement in the political process and only 10 percent are successful in meeting their goals. In short, moderation could be just as likely as radicalization in a life-cycle account.

This brief overview suggests the key problem with stage theories of radicalism, revolution, and terrorism – they are too deterministic. The social world is rarely so clean that every instance follows a common pattern. Rather, there are many paths to radicalism, many routes through revolution, and many destinations for terrorism. A life-cycle theory of radicalism thus might obscure more than it illuminates. But all is not lost. Like the psychology of radicalism, parts of this view can be saved and put into more fruitful perspective. This chapter focuses on two key areas of research: the role of repertoires of contention and innovation; and the dynamics of elite adaptation to and repression of contention. The chapter then concludes by considering the various outcomes of revolution that are possible.

Repertoires of contention and innovation

At any given time, the strategies that movements use are just one small subset of all the possible actions that a movement could engage in. Just as athletes have a signature move, so too do movements have tactical preferences that they use repeatedly – for instance, organizing a boycott or staging a mass demonstration. Charles Tilly (1977) originally introduced the idea of "repertoires of contention" in the 1970s to capture the patterns he saw in French history. Tilly recognizes that not only did particular movements have particular preferences, but also that the set of actions a movement engages in is roughly similar to other movements that exist at the same time (Tilly 1986; see also Hung 2011). Repertoire, at its root, thus had two meanings – what a single movement does, and what actions are used in a particular time period. Sidney Tarrow (1993a) expands this basic notion further, noting that Tilly suggests that repertoires are also what a movement knows how to do and what society expects it to do. In essence, we can think of collective action as a large kit with many possible tools that might be used, and a repertoire as the set of tools that are usually selected. In early modern times, the preferred tools of collective action were often based on existing local practices – the nineteenth-century barricading of streets to protest government evolved from the practice of stringing chains across a street at night to protect a neighborhood from thieves (Traugott 2010). As time wore on, repertoires became less particularistic and more "modular" (Tarrow 1993b), able to be applied to locales other than where they were first developed. While research on repertoires remains somewhat underdeveloped (Della Porta 2013b; Tilly 1993a), and many social movement scholars have forgotten the nuance of the idea – using it to refer just to what a movement does – it is a useful analytical tool for understanding all collective action, including radicalism.

Just as Tilly and Tarrow chart changes in the repertoires of movements over the past several centuries, so too have terrorism researchers noted changes in the tactics of terrorism over the last several decades. Enders and Sandler (1993) have shown that international terrorism shifted from hijackings of airplanes in the 1970s to a preference for kidnappings in the 1980s. More recently, terrorists have preferred to use suicide bombings rather than take hostages (Bloom 2005; Pape and Feldman 2010). Ongoing work by the National Consortium for the Study of Terrorism and Responses to Terrorism also documents changes in tactics over time (see Crenshaw 2012; LaFree, Yang, and Crenshaw 2009): over the last forty years, different sets of terrorist tactics have tended to rise and fall in use. What terrorists do, what they know how to do, and even what we expect them to do evolves. This suggests terrorism can be thought of as having repertoire-like features and, as this book tries to show, should not be analyzed in isolation from other types of collective action.

Thinking of radicalism in terms of repertoire leads to two analytically useful observations. First, repertoires are often linked to protest cycles, and thus change in one might yield change in the other. Second, innovative repertoires are more likely to be successful, and therefore, in the context of radicalism, more threatening. A protest cycle has three basic phases: ascension, peak, and decline. Within these phases are interrelated campaigns of collective action, where movements are often connected to each other and focused on similar goals (Della Porta 2013a). Protest cycles usually begin external to any particular movement, rooted in civil society and rising public consciousness of an issue (Tarrow 1989). This helps explain a commonly observed phenomenon – radicals and terrorist organizations often seem to "spin off" from larger movements. For instance, the Basque terrorist group ETA had its origins in Basque civil society in Spain, rather than emerging completely independently (Tejerina 2001), it was the strength of interwar Germany civil society that fueled the rise of the Nazi Party (Berman 1997; Riley 2010), and black nationalist groups like the Black Panthers were rooted in the civil rights movement (McAdam 1988). But what really gives impetus to a rise in contention is the innovation of new tactics or methods of mobilization. Innovative tactics tend to be more successful because they disrupt the cultural expectation of what a movement should do (part of the concept of repertoire) and elites and governments do not yet know how to counter them (McAdam 1983). Suicide terrorism using an explosive vest, for instance, was innovated by the Tamil Tigers in Sri Lanka in the 1980s and to this day is the among the most difficult form of terrorism to counter. Another key aspect of protest cycle ascension is borrowing – one movement learns a tactic from another and, as both employ it, contention overall may increase. The suicide vest has thus been adopted by Palestinian nationalist groups, Islamist insurgents in Iraq and Afghanistan, and even Marxist groups in Turkey (Bloom 2005). Further, collaboration between movement organizations is highly predictive of developing similar repertoires (Wang and Soule 2012), and imitation of tactics is much more likely than innovation (Biggs 2013). I discuss such diffusion processes in more detail in the next chapter, but for now this suggests that the innovation and spread of repertoires can lead to increases in the amount of contention and even radicalism.

But even innovative tactics lose their novelty, and contention subsides. Ruud Koopmans (1993) argues that the chance of success for a movement changes throughout the course of a protest cycle and this affects movement strategy. Hence, we would expect to observe a decline in a particular repertoire of contention and its replacement with other tactics over time. This is exactly what researchers on terrorism have shown, as noted above: hijacking became kidnapping which turned into suicide bombing. It is easy to imagine how to apply these insights to radical groups – the researcher could trace a terrorist tactic to its innovative source, follow the chain of imitation, and look for collaboration between various militant organizations that might explain how the repertoire developed. Radicalization itself could be considered an innovation that creates a new repertoire of contention and fuels a protest cycle. The key point here is that repertoires, even radical ones, are not static. Thus, even though the particulars will differ, we could expect cycles of radicalism and terrorism to emerge regularly – whether the anarchists of the nineteenth century or the Islamists of the twenty-first (Bergesen and Han 2005; Rapoport 2004). Adopting such a perspective does not mean that we have to argue for neat stages or a life cycle that all radicals must pass through. Rather, it means that we can be sensitive to the set of radical tactics that constitute the current repertoire and gauge their impact on the basis of their innovativeness.

Repression and elite adaptation

As suggested in the previous section, considering the repertoires of radicals also means considering how elites and governments adapt to them. State response is a primary dynamic that governs protest cycles (Della Porta 1995; Koopmans 1993). Nineteenth-century barricades in France may have emerged from local practices and been imitated even as recently as the 2014 Ukrainian Revolution in the Maidan, but governments have not stood still. In fact, the Paris we know today, with its broad boulevards like the Champs-Elysées, is a government response to the barricade. Under Napoleon III, Baron Haussmann redesigned Paris to remove the narrow cobblestone streets that were easily barricaded because of their size and of the amount of building material on hand (cobblestones themselves), and replace them with large thoroughfares that troops could march down and control with line of sight artillery. In short, repertoires are not just about tactics, but also about interactions between challenges, elites, and even counter-movements (Johnston 2014; Tilly 2008). And elites have a number of options available to them to repress a movement, even if they run the risk of sparking more protest.

As elites adapt, radicals must change tactics or face a diminishing chance of success. The shift in international terrorism from hijacking to kidnapping happened not just because of innovation, but because of the introduction of metal detectors into airports (Enders and Sandler 1993). More recently, terrorism has turned towards targeting private parties because counterterrorism efforts have made government targets harder to attack (Brandt and Sandler 2010). In these cases, counterterrorism interacts with existing tactics to shape the future of the terrorist repertoire. In revolutionary situations, repertoires are changed by government responses as well. The taking of the Bastille in the French Revolution began as a local action by a citizens' militia to seize gunpowder, but its success led Louis XVI to pull government troops out of Paris, turning reform into revolution (Sewell 1996). In Syria in 2011, the government's use of violence against protest marches led to the formation of armed insurgency, and, in the Color Revolutions, elite learning seemed to be the primary cause of the failure of later attempts at electoral revolution in the post-communist world (Beissinger 2007). Organizational flexibility in adopting new tactics is thus key to sustaining any type of movement over time (see Gamson 1975), and even more so for radical ones that may face violent coercion. This suggests that an interactional, evolutionary model of radicalism might be more fitting than a deterministic life-cycle, or even protest cycle, model.

Second, the possible repressive responses are as varied as the array of possible collective actions (see Earl 2011 for a review). This is true across regime type. Democratic governments are often the targets of terrorism (Chenoweth 2013), including suicide terrorism (Pape 2003) and hostage taking (Lee 2013), because the pressures of elections, public opinion, and free mass media provide an opportunity for terrorism to influence policy. We might think democracies have less leeway in their repressive responses owing to the rule of law and due process, but in fact this is not so (Davenport 2007). The current "long war" tactics of extraordinary rendition, waterboarding, and drone strikes demonstrate this well. Further, democratic states are able to use torture and other coercive means against violent opponents because such conflicts are somewhat immune to the effects of popular opinion and law (Davenport, Moore, and Armstrong 2007). In addition to outright violence and incarceration, governments can also channel contention into less threatening forms (Earl 2003). Even the threat of coercion can forestall violent contention (Ortiz 2007). Elite funding of movement organizations tends to favor moderates over radicals (Haines 1984; Jenkins and Eckert 1986), and governments often seek to compromise with reformers rather than extremists. For example, the Oslo peace process between Israel and the Palestine Liberation Organization (PLO) was in part an attempt to under-cut the more radical militancy of Palestinian groups like Hamas. But conciliation can also fail, particularly if it creates competition among organizations seeking to represent an aggrieved constituency. Competition breeds extremism (Della Porta 1995; Tarrow 1989). Tezcur (2010) argues that this has occurred in the ongoing conflict between Turkey and the PKK: the Turkish government has unwittingly eroded popular support for peace.

Sometimes a state's coercive responses develop in interaction with an opponent, just as repertoires do for challengers. For example, Dolores Trevizo (2006) charts the Mexican government's response to the 1968 student movement and subsequent peasant revolts. She concludes that the government's use of repression depended on the movements' different claim making. The peasant movements framed their cause in terms of national history, in contrast to the international communist frame of the students, and were more sympathetic to the public in general. Accordingly, the government responded with conciliation instead of force. Flexibility can benefit regimes as much as challengers. But it is almost a truism among sociologists that any large bureaucracy will become ossified and less flexible over time, and counterterrorism is likely no different. Governments, just like movements, run the risk of acquiring a tactical preference – a repertoire of repression, if you will – that may or may not work in all situations. The Ku Klux Klan and 1960s leftist groups were both targeted by the US government program COINTELPRO, but it saw much more success in the former case as the KKK was particularly vulnerable to this type of clandestine repression (Cunningham 2003). The good news is that the coercive apparatus in democratic states might be resistant to politicization (Deflem 2004). The bad news is that it is easy for them to miss emergent threats (Beck and Miner 2013). Further, elite learning does not always mean effective adaptation to a repertoire. For example, current counterinsurgency efforts in Afghanistan may be hampered because the American government learned incorrect lessons from prior British counterinsurgencies in 1950s Malaysia and Kenya (Branch 2010).

Thus, repertoires and repression evolve together, interacting across the phases of a protest cycle. This creates one of the most famous puzzles in studies of contention – the repression–protest paradox. A consistent finding in research on contention is that, if repression is used effectively, challengers will not be successful (Tilly 1978). For instance, the success of nonviolent revolutions hinges on the idea that pacifism undermines the use of repression by the state (Sharp 2010; Stephan and Chenoweth 2008). And the importance of elite schisms for revolution, discussed in chapter 4, is primarily due to the fact that a fractured elite is unable to martial an effective repressive response to challenges. Yet the use of repression can also spur further protest or undermine a regime (Goldstone 2001; Lichbach 1987). In Ukraine in 2014, the shooting of unarmed protestors in Kiev turned a declining protest into the successful overthrow of the Yanukovych regime. A similar dynamic is apparent in the Iranian Revolution of 1979, as the Shah's government wavered between conciliation and repression (Rasler 1996). The Islamist insurgency in Egypt in the 1990s was also exacerbated by the government's repressive response as both sides engaged in tit-for-tat escalation (Fielding and Shortland

2010). And in the Israeli–Palestinian case, repression by Israeli authorities spurred more collective action in the 1980s (Khawaja 1994), even though it does not seem to have had an effect on rates of terrorism more recently (Dugan and Chenoweth 2012). Repression can also have other unintended consequences, such as creating new coalitions of activists opposed to a regime that may mobilize at a later date (Chang 2008; Osa 2003). In short, repression appears to be like Goldilocks's porridge – the level needs to be just right for it to succeed in squashing opposition without creating more (see Lichbach and Gurr 1981). Charles Brockett (1993), by comparing civil wars in Central America, suggests that the paradox might be solved by linking repression's effect to the notion of the protest cycle. Repression during the upswing of a cycle spurs protest, he argues, while in the downswing it deters further contention. But since phases of protest cycles are already determined by the interaction of repertoires and repression, this explanation might be tautological. In any case, the repression–protest paradox remains one of the most important unanswered questions in the field (Beck forthcoming; Goldstone 2001). And the implications it has for current counterterrorism strategies means that it should be a foremost area for research on radicalism. Unfortunately, this has not been the case.

The two prior sections on innovation in repertoires and interactions with repressive responses suggest that there is some utility in thinking about the different phases in radical contention. Without claiming that some master template of common stages exists for all radical movements, suggestions for when certain dynamics are likely to be most important are summarized in Figure 6.1. In the initial stages of mobilization, innovation in the radical repertoire can be expected to play a key role, followed shortly by wider imitation as contention increases. Collective action ebbs as elites learn to respond to a repertoire, and repression sets in. Whether this ends further contention or leads to a second peak as repertoires evolve depends on the repression–protest paradox, and quite likely on the social and historical context as well. The model is not deterministic, but analytic – it suggests different ways to think about the evolution of repertoires and responses. The

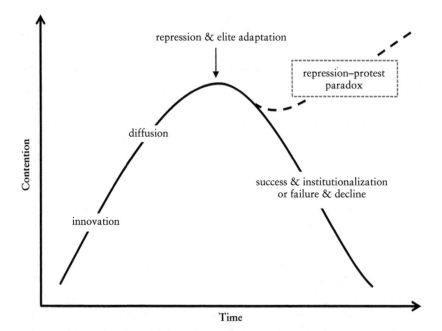

figure 6.1 The co-evolution of repertoires and repression in radicalism

analytical tool suggests that radicalism will taper off. Of course, all movements do end somehow. But it is agnostic about these endings; as the next section discusses, there are a variety of outcomes to terrorism, revolution, and radical contention.

Outcomes of radicalism

While radical political violence may not often achieve its stated aims (Abrahms 2006; Jones and Libicki 2008), it does have a number of effects on movements and societies. First, radical groups have many goals, not all of which are related to their political claims. These can include identity creation and maintenance, garnering resources, and attracting participants (Abrahms 2008; Krause 2013). Sometimes, there is a tension between these organizational-level goals and ultimate aims – organizational survival might undercut success (Acosta 2014). Della Porta (1995) documents this well for the European leftist terrorists of the 1960s; as the groups moved underground into survival mode, they reduced their chances of achieving their initial goals. The most successful terrorist groups are those that have the largest memberships and survive the longest (though religious terrorism does tend to last long but see less success than secular forms (Jones and Libicki 2008)). Ironically, organizational survival is predicted by higher amounts of violence (Blomberg, Engel, and Sawyer 2010), which belies the belief present in some life-cycle theories that violence undercuts a movement. There is thus great diversity in the group-level outcomes of terrorism. Audrey Ruth Cronin (2009) argues that four endings, besides success or full repression, capture most terrorist groups: the imprisonment or death of its leaders; transitions towards the political process; marginalization or self-implosion; and adoption of another modus operandi. She suggests that Al-Qaeda will continue even after its current leadership is removed, due to its fluid organizational structure. This is only partially borne out in the aftermath of bin Laden's death as its primary activities have shifted to local affiliates. The loose coupling of central leadership and active groups thus provides an opportunity for counterterrorism to reduce support for Al-Qaeda at a local level. As discussed before, it might be best to conceptualize Islamic terrorism as a civil war between globalists and nationalists (Kurzman 2011).

Even though a terrorist group might not reach its goals or even sustain itself in the long term, there are still a number of social and political impacts it can have. First, the psychological impact on a population lasts for a long period of time. This is particularly true of repeated acts of terrorism (Spilerman and Stecklov 2009). There is little evidence that a chronic experience of terrorism desensitizes the public to it (Stecklov and Goldstein 2010). Second, it is clear that terrorism impacts the political system, whether chronic or not. In the wake of the 2004 Madrid train bombings, the Spanish electorate surprisingly supported the opposition Socialist party in the national election three days later. Before the bombing, no one expected the opposition to win. The electorate's support for the opposition may have been due to the lack of transparency and response of the government in the attack's immediate wake. Chronic terrorism can also lead the public to point fingers. Kibris (2010) shows that voters in areas of Turkey that experienced PKK attacks were more likely to blame the government and support right-wing parties that promised a harder line against terrorism. Beyond electoral politics, the experience of terrorism in Israel has affected the adoption of human rights norms (Shor 2008). Ironically, however, counterterrorism legislation is decoupled from terrorist attacks – across the world, legislation seems to be passed in response to perceived threats rather than actual experiences (Shor 2011). This dovetails with my own research on terrorism designations by governments, where markers of terrorist threat seem to be more relevant for designation than actual activity (Beck and Miner 2013). Finally, terrorism is an economic detriment, both for the communities experiencing it and the communities from which it originates. Abadie and Gardeazabal (2003) analyze the economic conditions of the Basque areas in Spain and show that the economy declined by about 10 percent as a consequence of ETA's campaigns but picked up again in the late 1990s when a truce was declared. Interestingly, however, the socioeconomic environment of a terrorist organization does not seem to have a large impact on whether or not a radical group survives (Blomberg et al. 2010).

Revolutions have an even greater impact than terrorism, both on movements and societies. While full-scale revolutions are rare events, successful revolutionary movements do have the opportunity to remake social and economic structures substantially – a social revolution. Socially, revolutions can remake the relationships and routines of everyday life and have a lasting resonance in collective memory (Selbin 2010). Revolutions can also remake national economies, for instance, creating a transition to communism or away from it. However, the longer-term economic impact of revolution is often more ambiguous. Susan Eckstein is one of the few scholars to have explored this question. In a series of studies on Latin America (see Eckstein 1975, 1982, 1985), she shows that post-revolutionary states have trouble increasing social welfare generally. This may be because revolutions often occur in relatively underdeveloped societies, and thus the new state has few resources and little room to be more effective (see Foran 2005). We might thus speak of another development model – the post-revolutionary one – where martyrs are as important as markets, like the case of post-Shah Iran (Harris 2010).

The other obvious impact of revolution is political. While some revolutionary governments are able to sustain radicalism or even try to export it (see Halliday 1999; Katz 1997), others moderate their goals once in power. For instance, as we saw in the previous chapter, the post-Nicaraguan Revolution Sandinistas encouraged political pluralism and peacefully handed over power after losing an election. In fact, the degree of political change that a revolutionary movement can make may be inversely related to the breadth of participation in revolution (Domínguez and Mitchell 1977). This inclusion–moderation hypothesis is common in work on Islamist political parties (Kurzman and Naqvi 2010a; Moaddel 2002; Schwedler 2006). Yet moderation may only come from stability. If the uncertainty of a revolutionary situation continues, then radicalism can persist (Schwedler 2011), as the case of the still unfolding Egyptian Revolution of 2011 demonstrates. The uncertainty of revolutions also invites external intervention and influence. In March 2014, after Yanukovych fled Ukraine, Russia intervened in a dramatic fashion unprecedented in the post-Cold War world. Claiming that the right-wing nationalists of the new Ukrainian government were fascists, Russian forces moved into the Crimea. At first, the Russians retained "laughable" deniability by removing insignias from uniforms, and claimed that the armed groups were spontaneous local defense militias that just happened to be driving Russian military vehicles. But it quickly became apparent that intervention would lead to annexation, which was formally declared after a Crimean referendum passed with 97 percent of the votes. Presumably the other 3 percent voted for the only other option on the ballot – outright independence from both Ukraine and Russia. Such intervention tends to prolong conflicts (Cunningham 2010) and is more common when there is great-power conflict more generally (Kowalewski 1991). Both of these findings seem to hold true in Ukraine in 2014.

Like the endings of terrorist groups, the endings of revolution are thus quite varied. Think of the diversity in a list of countries like the United States, France, Poland, Serbia, Chile, Egypt, Iran, China, and South Africa – all post-revolutionary states and societies. Arthur Stinchcombe (1999) outlines the common political structures that are the outcome of revolutions, which can be updated for the contemporary world as follows. First, there is democracy, where the rule of law prevails and a regime can be supplanted by the citizenry only through legal means, usually through elections. Recent cases include some Eastern European post-communist states like Poland, South Africa after the end of Apartheid, and Serbia after the Bulldozer Revolution. Second is conservative authoritarianism, which is a "return to normalcy" that "incorporates much of the elite of the prerevolutionary regime" (Stinchcombe 1999: 54). This can be considered a reversed revolution with the triumph of reactionaries over revolutionaries. Examples include Franco's Spain and Pinochet's Chile. It often involves foreign intervention on the side of established elites. Next are anocracies or parliamentary authoritarianism (Stinchcombe's "revolutionary democracy"). Here, the new regime still relies on mobilization to maintain its power, but the system allows for limited political competition. This is a common contemporary outcome of the overthrow of purely autocratic states, with examples in post-1979 Iran and post-1992 Belarus. Fourth, *caudillismo* occurs when power is based on patrimonial arrangements and continuing competition for power, often from localized power structures, such as militias or tribes, or through revolving control of the coercive forces. While less common in the twenty-first century, earlier examples include Haiti pre-Aristide's 1994 restoration and Bolivia after 1952. Then there is true totalitarianism, characterized by the emergence of personalistic autocrats, who are charismatic leaders and use revolutionary mobilization and terror to maintain power. Classically, examples include Nazi Germany, Maoist China, and the Soviet Union. Sixth, an area may undergo fragmentation or independence from a central or foreign power

(Stinchcombe's category of "independence"). This includes the failure of centralized control over a territory, with emergence of new de facto or de jure authorities in a subregion. It often correlates with those countries considered to be failing or failed states, such as Puntland in Somalia, South Sudan, and the Kurdistan Regional Government in Iraq, both after 1991 and 2003. Finally, there is military occupation or defeat, which is rare in the contemporary world and usually represents a reversal of revolution entirely, as in Bahrain in 2011.

The variety of examples given here contradicts the notions of neat stages and endings advanced by the natural historians of revolution (see Brinton 1938; Pettee 1938; Sohrabi 1995). Yet it may be possible to create a model of path dependence in revolutionary situations and their outcomes if we think in terms of probabilities rather than predetermined stages.

A *modest* proposal:
From revolutionary coalitions to outcomes

Based on the observations of previous chapters, many, if not almost all, revolutions are accomplished by coalitions of challengers (Dix 1984; Foran 2005), who then compete with each other to institutionalize their power and ideological vision (Foran and Goodwin 1993; Goldstone 1991a; Selbin 1993). Logically, the eventual successor will have been a part of the winning coalition, unless the old regime or a foreign power is able to re-exert control. So the question might be: who makes up the coalition and what might they do? I propose that we can think of challengers in a revolutionary situation as coming from four different possible social locations. First, there are the actors of civil society, which include the formal yet independent organizations of social and political life, such as political parties, religious organizations, labor unions, and so on. Second, there are grassroots mobilizers who are primarily outside of existing institutions, taking the form of social movements, grassroots activists, and even some excluded or banned political oppositions. Next, there are non-state elites, such as landowners, business classes, and educated and intellectual elites. Fourth and finally, there is the state and regime itself, including its bureaucracy, judiciary, coercive forces such as the police and military, as well as regional and local authorities. The revolutionary coalition might develop from just one of these locations, but the most successful coalitions tend to incorporate various types of actors, for instance combining elites, movements, and elements of the state (Foran 2005; Goodwin and Skocpol 1989; Markoff 1996).

After the fall of the regime, the direction of revolution might be set by who emerges victorious in the ensuing power struggle (see Goldstone 1991b; Goodwin 2001; Skocpol 1979). While it is tricky to presume the interests of revolutionary actors or even that those interests are stable over time (see chapter 5), the type of dominant actor suggests with only minimal assumptions that some outcomes will be more likely than others. I suggest that there are four main possible pathways to Stinchcombe's outcomes listed in the previous section:

1. Civil society actors, in the contemporary period, lend themselves to democracy, particularly when formal social groups like religious institutions or trade unions play a role. This arrangement was crucial for Poland in 1989.
2. Mobilizers are most likely to yield democracy (when dominated by moderates as in Tunisia in 2011) or a form of anocracy (possible when radicals dominate as in Iran in 1979), as they combine with either civil society or elements of the elite and state.
3. Elite actors, generally, make a return to conservative authoritarianism more likely, particularly when joined with elements of the prior state, as we see in numerous postcolonial states like Malaysia, Indonesia, and Kenya. Anocracy is likely when elite oligarchs use their state for their own purposes, as in Ukraine after 2004.
4. State actors, depending on who they are, can combine with elites to form a conservative authoritarian government or an anocracy. These are more likely outcomes when hard-liners

dominate the coalition. The course of the 2011 Egyptian revolution suggests this may be occurring there.

However, depending on the specific actor within a type that emerges as dominant, other paths are possible. Specifically:

5. When paramilitary or armed rebel groups within a mobilizing coalition become dominant, the aftermath can yield *caudillismo*, totalitarianism, or fragmentation, dependent on conditions outside of the coalitional process. The aftermath of Libya's 2011 revolution displays the danger of this path as local militias continue to exert influence throughout the country.
6. If the primary elite actor is educated elites or professionals, then democracy may be more likely than other elite paths in the modern world. This pattern was common to the early twentieth-century constitutional revolutions.
7. Moderates within the state, either solely or through partnership with moderate mobilizers, can create the possibility for democracy and negotiated transfers of power as in South Africa in 1993 or Chile in 1991.
8. In cases of the coercive forces playing a dominant role, then the likelihood of *caudillismo* or totalitarianism increases, as organized force becomes the basis of power.
9. When non-central state actors, e.g., local and regional officials, play a central role, then fragmentation is more likely. This seems possible in the aftermath of the Arab Spring revolution in Yemen in 2011.
10. Outside of the coalitional process, independence, fragmentation, and military occupation are more likely when foreign intervention occurs, as the cases of Syria in 2011 and Ukraine in 2014 demonstrate.

As should be clear from Figure 6.2, which charts the pathways from dominant actors to outcomes, democracy has the most routes available in the modern world. This is primarily due to the central role that mobilizing and civil society actors play in modern

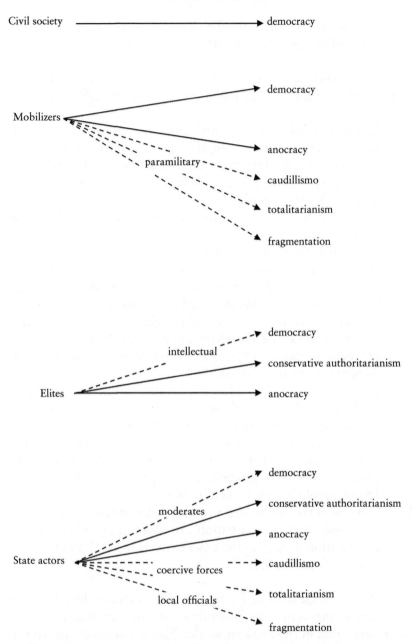

Figure 6.2 Dominant partners in coalitions and outcomes of revolutions

coalitions, and hence revolutions, and hence revolutionary aftermaths. Democracy is also sanctified by the current international system and encouraged both directly and indirectly by international norms (Meyer 2010). And, as Stephan and Chenoweth (2008) show, nonviolent revolutions have a higher success rate than violent ones, and nonviolence is both encouraged by and encourages democratic political goals. The second most likely outcome, anocracy, occurs when elements of the state maintain some control, and mix with inclusionary demands of mobilizers. However, an exclusionary and radical group, rather than broad-based mobilization, may also yield an anocracy. Conservative authoritarianism is the third most likely outcome, and occurs when conservative, often landed, elites and/or hard-liner elements of the state seek to maintain their roles and the privileges of the *ancien régime*. Finally, *caudillismo*, totalitarianism, and independence/fragmentation are less likely outcomes, occurring primarily when power based on coercive force or localized power structures is dominant. Fragmentation is the least likely outcome overall because foreign actors and the international system tend to preserve states as drawn on the map, even at the expense of stability (Hironaka 2005), notwithstanding the 2014 Russian intervention in the Crimea. For these three latter types, a large degree of contingency and the environmental context plays a role.

While this model is speculative, based on the underlying logic of previous research on revolutions, it does suggest a way that a stage theory of outcomes can be drawn in a probabilistic fashion. The examples given suggest its utility, but further research is needed to test its veracity. Given the importance of forecasting the outcome of revolutions (which will be discussed in the last chapter), I urge scholars of radicalism to consider it.[2]

Summary

There is an oft-asserted imagery that terrorism consumes itself, revolutions devour their own children, or that radicalism burns itself out. This chapter has considered why such life-cycle and natural-stage theories are attractive, mostly with a skeptical eye. As noted repeatedly, there are a great number of paths for radicalism and a wide array of outcomes and effects of it. This alone calls life-cycle imagery into doubt. Still, I have proposed that elements of life cycles can be made more analytically useful in two ways. First, it is possible that radicalism and terrorism are repertoires of contention, and thus affected by the dynamics of innovation and repression. Like other protest cycles, we can thus reasonably expect different mechanisms, both internal and external to a movement, to be in play at different times. Second, I have suggested that the outcomes of revolution might develop in a probabilistic path-dependent fashion as different actors dominate the revolutionary aftermath.

Both accounts require much more research to be substantiated. Even within existing studies of movements of all types, repertoires and cycles have not received the attention they need, and revolutionary aftermaths are the least studied aspect of the phenomenon. Thus, the key idea to take away is that radicalism is quite diverse in its development and impact. Anyone who asserts otherwise is either ignorant or selling something.

7

How and Why Does Radicalism Diffuse in Waves?

The mid-nineteenth century in Europe saw not only repeated revolution but the spread of radicalism more generally. Karl Marx's communism was only one of these philosophies. After the failure of the revolutions of 1848, different anti-authoritarian and socialist ideas coalesced into what we now know as anarchism. Anarchists, befitting a philosophy that defies authority, were from the very beginning factionalized. By the end of the 1860s, the First International (an international association of worker organizations) was riven by confrontations between the "mutualists" following the philosophy of Jean-Pierre Proudhon and the "collectivists" led by the Russian revolutionary Mikhail Bakunin. After the failure of the Paris Commune uprising and the imprisonment of many French anarchists, Bakunin split from Karl Marx, predicting that, if communists ever came to power, they would end up as a new ruling class: "the people will feel no better if the stick with which they are being beaten is labeled the 'people's stick'" (Bakunin 1990 [1873]: 23). The First International collapsed in 1873, and anarchists turned towards instigating a general revolution across the capitalist world. The tool for revolution was not a vanguard party, but "propaganda of the deed." While this included bank robberies and labor strikes, a common tactic was terrorism against symbolic targets. Anarchists assassinated numerous heads of state: Alexander II of Russia by a bomb in 1881; French president Sadi Carnot by knife in 1894; Spanish prime minister Antonio Canovas del Castillo by gun in 1897; Empress

Elizabeth of Austria-Hungary stabbed by a file in 1898; Umberto I of Italy by gun in 1900; US president William McKinley shot at point-blank range in 1901; Russian prime minister Pyotr Stolypin by gun in 1911; Spanish prime minister José Canalejas by gun in 1912; and George I of Greece by gun in 1913. (While the assassination of Archduke Franz Ferdinand that triggered World War I is popularly blamed on anarchist elements, it was actually carried out by Serbian nationalists. Then, as now, terrorism was a potent slander for enemies of the state.) The anarchists, enabled by the invention of dynamite, also targeted civilians, attacking theaters and cafés, and plotting against bankers and industrialists like John Rockefeller. In fact, the first "car bomb" in the history of the world was carried out in 1920 by anarchists driving a horse-drawn wagon full of explosives onto Wall Street. The anarchists were only loosely organized, composed of a plethora of independent groups and affiliated individuals whose primary inspiration was to resist the current social order. Activists, tactics, and ideologies spread across national borders, creating the first wave of international terrorism.[1]

As we saw in the previous chapter, radicalism seems to rise and fall with some regularity. Throughout this book, most exemplars of radicalism discussed have occurred as part of a larger wave of contention. In fact, the only major example I have used that does not seem to be part of a wave of radicalism is the contemporary Earth Liberation Front, and even that spread from its origins in Britain to the United States. This begs questions – does radicalism always diffuse, and why do waves of contention happen? This chapter provides an overview of how contention diffuses and what is known about revolutionary waves. The study of diffusion has its roots in late nineteenth-century sociology as a theoretical competitor to Emile Durkheim's (1895) science of "social facts." Gabriel Tarde (1903) proposed that social relations were primarily governed by lateral imitation among individuals, rather than social conditions that floated above human action. Tarde inspired Gustave Le Bon (1896, 1913), who used this as a basis to study the mob psychology of collective action and the "group mind" of rational people behaving irrationally. The metaphor here was one of contagion – like a virus, contact with an "infected" actor would further the diffusing item's spread. This way of thinking was picked up by mid-twentieth-century management scholars to explain how business innovations spread and new products were sold. Rogers (1962) influentially proposed that cumulative diffusion would resemble an S-curve, where early adoption was slow until a critical mass was reached, and then diffusion would rise steeply until the innovation had saturated the market. To this day, the social scientific language of diffusion resembles management speak.

Scholars of social movements also have researched the diffusion of collective action quite a bit, studying how tactics, models of organizations, claims, and so on spread across different movements and places. As discussed in the last chapter, such diffusion – what Tarrow (1993b) calls modular collective action – is crucial to the development of repertoires of contention. There are a number of syntheses of this large literature. Generally, a distinction is drawn between direct processes that involve the relations of persons or organizations and indirect or non-relational processes (Soule 2004; Tarrow 2005). Sometimes a dichotomy is drawn between diffusion within a particular population that is already connected, still called "contagion," and diffusion from one population to another, termed "broadcast diffusion" (Strang and Soule 1998). Even this two-sentence summary is awkward; diffusion research is fairly disorganized. Helpfully, McAdam and Rucht (1993: 59) propose that the diffusion of collective action has four elements:

> (1) a person, group, or organization that serves as the emitter or transmitter; (2) a person, group, or organization that is the adopter; (3) the item that is diffused, such as material goods, information, skills, and the like; and (4) a channel of diffusion that may consist of persons or media that link the transmitter and the adopter.

This suggests that diffusion involves actors who innovate and adopt, channels by which innovations are communicated or learned about, and items that can be innovated and adopted. In addition, the most crucial link in the diffusion process is what

David Strang and John Meyer (1993) call "theorization." A potential adopter does not just need to learn about something, they need to determine that it is relevant to their own situation. Without such a determination, nothing would be adopted and diffusion would not take place. Thus, the similarity, or theorized similarity (that is to say perceived), between the two actors or social sites governs the likelihood of diffusion.

So what can diffuse? The short answer is anything. Giugni (1995: 185–6) identifies five different items that diffuse in movements: a mobilization's goals, issues, ideas; forms of organization; tactics and types of action; general strategies for a movement; and information about the probable success and outcomes of mobilization. We see this diversity of diffusion in radicalism as well. The Tamil Tigers innovated the suicide bomber's belt and it is now widely used by militant organizations around the world. The anarchists pioneered the loosely affiliated international network of terrorism that we see today. And the goals and ideas of some radical movements, whether democracy or communism or Islamism, have spread around the world. In short, "protest makers do not have to reinvent the wheel at each place and in each conflict" (McAdam and Rucht 1993: 58). It is common to believe that only successful things spread (Connell and Cohn 1995; McAdam 1983; Myers 2000; Weyland 2009). For instance, it is difficult to imagine that the Arab Spring would have occurred if protest in Tunisia had not brought down the regime in January 2011. But even unsuccessful things diffuse (Soule 1999). Radicals have not successfully established a lasting Islamic state anywhere in the world, for example, but Islamist militants still try in Nigeria, Syria, and Somalia. And even sometimes seemingly innovative things are actually activations of latent ideas or strategies (Beck 2011), as France's repeated nineteenth-century revolutions demonstrate. This suggests the power of Strang and Meyer's theorization concept – when something is thought of as relevant and useful, it can spread even without a demonstration of its effectiveness. We thus do not need to try to explain diffusion by arguing for flawed information, cognitive heuristics, or Le Bonian irrationality (cf. Weyland 2014).

Advantages for movements are not the only things that can diffuse. As we saw in the last chapter, counter-movements, elites, and regimes also learn how to counter tactical innovations and thus the advantage of surprise decreases for later adopters (McAdam 1983, 1995). We see this in the policing of demonstrations in modern democracies. Over time, police forces around the world have learned how to effectively contain mass protests, and thus, while movements still use them, demonstrations tend to have less success than in the past (Della Porta and Reiter 1998; Earl 2003; Myers and Oliver 2008). Elites also learn to co-opt goals and claims of collective action by changing their behavior and giving some things away before movements are able to mobilize forcefully (Beissinger 2007). John Markoff (1996) has even argued that this dynamic is central to how democratization spread.

The next sections of this chapter examines the channels by which things spread and conditions under which determinations of relevance are made.

Channels of diffusion

The diffusion literature abounds in various "channels" that connect "transmitters" and "adopters." At its most basic, a channel of diffusion is just communication – what are the various ways a potential adopter may hear about the item of diffusion? Usually, the literature distinguishes between direct and indirect channels (Soule 2004), but this is less helpful as the direct category means only interpersonal networks and the indirect category becomes a catch-all for everything else. To address this, Andrews and Biggs (2006) propose a trichotomy of networks, movement organizations, and the news media. Tarrow (2005) distinguishes more clearly between relational channels, non-relational channels, and mediated channels. Yet, for clarity's sake, it is better to conceptualize channels that are as distinct as possible, rather than lumping together apples and orangutans. I thus draw a distinction between geographic-spatial channels, social-relational channels, brokerage, and mass-informational channels as detailed below.

One potential channel of direct diffusion is that of geographic proximity. Classically, it was assumed that mobilization would spread out from its point of origin with lessening effects in further populations (Connell and Cohn 1995). For instance, Rudé (1964) notes that collective action in eighteenth- and nineteenth-century France and England seemed to spread along major lines of transportation, and Hedström, Sandell, and Stern (2000) find that the growth of the Swedish Social Democratic Party followed the path of political instigators. Similarly, Earth Liberation Front attacks have been presumed to be the work of traveling activists, and court cases against ELF members have charged them with crimes in a variety of locales. Yet recent work that has examined geographic diffusion finds little role for it once other channels of diffusion are considered (Andrews and Biggs 2006; Braun and Vliegenthart 2009). Geographic proximity is more likely a stand-in for social proximity (Braun and Koopmans 2009; Myers 2000), particularly in eras with slower communication and transportation. Given the increasing interconnectedness of individuals, groups, and societies due to globalization and advances in technology, it is likely that geographic effects will continue to be overtaken by other channels. And, often, what we perceive as geography is actually social similarity, discussed in more detail in the next section. The Arab Spring and the post-communist Color Revolutions diffused within a region that shared similar regime types, cultural backgrounds, and social structures.

Another form of direct diffusion can be called social-relational. The key aspect here is social networks – individuals are obviously not isolated actors but connected to each other through various personal relationships. Previous research has shown that strong direct ties, such as friendship, are one avenue of participation in social movements (see chapters 2 and 3). Similarly, direct network ties can give individuals information about what others are doing and thus facilitate diffusion and adoption. For instance, Roger Gould (1991) finds that direct ties between neighborhoods in the Paris Commune uprising of 1871 diffused rebellion, particularly among the most interdependent groups. Different neighborhoods saw different levels of conflict and casualties, depending on how much social solidarity each neighborhood had. In addition to preexisting networks, direct ties can also be forged. In the Color Revolutions, youth activists in Serbia used the experience of their 2000 Bulldozer Revolution against Slobodan Milosevic to train other activists in Georgia and Ukraine (Kuzio 2006). As the Tunisian Revolution of 2011 got underway, activists there turned to their Eastern European counterparts for advice, translating their training manuals into Arabic. Activists from one movement can also become involved in another, carrying prior forms and actions with them (Meyer and Whittier 1994). An excellent study by Dan Wang and Sarah Soule (2012) uses network analysis to show that movement organizations who demonstrate together tend to adopt the same tactics. Collaboration is thus a social-relational channel for diffusion as well as for the development of repertoires. This is much of the story of contemporary Islamic radicalism – some mujahedeen who fought in the 1980s in Afghanistan helped spark Islamic revolts in places like Egypt and formed the early backbone of international Islamic terrorist groups.

Yet not all networks are direct. Many social relationships are formed by weak ties, where two individuals are linked by a third person they know in common. Weak ties have been found to have a strong role in various social pursuits as they bridge social networks and bring more information than any one set of relationships already has (Granovetter 1974). Thus, some individuals are "brokers" who bridge distinct social spheres. This is an important channel of diffusion which, while social-relational, deserves its own category.

Brokerage is "the linking of two or more previously unconnected social sites by a unit that mediates their relations with one another and/or with yet other sites" (McAdam et al. 2001: 26). Brokers are more than just participants in collective action; crucially, they leverage their network ties to create new relationships between multiple networks. As such, brokerage is a particularly effective indirect channel for diffusion and mobilization. For instance, Hillman (2008) finds that political mediators between multiple networks were critical in brokering the parliamentary coalitions that preceded the English Civil War of the 1600s, and Han (2009) argues that Paul Revere's famous Midnight Ride at the beginning of the American Revolution was made effective by his role as a broker (see chapter 3). Others have argued that revolutionary waves occur because revolutionary regimes consciously try to export their revolution (Halliday 1999; Katz 1997), but this is better seen as a version of brokerage. A revolutionary state finds like-minded activists in another society who then import the strategies and goals of revolution into their own country. These foreign-sponsored groups, whether radical, revolutionary, or terrorist, are brokers between two societies. For example, Hezbollah plays this role for the government of Iran and the Shiite community in Lebanon, and many communist revolutionaries like Ho Chi Minh and Che Guevara were brokers. In brokerage, influence creates diffusion and passivity can be turned into action. The previously mentioned case of Serbian activists in the group Otpor is one example. Brokers were crucial to translating and adopting western ideas such as the practice of nonviolent resistance advocated by Gene Sharp (Bunce and Wolchik 2006). International organizations, foreign governments, and groups like the Soros Foundation also played the role of brokers, encouraging activists and even financing mobilization (McFaul 2007). Thus, McAdam, Tarrow, and Tilly (2001) see brokerage as an important component in scale shift – a diffusion-like process in which local mobilizations transform into larger ones.

Finally, mass information is a crucial indirect channel of diffusion. I prefer the term "mass information" over the more common usage of "mass media" because of its historical and perhaps future flexibility (see chapter 4 as well). Thirty years ago, no scholar would have included the internet as a channel of diffusion but today it is a recognized mechanism. In the past, there were no news media, but pamphleteering and radical claims spread quickly after the development of the printing press. For instance, peasants in Southern Germany, Austria, and Switzerland in 1525 rose up against their overlords when a revolutionary tract, the Twelve Articles of Swabia, diffused ideas of limiting feudal exploitation that were legitimated by new common-language translations of the Bible (Blickle 1981). Thus, we should think of indirect mass communication as distinct from news media.

Mass information has been found to be a crucial predictor of diffusion (Andrews and Biggs 2006; Myers 2000), particularly the larger the media coverage of an event. Koopmans and Olzak (2004) find that right-wing anti-immigrant violence in Germany diffuses this way, and see the media as an opportunity for further articulation of claims and grievances. News coverage is also a mobilizing force. For instance, it brought participants to the streets in Ukraine's Orange Revolution (Beissinger 2011; McFaul 2005). It is also clear that sources of mass information are not domestic alone; Kern (2011) finds that foreign media were a major source of information in the collapse of East Germany in 1989. This is particularly noteworthy as the internet knows fewer broadcast constraints, and is increasingly a tool of social activists. But we should not overstate the role of the internet and social media in the diffusion of radical mobilization. While internet sites and forums provide a way to coordinate mobilization (like Polletta's (1999) "free spaces"), they also provide information to regimes about who the activists are. In fact, governments like Russia, Belarus, and China are known to target activists who post online. Further, the internet cannot replace the role of local face-to-face networks for creating and sustaining mobilization. In the Egyptian Revolution, protest took off *after* the internet and many cell services were shut down by the Mubarak regime, primarily due to the coalition with the Muslim Brotherhood.

In sum, then, diffusion can occur through many channels, including geography and proximity, relational and social networks, brokerage, and mass information. It should be clear from the previous review that diffusion is not forced into any one channel. Rather, each linkage can be used simultaneously and dynamically, reinforcing itself and others in a multiplicative fashion (see Myers 2000). But channels of diffusion are not the whole story. A channel only exists to the extent that it links two or more different social sites. Thus, to have a full understanding of diffusion, we need to examine the actors involved and their positions in social structure. This is the task of the next section.

Actors, social similarity, and relevance in diffusion

Every instance of diffusion involves at least two actors: a transmitter who innovates or pioneers an item of diffusion; and an adopter who implements the item in a different context. Either actor can have an active or passive role in diffusion. The actors can engage in "reciprocation" where both agents promote diffusion, "adaptation" where an active adopter intentionally copies from a passive transmitter, "accommodation" where an active transmitter customizes its content to the context of a passive adopter, or, finally, classic contagion where both actors are passive (Snow and Benford 1999). Not only is this language somewhat awkward, a focus on actors also downplays how relevant the diffusing item is to a potential adopter (Strang and Meyer 1993). As introduced above, relevance is the most crucial aspect of diffusion, even if it is often ignored.

Relevance can come from prior determinations by actors and is primarily related to place in social structure. Classically, diffusion research has emphasized hierarchical diffusion, the so-called "Harvard effect," where lower-status actors will imitate the practices of higher-status actors. For example, Braun and Vliegenthart (2009) find that soccer fans will copy the violence of the higher-status players on the pitch. However, Sarah Soule (1997) finds no evidence for hierarchical diffusion in the 1980s South African divestment movement led by American college students. Rather, student groups were more likely to adopt from groups at similar institutions. While such "structural equivalence," a general term for social structures or groups that are largely similar to each other, is often considered another channel of diffusion, it makes more sense to see it as part of the actors' relationship to social structure.

First, structural equivalence can be created by factors outside of the actors' control. For instance, Tarrow (1993a, 1993b) argues that state building and centralization in early modern Europe created structurally equivalent societies with similar actors in which diffusion could take place. Such state-centered factors also have been found to be important in the collapse of the Soviet Union (Beissinger 1998). In the present era, globalization and increasing standardization of social practice may also be increasing structural equivalence (Giugni 1998). Thus, some argue that international terrorism may actually be a counterpart to globalization (Barber 1995; Eisenstadt 1999; Moghaddam 2008). Further, Goldstone (2004) argues that protest and social movements spread as democratization spreads. As we saw in chapter 4, we might thus expect radicalism to increase in turn. In short, changes in political institutions can create structural equivalence and social similarity, and it should be no surprise that collective action, whether radical or not, increases as a result.

Second, the creation of cultural categories and identities can also generate social similarity. In a wonderful, but non-radical example, once autism and the autistic became identified as a category, practices for autistic care and diagnosis quickly spread (Eyal 2010). Similarly, the growth of the activist identity in New Left movements allowed them to borrow from one another (McAdam and Rucht 1993; Soule 2004), even to the extent of radicalism like that of the American Weather Underground and the German Red Army Faction. Social similarity has also been found to outweigh the effects of particular channels of diffusion (Braun and Koopmans 2009). For example, labor unions in one country will closely follow the actions of labor unions in another country because they occupy the same role in both societies (Giugni 1998). And Kurzman (2008) argues that intellectuals in various societies imitated and drew on one another's experience in the early twentieth-century wave of constitutional revolutions as their identity as a distinct social class emerged. This also seems to be part of the story of the Arab Spring (Beck 2014). In short, the determination of relevance can predate the diffusion process – actors will pay attention to the innovations and practices of actors they deem socially similar, even in the absence of other channels.

Yet relevance can also be a more active process. Pamela Oliver (1989) has argued that hearing about contentious events allows for a "moment of decision" in which individuals are given the opportunity to consider their own positions and possible support or participation. Diffusion researchers tend to emphasize that these decisions are based on judgments of relative advantage. For instance, Weyland (2009) argues that the revolutions of 1848 displayed bounded rationality where mobilizing groups weighed, and sometimes mis-weighed, the advantages of rebellion. Kuran (1995) also assumes rationality on the part of actors and suggests that surprising events occur because individuals hide their real preferences until a mobilization is underway. However, DiMaggio and Powell (1983) argue that actors are most likely to adopt a new approach wholesale without consideration as they are unable to calculate rationally the costs and benefits. Further, instances of collective action are often confusing and ambiguous events. Kurzman (2004b) argues that such ambiguity led people into the streets during the Iranian Revolution as they did not know what else to do, and Ermakoff (2009) has argued that in times of confusion actors will try to determine and then follow what they perceive the collective will to be. In short, while rational adoption certainly does exist, it is not the only process by which a determination of relevance is made. Actors can and do make seemingly irrational choices and miscalculate benefits of adoption. The diffusion process as a whole is summarized in Figure 7.1.

The importance of social similarity and perceptions of relevance in diffusion points to another issue. Diffusion occurs not just among actors but also under particular social conditions. We might thus expect diffusion and waves of radicalism to be more or less likely at different times or in different contexts. This is the focus of the next section and the second question that this chapter addresses.

Time, space, and context of radical waves

As we saw in chapter 6, diffusion is one aspect of protest cycles. But a rise in average protest rates does not a true wave of contention make. Thus, we need to distinguish between cycles and waves, and further differentiate them from spikes in contention. Collective action may occur in a rapid spurt and, with little further

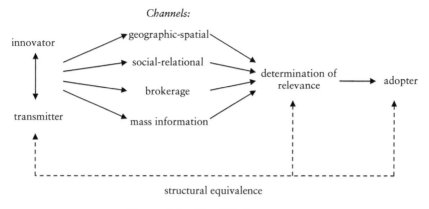

Figure 7.1 The diffusion process

diffusion, resemble a short-lived spike. Or collective action can peak more slowly and constitute a cycle sustained by diffusion over time. Or collective action can take longer and spread further and constitute a wave of contention that can last for years or even decades. In short, we need to recognize that contentious events are rarely isolated, but occur in sequences of prior and subsequent events (Koopmans 1993, 2004).

If diffusion is fast, a surge in collective action is also likely to be fast. These shorter peaks may be fundamentally governed by dynamics internal to collective action. Biggs (2003, 2005) argues that positive feedback, whereby the diffusion of collective action builds on itself ever more intensely, is a product of the interdependence of activists. The more dependent actors are on one another, as in a labor union considering a strike, the more likely it is that positive feedback will occur. Recall that Gould (1991) found just such a process in the Paris Commune rebellion. Protest cycles, however, display sustained collective action over time, which requires more organization and strategy than a short-lived spurt. This is often promoted by movement organizations and their own dynamics of competition in interaction with the larger political environment (Tarrow 1998). Spikes and cycles may tend to burn themselves out from exhaustion effects and resource constraints (Olzak 1994), as well as counter-adaptation as we have seen.

On the other hand, waves of contention seem to be built out of dynamics that are primarily outside the process of collective action. Repertoires of contention are long-standing and build slowly (Tilly 1977), and mark long-lasting shifts in an entire social system (Beck 2011). Here, diffusion may be much slower and more likely related to changes in social structure. In fact, diffusion may be so slow that it makes less sense to speak of it as a process fundamental to waves of contention, as I discuss below. Rather, waves are distinct in that they are driven by underlying economic, social, and political realities far beyond the control of any given actor or movement. This is true even when diffusion is quite fast – the Arab Spring occurred because the fundamental contradictions of authoritarian regimes made them susceptible to challenge (Beck 2014; Goldstone 2013). Recently, revolution seems to be a dirty word. Social scientists have avoided calling contemporary waves revolutions, preferring "democratization" (Markoff 1996; Weyland 2014) or the conceptual tongue twister "regime change cascades" (Hale 2013). Such terms obscure more than they illuminate. I think the aversion is because the term "revolution" has taken on a negative connotation. In my current research on the empirical basis of revolution studies, I find that leftist, guerrilla-war-type insurgencies are the most popular cases to study, even though they are not the most common type of revolution. For instance, the Nicaraguan Revolution of 1979, while neither generally memorable nor historically important, is the most studied event. No wonder there are so many competing interpretations of it as outlined in chapter 5. In any case, let us call a revolutionary wave a revolutionary wave, and not make the mistake of France's Louis XVI in 1789 and ask if it is just a regime-change cascade.

As we saw in chapter 4, some social and political conditions make different types of radicalism, revolution, or terrorism more likely. The favorable conditions that exist transnationally, that is to say, above and beyond any one state, cause a wave of contention as they create social similarity and intensify diffusion processes. Thus, in a wave of radicalism, diffusion is usually a mechanism or secondary cause (what sociologists sometimes call proximal causation). We thus need to consider the "permissive world context" for radicalism (Goldfrank 1979). There are three primary areas to examine: economic conditions, geopolitical competition, and sociocultural contexts.

One line of thought about revolutionary waves is that they are the product of global economic shifts, particularly during times of recessions or decreasing prices for exports (Paige 1975; Wallerstein 1980). The imagery here is not one of diffusion from an initiating event to subsequent ones. Rather, economic strain is argued to affect many states simultaneously, creating the potential for near simultaneous mobilizations (Arrighi and Silver 1999; Foran 2005; Tilly 1993b). This logic typifies much of the extant research on clusters of revolution (e.g., Goldstone 1991b), even if it does not provide a true theory of waves as a distinct phenomenon. While such a process was noted by early twentieth-century scholars of revolution (e.g., Merriman 1938), research in this vein has its roots in 1980s attempts to unify state-centered theories of revolution with world systems analysis, starting with an article by Walter Goldfrank (1979). The first attempt emphasized the economic dependency of a peripheral, resource-producing state on a core, manufacturing state. In a series of studies, Terry Boswell and William Dixon (1990, 1993) find that such dependency increases rates of rebellion in economically peripheral societies. Their logic is purely Marxist – dependency heightens economic exploitation and class conflict, which builds into rebellion as Marx would have anticipated. Jeffrey Paige (1975, 1997) uses a similar logic in his studies of agrarian revolutions, as does John Foran's (2005) five-factor framework – one of which is dependency – for explaining Third World revolutions. A review of evidence for the link between transnational conditions and protest by Maney (2001) concludes that dependency heightens political exclusion but also divides elites. As we well know from chapter 4, these two conditions are common to the beginnings of revolutionary situations.

Economic conditions can also generate waves of contention through another process. World systems analysis stresses the cyclical nature of the global economy. Fortunes rise and fall with some regularity, and recessions seem to correlate with a variety of political phenomenon, like war (Goldstein 1988). Radicalism and revolution also seem to fall in line with economic depression, as the recent resurgence of ultra-nationalists in Europe and the Arab Spring revolutions demonstrate. Arrighi, Hopkins, and Wallerstein (1989) argue that economic shifts create the potential for "anti-systemic movements" (see also Arrighi and Silver 1999), which are mobilizations directed against the very nature of the international system and world economy. They see the New Left movements of the 1960s as the first expression of a contemporary trend of anti-systemic mobilization. Currently, world systems scholars are more obsessed with the World Social Forum, an annual international conference of activists that is intended as a counterpart to neoliberal capitalism (Byrd and Jasny 2010; Chase-Dunn et al. 2008; Reese et al. 2008; Smith 2004; Smith et al. 2012). While I do not believe that a conference constitutes radicalism, it is a sign of international learning and coordination among activists who may someday become radicals. The growth of contemporary anti-systemic movements correlates with the general shift of the center of the global economy from North America and Europe to Asia. Wallerstein (2000) argues that much of what we call globalization now is actually an expression of this change. In short, from this view, radical waves are expressions of economic shifts and come regularly in the world system, whether in the form of radical Calvinists of the sixteenth century (Bergesen and Lizardo 2004), communists of the nineteenth century (Arrighi et al. 1989), international terrorists of the twentieth century (Moghaddam 2008), or the nonviolent activists of the twenty-first century (Smith and Wiest 2012).

World systems analysis also focuses on phases within geo-political power. In Wallerstein's original formulation, unrivaled hegemonic power is dependent on the economic growth that enables military supremacy (Hopkins and Wallerstein 1979; Wallerstein 1983). Hegemons provide stability in the international system and coordinate coalitions of great and lesser powers that suppress challenges to the international order (Modelski and Thompson 1988; Modelski 1987). We thus would expect the relative decline of the hegemon and growing geopolitical competition to correspond with an increase in radical challenges. Terry

Boswell (2004), in his last, uncompleted research project before his early death, had begun to find evidence for this proposition. The idea has made it into other studies of revolution as well, even if waves are not the object of study (e.g., Foran 2005). Again, the logic here is of simultaneous pressure creating simultaneous rebellion. For example, Timothy Wickham-Crowley (1992) examines radical mobilizations in post-World War II Latin America and finds that they were part of the Soviet and American struggle for influence in the region. Geopolitics is thus a political opportunity for radicals. But revolutions themselves also create geopolitical competition (Halliday 1999; Walt 1996). Both Mark Katz (1997) and Michael Mann (2013) argue that revolutionary waves are products of a central successful revolution. The post-revolutionary state can try to export its model or have demonstration effects on other societies in the region. From this viewpoint, we would expect to see revolutionary and radical waves during times of a shift in the locus of global power, and perhaps even presaging it as core great powers exhaust themselves militarily and financially in war and intervention. As I noted before, the second Iraq War and NATO intervention in Afghanistan seem to have done just that (C. Johnson 2001; Mann 2005; Wallerstein 2003).

As we saw in chapter 4, economic and political conditions are not the only context of radicalism. Sociocultural shifts can also make revolution, radicalism, and terrorism more likely. Historians of revolutionary waves have long noted this dynamic and stressed the role of cultural change in creating similar ideological claims in a particular era. Most of the research here is based on studies of the Enlightenment revolutions at the end of the eighteenth century (see Chartier 1991; Godechot 1965; Palmer 1954, 1959), but the idea is generalizable to other times and places (Sewell 1985; Wuthnow 1989). Each era has its own cultural mentality and model of politics (Goldstone 2002; Sohrabi 1995), and these can promote radical collective action. In my own research on revolutionary waves, I have stressed how waves seem to be distinctly cultural events. My first study of revolutionary waves analyzes data on Europe from the 1500s to the 1900s with a focus on the changes in transnational conditions and the beginning of revolutionary wave events (Beck 2011). I find that waves seem to be explained best by broader cultural change and integration within Europe, rather than other factors. I have also extended this model to the Arab Spring (Beck 2014). I argue that revolutionary waves are more likely when a society is relatively connected to world society, and thus its cultural content, but its local political structures are incongruent with transnationally legitimated practices. This dynamic also creates schisms between elites, elements of the state, and the regime. Authoritarian Middle Eastern regimes were clearly in contradiction with the international ideals of political participation and human rights, and the relative global connectedness of these societies allowed for the diffusion and incorporation of claims and tactics developed elsewhere, like in the Color Revolutions. The evidence I analyze supports this story. I also suggest in the article that we need to make our theories of radical waves better. Rather than making a false choice between lateral diffusion and simultaneous transnational pressures, I propose that we should create theories that account for both. Transnational conditions create social similarity between societies and this allows a greater chance that random events, like a Tunisian fruit-seller's self-immolation, will instigate a wave of contention. How this might work for each of the conditions surveyed is presented in Table 7.1.

Even if you agree with the thrust of this section – that transnational conditions matter for waves – the question remains as to which condition is the most important. In my study of European waves, I find no significant correlation between revolution and world economic conditions, but some correlation with geopolitical competition and cultural changes. In contrast, Ho-Fung Hung's (2009, 2011) studies of contentious waves in early modern China find that the protest corresponds to economic changes and state formation with the only effect of cultural idioms being on the target of contention. I remain agnostic as to which condition is primary. All transnational processes are highly interrelated – hegemony depends on economic growth, political ideologies determine the legitimate bounds of power, and economic and cultural shifts tend to go hand in hand. These dynamics, which we now experience as globalization, have also been bundled together in other eras such

Table 7.1 Transnational conditions, diffusion, and radical waves

Transnational condition	Direct effects on mobilization (simultaneous conditions)	Indirect effects on mobilization (diffusion processes)
Economic dependency	(1) Increases class exploitation and grievances (2) Creates exclusionary and personalist regimes	(1) Increases structural equivalence among peripheral societies
World economic downturn or shift	(1) Increases grievances (2) Strains state capacity	(1) Creates opportunity for transnational "anti-systemic" movement
Geopolitical competition	(1) Creates political opportunity for contention (2) Weakens regimes reliant on foreign powers	(1) Increases perception of probable success of mobilization in "unsettled time"
Successful revolution	(1) Heightens regional instability (2) Increases likelihood of international war	(1) Demonstration effect of success (2) Creates sponsor and broker for further contention
World cultural change	(1) Delegitimates incongruent regimes (2) Reduces elite unity (3) Changes role of non-state actors	(1) Heightens "theorization" of cross-national similarity (2) Provides innovative models and increases channels of diffusion

as the "first" wave of globalization at the end of the nineteenth century. This suggests that, if transnational changes yield radical waves, we should be able to discern them in these two times. In fact, this is my next research project – to compare waves in different eras of globalization. As this book stated at its very beginning, some of the parallels are quite eerie: the early twentieth-century constitutional revolutions as compared with the nonviolent ones of today, or the nineteenth-century anarchists as compared with current Islamist terrorists. And I do not think it is a coincidence that the Enlightenment revolutions occurred at the same time as mercantile capitalism emerged within the Atlantic system or that the Protestant Reformation and its attendant radical violence and rebellion happened shortly after the beginning of European colonization of the globe. So I recommend the interested reader to look for my book on the subject, hopefully sometime in the next decade.

Summary

This chapter has surveyed the research on how radicalism spreads and waves of contention form. There are two ways of approaching the issue. The first stresses an actor-centric diffusion process, where channels link innovators and adopters, and their similarities to one another affect the likelihood of imitation. The second focuses on the conditions that are outside of actors and their societies – how transnational conditions can create the potential for radicalism in multiple places at the same time. I have proposed that we can and should unify the two imageries and build theories and research studies that show how the two are related. This is the key idea of the chapter – when a diffusion or wave account of an event or movement is encountered, the reader should be able to identify which imagery the author relies on and how the theory might be improved if the author considered the other dimension.

I want to end with one further thought about diffusion and waves that was inspired by the students in my 2012 class of the same name as this book. Could what we perceive as diffusion often just be political opportunity? At the 2011 American Sociological Association conference, one sociologist recounted a conversation with a member of the Syrian opposition a few years earlier. The Syrians wanted expert advice on how the Assad regime might be overthrown. The sociologist advised: "wait for an opportunity." A diffusion story of waves like the Arab Spring would stress imitation, and assume that there would be no mobilization without previous innovation and success. But, as we saw in the first part of this book, radicals constantly have grievances and do not need a demonstration of them to desire to mobilize. Rather, they may just be taking advantage of the opportunity that a prior event provides through priming public and international support for mobilization. And, in fact, this does seem to have happened in the Arab Spring as protestors in Egypt, Bahrain, and Syria drew on existing mobilizing networks and prior attempts (Beck 2014; Clarke 2011; Leenders 2012). In this sense, what looks like imitation might actually just be good strategy. This hypothesis is easily testable. A study could examine well-known waves of contention and look for evidence of prior organization by activists. If there was little to none, then a diffusive view of imitation would be supported. But if there was quite a bit, then perhaps it is only the spread of opportunity.

8

What is the Past and Future of Radicalism?

It is common in the last chapter of a book to summarize all that has come before and provide prognostication about the future direction of the subject matter at hand. I shall not disappoint. But why just prognosticate, when I can discuss what social scientists think of prediction of political instability in general, and why just summarize, when each chapter ends with a brief conclusion about the main point and can be consulted again? Instead, there is more utility in surveying what we have learned about the numerous examples of radicals, revolutionaries, and terrorists used throughout – by my count, more than fifty different events and groups. And when these examples are organized in rough chronological order, perhaps more general observations can be made.

The earliest examples of radicalism given come from the early modern world. The sixteenth century in Europe saw the diffusion of radical ideas, enabled by the printing press. Contention had religious overtones as Luther created a schism within the Catholic Church, German peasants fought their masters in 1525, and radical Calvinists instigated revolt in Switzerland and the Netherlands. The English Civil War and resulting Glorious Revolution of the 1600s displayed these continued religious conflicts, but also developed when marginal elites were excluded from the benefits of power and brokers formed competing political factions. Other parts of the early modern world, too, saw radicalism – Chinese movements fought against the imperial state and local officials as economic and political shifts occurred. By the eighteenth century, in the next set of examples, the template for modern revolutions emerged. American Patriots, organized through networks of secret associations, launched a war of independence against the British state. Their success helped inspire the natural historians' most favored case of a social revolution – France in 1789. The French monarchy, strained by competition with other great powers and in increasing financial straits, accidentally enabled revolution by calling the Third Estate to meet. This brought the Enlightenment radicals with their philosophy of natural rights into conflict with the regime, and elite schisms resulted. The liminality of events such as the taking of the Bastille turned instability into revolution and helped inspire a revolutionary wave across the Atlantic system. By Napoleon's last march, the map of Europe and the Americas had been remade by revolutions, counterrevolutions, and war.

The nineteenth century saw the development of modern social movements and repeated revolutionary attempts in Europe and elsewhere. The failed revolutionaries of 1848 borrowed from each other, developing the tactic of barricading a street into a repertoire of contention. 1848 also gave new life to radical ideas, reactivating the notion of individual rights against tyranny and reshaping it into revolutionary ideologies like communism and anarchism. Anti-systemic ideas combined with loosely organized affiliates that knew no borders, as both a cause of radicalism and an outcome of it. While immediate attempts at revolution such as the Paris Commune of 1871 would fail (though demonstrating the role of network mobilization and solidarity of participants in revolution), the radicals hung on. Anarchists stalked government officials with knives, guns, and bombs and created the first modern wave of international terrorism. With the world facing the challenge of trade globalization that standardized national economies, created cross-national similarities, and instituted new models of political action and governance, the remaining monarchies faced a new revolutionary challenge. Early twentieth-century republican reformers in Russia, Persia, Turkey, and elsewhere sought to limit monarchal authority and put in place national constitutions that enshrined some citizenship rights. This instituted a new model of revolution, the democratic one, accomplished as much from within the state as from without. Reformers saw initial success due to their coalitions with intellectuals, bureaucrats, and members of the regime, but had their gains rolled back as monarchs reasserted themselves and international support waned.

But repression of revolution – even a moderate, inclusive revolution – often sets the stage for more radical attempts in the near future. In 1917, the Russian Empire was exhausted by the grinding warfare of World War I. With an organizational home in the Communist Party and workers' associations, the revolutionaries successfully created an instance of dual power, as coined by Trotsky, and overthrew the tsar. The resulting civil war established the Soviet Union in the world's second great social revolution, and created a sponsor of revolution worldwide. The communists were not the only radicals to seize on the opportunities that world war and its devastating economic and social dislocation provided. Nationalist and democratic reformers tried to establish new governments in the old colonial empires, but their efforts were eclipsed by the rise of fascism. Using shirts as displays of solidarity, fascists gained popularity due to the social environment of the time, their friendliness to business interests, and their effective use of civil society organizations. They saw a quick rise to power in Italy and Germany and electoral influence elsewhere. By the 1930s, Spanish Civil War, fascism and communism seemed to be the only alternatives for political organization as democratization faltered. World war again changed the direction of radicalism, ending sympathy for fascism, but also creating new opportunities for revolutionaries. In 1948, Chinese communists overcame the remnants of the nationalist state that had been smashed by the Japanese invasion. While the early communists gained a foothold by taking over student movements, it was Mao's organizational structure of a guerrilla army that successfully brought them to power. This ended a decades-long series of rebellions in China that began with Sun Yat-Sen's constitutional revolution against the faltering imperial state in 1911. Throughout the postwar years, communism remained a potent ideological and organizational weapon for revolutionaries. Fidel Castro, like Mao before him, led a group of guerillas to victory against a personalistic dictator in

Cuba. He, like other Latin American guerilla leaders, commanded a group made up of people from diverse backgrounds. Radicals joined the revolution due to their own biographical availability and network ties, like Ernesto Che Guevara. Guevara would go on to become a symbol of resistance and radicalism, even though his revolutionary attempts in Africa and Bolivia led only to his death.

Yet even communist revolutionaries rarely adopted ideology blindly. In the Nicaraguan Revolution of 1979, socialism mixed with the liberation theology of the Catholic Church and a history of resistance against the state to create a uniquely pluralist socialist revolution. Similarly, many of the other post-World War II radicals were more nationalist than they were Marxist, fighting for independence from colonial empires or to establish ethnic homelands. The activists of the FLN fought French authority in Algeria with a pyramidal structure of cells that allowed for coordinated action but kept information compartmentalized. Northern Irish nationalists organized themselves in a bifurcated fashion, with militant and political wings, and drew most of their participants by appealing to identity, family honor, and personal dignity. Nationalism was not always a success, however. Basque separatists, emerging from the region's civil society, failed to establish effective territorial control and began a campaign of terrorism against the Spanish state that left scars on the region's economy. The PKK did not form a Kurdish state in Turkey but did create support for right-wing opposition parties because the government got the blame for not preventing their attacks. And even the formidable Tamil Tigers of Sri Lanka – who had established a quasi-government in part of the country and created the modern suicide bomber – were defeated by the government in 2009.

The 1960s and 1970s also saw the emergence of the New Left social movements who spun off their own radicals. New Left groups, like labor unions, student groups, and identity movements, borrowed tactics and ideas from each other cross-nationally and contributed to a growing sense that anti-systemic contention could change the world. Activists, when faced with a failure to influence their governments' policies, became more radical. In Europe, the German Red Army Faction and the Italian Red Brigades engaged in terrorist attacks and displayed a classic life cycle of radicalization as they became more isolated and fetishized violence. In the United States, Black Panthers spun off from the civil rights movement, and the Weather Underground broke from the student anti-Vietnam War movement. Weathermen and -women were young, often students, and came predominantly from the educated middle and upper classes, but had prior nonviolent activist experience. Thus, they needed to socialize themselves into the possibility of using violence and consciously broke social norms to create in-group solidarity. Even though the Weather Underground did not end the Vietnam War or succeed at any of its other goals, the group displayed a different path to their European counterparts. They were self-moderating radicals, preferring property damage to bodily harm, and were able to emerge from the underground without serving years in prison.

The failure of nationalist and leftist organizations created an opportunity for another important form of twentieth-century radicalism. By the 1970s, Islamist organizations across the Middle East were engaged in struggles against authoritarian dictatorships and monarchies. In 1979, a broad coalition of Iranians brought the seemingly permanent Pahlavi state to its knees. The regime was made vulnerable by a patrimonial structure that excluded many elites and by weakening oil prices, and its vacillating response of conciliation and repression only fueled the street protests. During the course of the revolution, Shiite political Islam gained more support and, after the Shah fled the country, Khomeini and his followers quickly outmaneuvered other factions to establish an Islamic republic. Islamism became a powerful weapon for radicals elsewhere – the mujahedeen of Afghanistan fought the Soviet Union with American support and later evolved into the Taliban and Al-Qaeda. Al-Qaeda's hybrid organizational structure – part hierarchy, part affiliation network – allowed it to become an umbrella organization for Islamist resistance against the West and its client regimes in the region. While support for Islamists varied widely by country and with little correlation to any particular demographic or grievance, the ideology was flexible enough to work as an identity, a religious philosophy, and a revolutionary platform. In fact, Islamism was rather more modernist than fundamentalist. Accordingly, Islamism penetrated into formerly nationalist struggles, like the Israeli–Arab conflict or the Chechen insurgency against the Russian state. Hamas began as an Islamic counterweight to the secular PLO, and employed a bifurcated organizational structure to great success, so much so, in fact, that nationalist Palestinian groups copied its tactics, developing a network of suicide bombers to fight Israeli occupation and military actions. In Lebanon, Hezbollah acted as a local broker between Lebanon and Iran. And both Hamas and Hezbollah struggled for political legitimacy, particularly given media depictions of them as terrorist organizations. After the spectacular attacks on September 11th, fighting terrorism became the new imperative. Failing states like Afghanistan and Somalia saw increasing intervention as other powers sought to deny Islamist organizations safe harbor. While Al-Qaeda central had been rendered mostly impotent by the "war on terror" and the death of its figurehead bin Laden, small groups of sympathizers staged attacks in places like Madrid, London, and Boston, unknowingly copying the template of the anarchists a century before.

The end of the twentieth century also saw resurgent radicalism on both the left and the right side of the political spectrum in democracies. In the United States, social movements spawned abortion clinic bombers, white-power activists, and militia movements. Some of these right-wingers engaged in terrorism, most notably Timothy McVeigh's bombing of the Oklahoma City Federal Building in 1995. On the left, animal rights and environmental activists began campaigns of arson against corporate and government targets. Both sets of radicals organized through leaderless resistance and engaged in their contention as a form of identity work. In the Earth Liberation Front, activists seemed to come from relatively affluent backgrounds, while the militia movement found its support in communities affected by the economic restructuring. In general, radicalism of this era was rooted in local politics but oriented towards the globe. For example, the Zapatistas harnessed a long-standing culture of rebellion to draw the world's attention to the grievances of Mexico's rural poor.

And in the European Parliament elections of 2014, radical parties from the anti-immigrant right and socialist left had unprecedented victories. The entire future of EU integration was cast into doubt.

The cusp of the twenty-first century also generated a new type of revolution – the nonviolent one. Beginning with mass protests in the 1980s in favor of democracy in the Philippines and South Korea, activists learned that nonviolence was one way to overcome the repression of the state. In Poland, members of the trade union Solidarity were able to withstand suppression as they organized in sympathetic organizations like the Church. By 1989, under economic and geopolitical strain, the Soviet Union stopped guaranteeing the power of its Eastern European satellites. Regimes across the region quickly fell to mass demonstrations or negotiated transfers of power, and the Soviet Union itself dissolved in 1992 under nationalist pressure. The aftereffects of this revolutionary wave continued for more than two decades. Many of the first post-communist states were only partly democratic, with elections frequently stolen by those in power. In 2000, Serbian youth activists successfully used nonviolent protest to oust their dictator, and then trained activists in Georgia, Ukraine, and elsewhere. The resulting wave of Color Revolutions had mixed success. For instance, Ukraine's 2004 Orange Revolution brought a new party to the presidency but the old one, led by Victor Yanukovych, regained power in 2010. After a series of failed negotiations with the European Union and increasing anti-democratic moves, activists (including ultra-nationalists like Right Sector) again took to the streets of Kiev and successfully overthrew the government in 2014. In the resulting instability, Russia intervened and seized the region of Crimea.

Nonviolent tactics also saw success elsewhere, dependent on extant mobilizing structures, state-centered strains, and connections with the international system. At the end of 2010, a series of protests brought down the Ben Ali regime when his military chief refused to suppress demonstrators. Quickly thereafter, activists across the Arab countries took advantage of the opportunity. A coalition of urban classes, youth, intellectuals, and the Muslim Brotherhood took to the streets in Egypt, enabled in part by the ability to organize online and powerful symbols of solidarity like "We are all Khaled Said." After police repression failed and the army remained neutral, Mubarak quickly resigned (though the counterrevolution would return as the military removed the popularly elected Muslim Brotherhood president Mohammed Morsi in 2013). Protests in Bahrain imperiled the monarchy until Saudi intervention, and Libyan and Syrian protests turned into civil war in the face of government repression. In Libya, NATO intervention helped overthrow Qaddafi, but in Syria the civil war dragged on with increasing concern about the influx of Islamist militants into the opposition's ranks and the growth of the Islamic State.

The examples of this book thus cover most regions of the world across the last five centuries, even if the last century of Euro-American history dominates, a common problem in contemporary social science. This by itself is a challenge to the view that the social science of radicalism is not generalizable. But, in general terms, where do these examples fall? The book begins with definitions of terrorism, revolution, and radicalism. I have used the terms defined in the first chapter somewhat loosely, often calling everyone a radical, and so it is now time to revisit the definitions and place our examples. Radicals are those who engage in non-routine collective action with the goal of change. Revolutions are not only outcomes of regime or social change, but situations involving dual claims to power. And terrorism involves the illegitimate use of non-routine violence intended to influence someone beyond the immediate victim. I suggest at the beginning of the book that these form a Venn diagram with varying degrees of overlap. Figure 8.1 locates the examples within these areas.

The majority of the examples fall between revolution and radicalism. Since radicalism is about change, and revolutionaries often desire to change not only governments but also social and economic structures, it is logical that most of what we call revolutions would fit here. Arguably, cases that did not have extensive social restructuring as a goal, perhaps like the American Revolution or some of the contemporary nonviolent mobilizations, would lean towards the revolution category alone. On the other hand, there

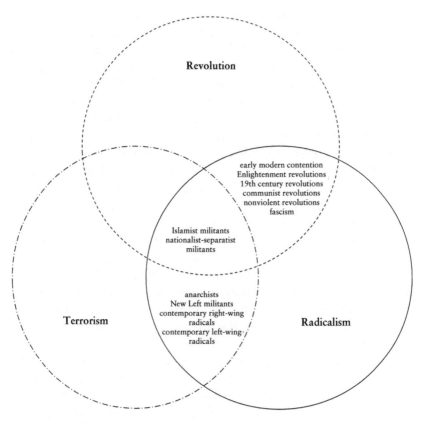

early modern contention
Enlightenment revolutions
19th century revolutions
communist revolutions
nonviolent revolutions
fascism

Revolution

Islamist militants
nationalist-separatist
militants

anarchists
New Left militants
contemporary right-wing
radicals
contemporary left-wing
radicals

Terrorism

Radicalism

Figure 8.1   Radicals, revolutionaries, or terrorists?

are also radical terrorists. The anarchists may edge slightly towards the borders of revolution, and contemporary groups like the ELF towards radicalism. However, the groups here tend to be the less effective ones, which suggests that sustained movements directly seek political power, rather than just social, economic, or cultural change. Then there is the area of overlap of all three. Radical, revolutionary, and terrorist movements are those that come to mind when we think of terrorism – nationalist-separatist groups and Islamic militants. Many of these have sought state power and social change, and used terrorism to get there (though Al-Qaeda central might trend towards radicalism-terrorism since the group's revolutionary attempts seem to come from local affiliates more than from the core hierarchy). Tellingly, the fields for pure radicalism, revolution, and terrorism are empty. This is a good sign that I did not stray from my promise to only investigate combinations of the three. But there are possible examples for each "pure" type. For example, reactionary revolutions or those instituted by elites, such as Meiji Japan or Pinochet's Chile, could be considered revolutions alone. Religious movements or cults that reject the political realm could also be considered just radicals, like the "revolutionary suicide" of the Jonestown cult in 1978. And lone wolves like Anders Behring Breivik or Ted Kaczynski, known as the Unabomber for sending mail bombs to universities and airlines, perhaps could be considered purely terrorists as their goals, even if articulated, are not shared widely enough to be considered radical ideology. More importantly, the field of revolution-terrorism is completely empty. I cannot think of a single example from this book that fits better here than anywhere else. Our revolutionary terrorist would use political violence to influence others and take power but would not have goals associated with social, political, economic, and/or cultural change. In other words, he or she would be Machiavellian – interested only in power for power's sake and willing to use any means to get there. In that sense, it is possible that this is the field of military juntas and coups, such as the many initiated by the Thai military, most recently in 2014. Or perhaps here are authoritarian regimes and dictatorial strongmen that use state terrorism to keep populations in line, common to post-revolutionary societies like Jacobin France, Nazi Germany, or Stalinist Russia. It is a puzzle that I cannot resolve easily.

The future of radicals, revolutionaries, and terrorists

If the scope of the examples of revolution, terrorism, and radicalism suggests some recurrent features of the phenomena, the question is whether or not these patterns add up to predictability. Prediction generally, and of revolution in particular, has been hotly debated by social scientists for decades. And the history of social science is littered with predictions that did not pan out. For instance, Karl Marx famously predicted that capitalism would lead to socialist revolution as industrial production brought workers together and they developed class consciousness. And one of Marx's contemporary heirs, Immanuel Wallerstein, has anticipated the demise of the global capitalist system for much of his career. In February 2001, Larry Johnson (2001) published an article that proclaimed the era of international terrorism over because counterterrorism had succeeded and fatalities had declined. He, like the Bush Administration, had not seen the infamous memo of August 2001: "Bin Laden Determined to Strike the United States."

Some of the most extensive work on prediction has been done by Philip Tetlock. He examines the predictions of hundreds of experts and finds that on average the experts did little better than random chance (2005). He argues further, drawing on an essay by Isaiah Berlin, that expertise comes in two forms – foxes, who know a little about a lot and have an understanding of a variety of theories, and hedgehogs, who have deep knowledge about a particular thing, primarily from one perspective. Since foxes are more likely to be open to disconfirming evidence, Tetlock argues that these experts will be the better predictors. With such a description, who would not want to be a fox? Accordingly, the study of revolution does have some scattered successes in prediction. Randall Collins (1986; see also 1995), analyzing Russia in 1980, predicted that the Soviet Union would face geopolitical overextension and collapse within 30–50 years. Perhaps we can forgive him for being off by two decades, even if Timur Kuran (1995) argues that prediction without timing is hardly a prediction at all. Jack Goldstone also claims some successes in his contribution to a debate over the prediction of revolution (see Keddie 1995). Goldstone states that the year before the People Power Revolution of 1986, he believed that Marcos's regime was unlikely to last more than a few years, that he anticipated more uprisings in Eastern Europe while planning his reader on revolutions in 1986, and that he said the Tiananmen Square uprising of 1989 would not overthrow but contribute to the liberalization of the Chinese state.

I would also like to claim some prescience. Before the American invasion of Iraq in 2003, my fellow PhD student, Reuben (Jack) Thomas, and I debated possible effects. I predicted that the breaking of the Baathist state would lead to general, communal conflict and that it would become a focus for Islamic militants. I had forgotten this conversation until the Iraqi insurgency was well underway, and Jack remarked that if a second-year graduate student in sociology could have seen this, then the American government had no excuse. In the conclusion to my dissertation on revolutionary waves (Beck 2009a), I noted that the present era was only one of many that had "alarums of war and revolution" (Brinton 1938: 5) and that we were in a period of revolutionary waves. The Arab Spring fit my expectations to a T (see also Beck 2014: 208). But lest you think me a sage, I will gladly admit failures. When I first started researching the Earth Liberation Front in the early 2000s, I noted the escalation in tactics and attacks, and would joke with dark humor in scholarly presentations that we might soon face the possibility of "vegans who kill." But the ELF turned out to be self-moderating and more ephemeral than I had supposed. Also, in early February 2011, I told the students of my class on revolution that I expected Mubarak would weather the protests in Tahrir Square. I had assumed that elite learning and adaptation had taken place; after Tunisia, Mubarak must have assured himself of the loyalty of the security services, military, and political elites. Clearly, I was wrong.

Policy makers, too, are particularly interested in the prediction of political instability. In 2003, DARPA, the research wing of the American Department of Defense, proposed a futures market for event prediction. Futures markets, like those of financial instruments or betting pools on sporting events, have proven to be efficient predictors of outcomes when knowledge is diffusely held. The average of all bets made tells us what participants as a whole know. DARPA's logic was that terrorist attacks could be predicted in such a fashion. There were two problems with this, however. First, knowledge about terrorist attacks is not widely spread but rather kept a close secret among terrorist planners. If the population at large had this knowledge, prediction would not be needed to stop terrorists. Second, the futures market created the possibility that terrorists could earn money off their activities by betting for or against predicted events. The second criticism led to a small uproar and the project was canceled.

Another government project on prediction was started in the 1990s. Called the Political Instability Task Force (PITF) and directed by the Central Intelligence Agency, the goal of the project is to develop statistical models for predicting state failure and political instability of various types. The PITF uses the logic of forecasting rather than prediction. Forecasting, like long-range weather reports, seeks to determine the likelihood of an event occurring within a particular time frame and at a specific place. The models built are thus less of prediction and more of probability. The PITF does claim some success in its statistical modeling of conflict (see Goldstone et al. 2010; Ulfelder and Lustik 2007). This logic has begun to permeate political science more generally, such as in the work of Bruce Bueno de Mesquita (2009b) who develops game theory models of politics to predict the future. And members of the PITF, such as Jay Ulfelder and Barbara Harff, are involved in developing predictions of the likelihood of genocides.

Even so, the conventional wisdom of social science is that prediction is essentially futile (Hechter 1995). While revolutions might be deterministic, in that they are a sequence of events in which one causes the next (Keddie 1995), they are also times of general confusion (Kurzman 2004a). Thus, the outcome of contention is unknowable even to the participants as random decisions and events can change the course dramatically. For example, Charles Kurzman and his co-author Aseem Hasnain (2014) examine tit-for-tat violence between Israel and the Palestinians and conclude that the escalation of any particular conflict cannot be predicted. This, however, misses the point that these episodes of violence are structured by the long-term Israeli–Palestinian conflict. We may not be able to forecast the degree of violence but we can readily suspect there will be some. Therefore, we should not conclude, as Kurzman and Hasnain do, that conflict cannot be explained at all.

I am not satisfied with the position that prediction is futile. Based on the logic of Charles Tilly (1995) – that different combinations of mechanisms, rather than unchanging causes, create events – I argue that social scientists should adopt a process-oriented view. We might call this the social science of anticipation, rather than prediction. This approach has two features. First, it rejects thinking of the average of cause and effect within some population of cases as in a statistical model. Different events are constructed differently, and multiple interactions of causes should be the focus. Second, it also rejects the position that there are no generalizable patterns. As seen throughout this book, different things reoccur in radicalism with a high amount of regularity. The task then is to identify which patterns possibly lead to which outcomes and develop benchmarks that can, in real time, allow us to anticipate the course of events underway.

An example of this type of thinking was presented in chapter 6. Here, I proposed that we might be able to anticipate the possible directions of a revolutionary situation by examining the partners of a revolutionary coalition. Within the scope condition of the contemporary world, each partner is more likely to lead to some paths than others. For instance, if we had had this model in February 2011, we would have noticed that the coalition of young, urban elites, the Muslim Brotherhood, and the military had ousted Mubarak. This made three paths most likely – respectively democracy, anocracy, or conservative authoritarianism. The chances for democracy lessened with the election of Morsi, and, with his ouster, conservative authoritarianism remains the most likely settlement for the time being. Not prediction, nor really forecasting, but process-oriented anticipation of the future.

There are also more general analytical tools that can help with this task. Charles Ragin (2008) has developed a method called qualitative comparative analysis which combines the advantages of case knowledge with the precision of logical reasoning (in essence, making a hedgehox or foxhog of social scientists). Crucially, the absence of a cause is taken to be just as important as its presence, and the classification can be "fuzzy" – neither all in nor all out, unlike in a statistical model. The method then relies on the interactive combination of factors to detail the possible "recipes" for a particular outcome. An outcome might have numerous different causal paths that lead to it, but using logic we can reduce the number of factors from many to few and try to cover as many cases as possible. I use this tool in my study of the Arab Spring (see Beck 2014) and am able to account for three of the four regime transitions with only two combinations of factors: relative embeddedness in world society and political exclusion in all cases, combined with a lack of demographic pressure (Tunisia) or a history of opposition against the state (Egypt and Yemen). My model, in its illustrative form, could not anticipate the case of Libya where the contingency of NATO intervention turned the tide.

Using this logic, I have developed my own personal benchmarks for anticipating when protest might turn to revolution, based on my understanding of recurrent patterns. I have been presenting this "minimal formula" in my classes for a few years: mobilization sustained over time + repression failing to stop protest + evidence of elite/regime schisms. Each of these factors is interactive – protest can only be sustained if repression fails (or is not tried), failing repression creates elite schisms, regime fragmentation makes repression less effective, and elite involvement sustains movements. This does not predict when and where a revolution will occur, but it does provide a way of analyzing a movement or contentious event and anticipating whether its path is revolution or not.

But what of terrorism and radicalism? These are more difficult to anticipate because, many as are the causes of revolution, those of political violence are even more numerous. In general, I see terrorism as a strategy that groups turn to when institutional means of political participation or action are not present. But that alone is not enough. I agree with Jeff Goodwin (2006) that terrorism also occurs when the populace at large is seen as complicit with the target of a movement, be it a government, foreign power, or competitor. Terrorism's minimal formula might thus be: frustrated political participation + categorization of complicity. Radicalism is even more difficult. While I do not believe that radicalism is always a feature of protest cycles, I do agree with Jack Goldstone

(2004) that they are generally an outgrowth of social movements. Further, radicalism is more likely when new ideas, claims, and goals are legitimated externally by world cultural scripts (Beck 2011, 2014) or internally by state practices (Beck 2009b). Who says social movements, says radicalism, particularly during times of rapid cultural change.

So this leads me back to my first work on revolution. Radicalism, revolution, and terrorism seem to be common features of world history and reoccur with regularity. Currently, we live in such a radical era – as globalization restructures economies, changes cultural practices, and undermines existing political arrangements, it is no surprise to me that international terrorism, revolution, and movement radicalism in general have resulted. Radical contention comes from both the political right and the political left and is more than just politics as usual. It is an almost necessary expression of the Zeitgeist. Yet waves of revolution, even long ones, do subside just as the Enlightenment ones did two hundred years ago. International terrorism cannot sustain itself forever, as the history of the anarchists shows. And radicalism comes and goes in fashion, like Black Shirts or Che shirts. Thus, this era of alarums of wars and revolution, too, will pass as a new international order emerges, likely with either China or a resurgent United States as the predominant power. Today's global threats to stability in the form of climate change, population growth, and technological advancement and disruption may seem unprecedented (Beck 2000; Lachmann 2013). But, relatively speaking, they are not. So just as in previous periods of dramatic change – like Europe in 1450 on the cusp of plagues, cultural renaissance, the printing press, and expansion across the globe – radicalism, revolution, and terrorism could last for a very long time. Welcome to the long twenty-first century. We are in for a bumpy ride.

Notes

Chapter 1   What is Radicalism?

1 There are many other definitions of social movements and collective action. For a book-length treatment of the issue, I recommend Hank Johnston's *What is a Social Movement?* (2014).

2 Calculation of Pearson's correlation coefficients shows that the proportion of attention to revolution and terrorism is actually negatively correlated, while radicalism is positively correlated with terrorism and has little relationship with revolution. In other words, revolution and terrorism compete with each other for scholarly attention, while radicalism seemingly is considered more an aspect of terrorism than revolution.

3 We could go even as broad as Paige (2003: 24) to include any social or political change that results from "widespread popular acceptance of a utopian alternative to the current social order," but so far most revolution scholars have not adopted this view.

4 The titles of the book's parts take their names from remarks by US Defense Secretary Donald Rumsfeld at a February 12, 2002 press conference on the lack of evidence for Iraq's weapons of mass destruction. I would have enjoyed writing a third part on unknown unknowns, but I would not even know what to cover in it.

Chapter 2   Who is Radical?

1 Mark Rudd's memoir *Underground* (2009) is an excellent source for understanding the Weather Underground. Other good sources include Jeremy Varon's *Bringing the War Home* (2004) and Todd Gitlin's *The Whole World is Watching* (1980).

2 The most definitive biography of Che is John Lee Anderson's *Che Guevara: A Revolutionary Life* (1997). The 2004 film *The Motorcycle Diaries* also does

an excellent job of dramatizing young Ernesto's transformation, and is based on his own writings.

Chapter 3   How Do Radical Movements Organize?

1 Among the best popular accounts of early Al-Qaeda are Lawrence Wright's *The Looming Tower* (2006), Jason Burke's *Al-Qaeda: The True Story of Radical Islam* (2004), and Peter Bergen's *Holy War, Inc.* (2001). Terry McDermott's *Perfect Soldiers* (2009) focuses on biographies of the September 11th hijackers, and the official US government report on September 11th is quite detailed (United States National Commission on Terrorist Attacks upon the United States 2004).
2 There is little rigorous scholarly work on the ELF, but two good first-hand accounts of radical environmentalism are Craig Rosebraugh's memoir *Burning Rage of a Dying Planet* (2004) and Dave Foreman's manifesto *Confessions of an Eco-Warrior* (1991). The 2011 documentary *If a Tree Falls* charts the involvement and prosecution of one cell of ELF members. For the general spirit of the movement, Edward Abbey's novel *The Monkey Wrench Gang* (1975) is still relevant.
3 Given the significant lag time in scholarly study, at least three to five years from event to publication, the best work on the Arab Spring has yet to arrive. For now, Marc Lynch's *The Arab Uprising* (2013) provides a good overview. Jeffrey Alexander's *Performative Revolution in Egypt* (2011) provides an analysis of key discourses during the revolution, and Hazem Kandil's *Soldiers, Spies, and Statesmen* (2012) is an interesting history of competing power blocs in modern Egypt.

Chapter 4   When and Where Does Radicalism Occur?

1 While there are voluminous histories of fascism, and Nazism in particular, two recent works stand out for their social scientific contributions. Michael Mann, in *Fascists* (2004), provides a good synthetic conceptualization and history of fascism, and Dylan Riley's *The Civic Foundations of Fascism in Europe* (2010) is a novel comparative study of the movement's origins.

Chapter 6   Is There a Life Cycle of Radicalism?

1 An excellent account of the early phases of 1990s separatism in the Caucasus is given by Georgi Derluguian in *Bourdieu's Secret Admirer in the Caucasus* (2005).
2 Special thanks are owed to Mark Kramer, Doug McAdam, and Steve Fish for their comments on previous versions of this model.

Note to p. 132

Chapter 7   How and Why Does Radicalism Diffuse in Waves?

1 James Joll's classic history of anarchism *The Anarchists* (1964) is still an authoritative account, and Beverly Gage's book on the Wall Street bombing, *The Day Wall Street Exploded* (2008), is a compelling history of American anarchists. Works by anarchist thinkers such as Proudhon, Bakunin, and Emma Goldman remain some of the most accessible and passionate radical tracts ever written.

References

Abadie, Alberto, and Gardeazabal, Javier. 2003. "The Economic Costs of Conflict: A Case Study of the Basque Country." *American Economic Review* 93(1): 113–32.

Abbey, Edward. 1975. *The Monkey Wrench Gang*. Philadelphia, PA: Lippincott Williams & Wilkins.

Abrahamian, Ervand. 1982. *Iran Between Two Revolutions*. Princeton, NJ: Princeton University Press.

Abrahms, Max. 2006. "Why Terrorism Does Not Work." *International Security* 31(2): 42–78.

Abrahms, Max. 2008. "What Terrorists Really Want: Terrorist Motives and Counterterrorism Strategy." *International Security* 32(4): 78–105.

Acosta, Benjamin. 2014. "Live to Win Another Day: Why Many Militant Organizations Survive Yet Few Succeed." *Studies in Conflict and Terrorism* 37(2): 135–61.

Alexander, Jeffrey C. 2004. "From the Depths of Despair: Performance, Counterperformance, and 'September 11.'" *Sociological Theory* 22(1): 88–105.

Alexander, Jeffrey C. 2011. *Performative Revolution in Egypt: An Essay in Cultural Power*. New York: Bloomsbury Academic.

Alexander, Jeffrey C., and Smith, Philip. 1993. "The Discourse of American Civil Society: A New Proposal for Cultural Studies." *Theory and Society* 22(2): 151–207.

Alinsky, Saul. 1971. *Rules for Radicals*. New York: Vintage Books.

Allardt, Erik. 1971. "Culture, Structure and Revolutionary Ideologies." *International Journal of Comparative Sociology* 12(1): 24–40.

Althusser, Louis. 1971. *Lenin and Philosophy, and Other Essays*. New York: Monthly Review Press.

Anderson, Jon Lee. 1997. *Che Guevara: A Revolutionary Life*. New York: Grove Press.

References

Anderson, Lisa. 1991. "Absolutism and the Resilience of Monarchy in the Middle East." *Political Science Quarterly* 106(1): 1–15.

Andrabi, Tahir, Das, Jishnu, Khwaja, Asim Ajaz, and Zajonc, Tristan. 2006. "Religious School Enrollment in Pakistan: A Look at the Data." *Comparative Education Review* 50(3): 446–77.

Andrews, Kenneth T., and Biggs, Michael. 2006. "The Dynamics of Protest Diffusion: Movement Organizations, Social Networks, and News Media in the 1960 Sit-Ins." *American Sociological Review* 71(5): 752–77.

Arrighi, Giovanni, and Silver, Beverly J. 1999. *Chaos and Governance in the Modern World System*. Minneapolis, MN: University of Minnesota Press.

Arrighi, Giovanni, Hopkins, Terence K., and Wallerstein, Immanuel Maurice. 1989. *Anti-Systemic Movements*. London: Verso Books.

Asal, Victor, and Rethemeyer, R. Karl. 2008. "The Nature of the Beast: Organizational Structures and the Lethality of Terrorist Attacks." *Journal of Politics* 70(2): 437–49.

Austin Holmes, Amy. 2012. "There are Weeks When Decades Happen: Structure and Strategy in the Egyptian Revolution." *Mobilization: An International Quarterly* 17(4): 391–410.

Bail, Christopher A. 2012. "The Fringe Effect: Civil Society Organizations and the Evolution of Media Discourse about Islam since the September 11th Attacks." *American Sociological Review* 77(6): 855–79.

Bakunin, Mikhail Aleksandrovich. 1990 (1873). *Statism and Anarchy*. Cambridge: Cambridge University Press.

Barber, Benjamin. 1995. *Jihad vs. McWorld: Terrorism's Challenge to Democracy*. New York: Random House.

Bearman, Peter S. 1993. *Relations into Rhetorics: Local Elite Social Structure in Norfolk, England, 1540–1640*. New Brunswick, NJ: Rutgers University Press.

Beck, Colin J. 2007. "On the Radical Cusp: Ecoterrorism in the United States, 1998–2005." *Mobilization: An International Quarterly* 12(2): 161–76.

Beck, Colin J. 2009a. "Ideological Roots of Waves of Revolution." Dissertation, Stanford University, Stanford, CA.

Beck, Colin J. 2009b. "State Building as a Source of Islamic Political Organization." *Sociological Forum* 24(2): 337–56.

Beck, Colin J. 2011. "The World-Cultural Origins of Revolutionary Waves: Five Centuries of European Contention." *Social Science History* 35(2): 167–207.

Beck, Colin J. 2014. "Reflections on the Revolutionary Wave in 2011." *Theory and Society* 43(2): 197–223.

Beck, Colin J. Forthcoming. "Revolutions: Robust Findings, Persistence Problems, and Promising Frontiers," in Michael Stohl, Mark Lichbach, and Peter Grabosky (eds), *Handbook of Political Conflict*. New York: Paradigm Publishers.

Beck, Colin J., and Miner, Emily. 2013. "Who Gets Designated a Terrorist and Why?" *Social Forces* 91(3): 837–72.

References

Beck, Colin J., Drori, Gili S., and Meyer, John W. 2012. "World Influences on Human Rights Language in Constitutions: A Cross-National Study." *International Sociology* 27(4): 483–501.

Beck, Ulrich. 2000. *What is Globalization?* Cambridge: Polity.

Becker, Jaime, and Goldstone, J. 2005. "How Fast Can You Build a State? State Building in Revolutions," in Matthew Lange and Dietrich Rueschemeyer (eds), *States and Development: Historical Antecedents of Stagnation and Advance.* New York: Palgrave Macmillan, pp. 183–210.

Beissinger, Mark R. 1998. *Nationalist Mobilization and the Collapse of the Soviet State.* New York: Cambridge University Press.

Beissinger, Mark R. 2007. "Structure and Example in Modular Political Phenomena: The Diffusion of Bulldozer/Rose/Orange/Tulip Revolutions." *Perspectives on Politics* 5(2): 259–76.

Beissinger, Mark R. 2011. "Mechanisms of Maidan: The Structure of Contingency in the Making of the Orange Revolution." *Mobilization: An International Quarterly* 16(1): 25–43.

Bell, J. Bowyer. 1971. *The Myth of the Guerrilla: Revolutionary Theory and Malpractice.* New York: Knopf.

Benford, R. D., and Snow, D. A. 2000. "Framing Processes and Social Movements: An Overview and Assessment." *Annual Review of Sociology* 26(1): 611–39.

Ben-Yehuda, Nachmann. 2005. "Terror, Media, and Moral Boundaries." *International Journal of Comparative Sociology* 46(1–2): 33–53.

Bergen, Peter L. 2001. *Holy War, Inc.: Inside the Secret World of Osama Bin Laden.* New York: Free Press.

Bergesen, Albert J. 1995. "EcoAlienation." *Humboldt Journal of Social Relations* 21(2): 111–26.

Bergesen, Albert J. 2007. "Three-Step Model of Terrorist Violence." *Mobilization: An International Journal* 12(2): 111–18.

Bergesen, Albert J., and Han, Yi. 2005. "New Directions for Terrorism Research." *International Journal of Comparative Sociology* 46(1–2): 133–51.

Bergesen, Albert J., and Lizardo, Omar. 2004. "International Terrorism and the World System." *Sociological Theory* 22(1): 38–52.

Berman, Sheri. 1997. "Civil Society and the Collapse of the Weimar Republic." *World Politics* 49(3): 401–29.

Berrebi, Claude. 2007. "Evidence about the Link Between Education, Poverty and Terrorism among Palestinians." *Peace Economics, Peace Science and Public Policy* 13(1): 1–36.

Biggs, Michael. 2003. "Positive Feedback in Collective Mobilization: The American Strike Wave of 1886." *Theory and Society* 32(2): 217–54.

Biggs, Michael. 2005. "Strikes as Forest Fires: Chicago and Paris in the Late Nineteenth Century." *American Journal of Sociology* 110(6): 1684–1714.

Biggs, Michael. 2013. "How Repertoires Evolve: The Diffusion of Suicide Protest in the Twentieth Century." *Mobilization: An International Quarterly* 18(4): 407–28.

Blickle, Peter. 1981. *The Revolution of 1525: The German Peasants' War from a New Perspective*. Baltimore, MD: Johns Hopkins University Press.

Blomberg, S. Brock, Engel, Rozlyn C., and Sawyer, Reid. 2010. "On the Duration and Sustainability of Transnational Terrorist Organizations." *Journal of Conflict Resolution* 54(2): 303–30.

Bloom, Mia. 2005. *Dying to Kill: The Allure of Suicide Terror*. New York: Columbia University Press.

Boli, John, Ramirez, Francisco O., and Meyer, John W. 1985. "Explaining the Origins and Expansion of Mass Education." *Comparative Education Review* 29(2): 145–70.

Borum, Randy. 2011. "Radicalization into Violent Extremism I: A Review of Social Science Theories." *Journal of Strategic Security* 4(4): 7–36.

Bosi, Lorenzo. 2012. "Explaining Pathways to Armed Activism in the Provisional Irish Republican Army, 1969–1972." *Social Science History* 36(3): 347–90.

Boswell, Terry. 2004. "Hegemonic Decline and Revolution: When the World is Up for Grabs," in Thomas Reifer (ed.), *Globalization, Hegemony, & Power: Anti-Systemic Movements and the Global System*. New York: Greenwood Press, pp. 149–62.

Boswell, Terry, and Dixon, William J. 1990. "Dependency and Rebellion: A Cross-National Analysis." *American Sociological Review* 55(4): 540–59.

Boswell, Terry, and Dixon, William J. 1993. "Marx's Theory of Rebellion: A Cross-National Analysis of Class Exploitation, Economic Development, and Violent Revolt." *American Sociological Review* 58(5): 681–702.

Branch, Daniel. 2010. "Footprints in the Sand: British Colonial Counterinsurgency and the War in Iraq." *Politics & Society* 38(1): 15–34.

Brandt, Patrick T., and Sandler, Todd. 2010. "What Do Transnational Terrorists Target? Has It Changed? Are We Safer?" *Journal of Conflict Resolution* 54(2): 214–36.

Brannan, David W., Esler, Philip F., and Strindberg, N. T. Anders. 2001. "Talking to 'Terrorists': Towards an Independent Analytical Framework for the Study of Violent Substate Activism." *Studies in Conflict and Terrorism* 24(1): 3–24.

Braun, Robert, and Koopmans, Ruud. 2009. "The Diffusion of Ethnic Violence in Germany: The Role of Social Similarity." *European Sociological Review* 26(1): 111–23.

Braun, Robert, and Vliegenthart, Rens. 2009. "Violent Fan Fluctuations: A Diffusion Perspective to Explain Supporters' Violence." *Mobilization: An International Quarterly* 14(1): 23–44.

Brinton, Crane. 1938. *The Anatomy of Revolution*. New York: Prentice-Hall.

Brockett, Charles D. 1993. "A Protest-Cycle Resolution of the Repression/Popular-Protest Paradox." *Social Science History* 17(3): 457–84.

Brustein, William. 1988. "The Political Geography of Belgian Fascism: The Case of Rexism." *American Sociological Review* 53(1): 69–80.

Brustein, William. 1991. "The 'Red Menace' and the Rise of Italian Fascism." *American Sociological Review* 56(5): 652–64.

Brustein, William. 1996. *The Logic of Evil: The Social Origins of the Nazi Party, 1925–1933.* New Haven, CT: Yale University Press.

Bunce, Valerie J., and Wolchik, Sharon L. 2006. "International Diffusion and Postcommunist Electoral Revolutions." *Communist and Post-Communist Studies* 39(3): 283–304.

Burke, Jason. 2004. *Al-Qaeda: The True Story of Radical Islam.* London: I.B.Tauris.

Burns, Gene. 1996. "Ideology, Culture, and Ambiguity: The Revolutionary Process in Iran." *Theory and Society* 25(3): 349–88.

Burns, Tom R., and Dietz, Thomas. 2001. "Revolution: An Evolutionary Perspective." *International Sociology* 16(4): 531–55.

Byrd, Scott C., and Jasny, Lorien. 2010. "Transnational Movement Innovation and Collaboration: Analysis of World Social Forum Networks." *Social Movement Studies* 9(4): 355–72.

Carley, Kathleen M. 2006. "Destabilization of Covert Networks." *Computational & Mathematical Organization Theory* 12(1): 51–66.

Cesari, Jocelyne. 2004. *When Islam and Democracy Meet: Muslims in Europe and in the United States.* Basingstoke: Palgrave Macmillan.

Chang, Paul Y. 2008. "Unintended Consequences of Repression: Alliance Formation in South Korea's Democracy Movement (1970–1979)." *Social Forces* 87(2): 651–77.

Chartier, Roger. 1991. *The Cultural Origins of the French Revolution.* Durham, NC: Duke University Press.

Chase-Dunn, Christopher et al. 2008. "North–South Contradictions and Bridges at the World Social Forum," in Rafael Reuveny and William R. Thompson (eds), *North and South in the World Political Economy.* Oxford: Blackwell, pp. 341–66.

Chenoweth, Erica. 2013. "Terrorism and Democracy." *Annual Review of Political Science* 16(1): 355–78.

Chermak, Steven, Freilich, Joshua, Duran, Celinet, and Parkin, William. 2013. "An Overview of Bombing and Arson Attacks by Environmental and Animal Rights Extremists in the United States, 1995–2010". College Park, MD: START, University of Maryland.

Clarke, Killian. 2011. "Saying 'Enough': Authoritarianism and Egypt's Kefaya Movement." *Mobilization: An International Quarterly* 16(4): 397–416.

Coggins, Bridget L. Forthcoming. "Does State Failure Cause Terrorism? An Empirical Analysis (1999–2008)." *Journal of Conflict Resolution.* Accessed March 29, 2014 (http://jcr.sagepub.com/content/early/2014/03/05/00220027 13515403).

References

Cole, Wade M. 2005. "Sovereignty Relinquished? Explaining Commitment to the International Human Rights Covenants, 1966–1999." *American Sociological Review* 70(3): 472–95.

Collard-Wexler, Simon, Pischedda, Costantino, and Smith, Michael G. 2014. "Do Foreign Occupations Cause Suicide Attacks?" *Journal of Conflict Resolution* 58(4): 625–57.

Collins, Kathleen. 2007. "Ideas, Networks, and Islamist Movements: Evidence from Central Asia and the Caucasus." *World Politics* 60(1): 64–96.

Collins, Randall. 1986. *Weberian Sociological Theory*. Cambridge: Cambridge University Press.

Collins, Randall. 1995. "Prediction in Macrosociology: The Case of the Soviet Collapse." *American Journal of Sociology* 100(6): 1552–93.

Collins, Randall. 2004. "Rituals of Solidarity and Security in the Wake of Terrorist Attack." *Sociological Theory* 22(1): 53–87.

Collins, Randall. 2007. "Turning Points, Bottlenecks, and the Fallacies of Counterfactual History." *Sociological Forum* 22(3): 247–69.

Connell, Carol, and Cohn, Samuel. 1995. "Learning from Other People's Actions: Environmental Variations and Diffusion in French Coal Mining Strikes." *American Journal of Sociology* 101: 366–403.

Crenshaw, Martha. 1978. *Revolutionary Terrorism: The FLN in Algeria, 1954–1962*. Stanford, CA: Hoover Institution Press.

Crenshaw, Martha. 1981. "The Causes of Terrorism." *Comparative Politics* 13(4): 379–99.

Crenshaw, Martha. 2011. *Explaining Terrorism: Causes, Processes, and Consequences*. New York: Routledge.

Crenshaw, Martha. 2012. "The Causes and Consequences of Interactions among Militant Groups: A Research Agenda." San Diego, CA: International Studies Association.

Cronin, Audrey Kurth. 2009. *How Terrorism Ends: Understanding the Decline and Demise of Terrorist Campaigns*. Princeton, NJ: Princeton University Press.

Cunningham, David. 2003. "Understanding State Responses to Left- versus Right-Wing Threats: The FBI's Repression of the New Left and the Ku Klux Klan." *Social Science History* 27(3): 327–70.

Cunningham, David E. 2010. "Blocking Resolution: How External States Can Prolong Civil Wars." *Journal of Peace Research* 47(2): 115–27.

Danzell, Orlandrew E. 2010. "Political Parties: When Do They Turn to Terror?" *Journal of Conflict Resolution* 55(1): 85–105.

Davenport, Christian. 2007. "State Repression and Political Order." *Annual Review of Political Science* 10(1): 1–23.

Davenport, Christian, Moore, Will H., and Armstrong, Dave. 2007. *The Puzzle of Abu Ghraib: Are Democratic Institutions a Palliative or Panacea?* Rochester, NY: Social Science Research Network. Accessed December 8, 2010 (http://papers.ssrn.com/sol3/papers.cfm?abstract_id=1022367).

References

Davies, James C. 1962. "Toward a Theory of Revolution." *American Sociological Review* 27(1): 5–19.

Deflem, Mathieu. 2004. "Social Control and the Policing of Terrorism: Foundations for a Sociology of Counterterrorism." *American Sociologist* 35(2): 75–92.

Della Porta, Donatella. 1995. *Social Movements, Political Violence, and the State: A Comparative Analysis of Italy and Germany*. Cambridge: Cambridge University Press.

Della Porta, Donatella. 2013a. "Protest Cycles and Waves." in David A. Snow, Donatella della Porta, Bert Klandermans, and Doug McAdam (eds), *The Wiley-Blackwell Encyclopedia of Social and Political Movements*. Hoboken, NJ: Blackwell Publishing.

Della Porta, Donatella. 2013b. "Repertoires of Contention," in David A. Snow, Donatella della Porta, Bert Klandermans, and Doug McAdam (eds), *The Wiley-Blackwell Encyclopedia of Social and Political Movements*. Hoboken, NJ: Wiley–Blackwell.

Della Porta, Donatella, and Reiter, Herbert. 1998. *Policing Protest: The Control of Mass Demonstrations in Western Democracies*. Minneapolis, MN: University of Minnesota Press.

de Mesquita, Ethan Bueno. 2009a. *Correlates of Public Support for Terrorism in the Muslim World*. Washington, DC: United States Institute of Peace.

de Mesquita, Ethan Bueno. 2009b. *Predictioneer's Game: Using the Logic of Brazen Self-Interest to See and Shape the Future*. New York: Random House.

Derluguian, Georgi M. 2005. *Bourdieu's Secret Admirer in the Caucasus: A World-System Biography*. Chicago, IL: University of Chicago Press.

DiMaggio, Paul J., and Powell, Walter W. 1983. "The Iron Cage Revisited: Institutional Isomorphism and Collective Rationality in Organizational Fields." *American Sociological Review* 48(2): 147–60.

Dix, Robert H. 1984. "Why Revolutions Succeed and Fail." *Polity* 16(3): 423–46.

Domínguez, Jorge I., and Mitchell, Christopher N. 1977. "The Roads Not Taken: Institutionalization and Political Parties in Cuba and Bolivia." *Comparative Politics* 9(2): 173–95.

Drakos, Konstantinos, and Gofas, Andreas. 2006. "The Devil You Know but Are Afraid to Face: Underreporting Bias and Its Distorting Effects on the Study of Terrorism." *Journal of Conflict Resolution* 50(5): 714–35.

Dugan, Laura, and Chenoweth, Erica. 2012. "Moving Beyond Deterrence: The Effectiveness of Raising the Expected Utility of Abstaining from Terrorism in Israel." *American Sociological Review* 77(4): 597–624.

Durkheim, Emile. 1895. *Rules of Sociological Method*. New York: Simon and Schuster.

Earl, Jennifer. 2003. "Tanks, Tear Gas, and Taxes: Toward a Theory of Movement Repression." *Sociological Theory* 21(1): 44–68.

References

Earl, Jennifer. 2011. "Political Repression: Iron Fists, Velvet Gloves, and Diffuse Control." *Annual Review of Sociology* 37(1): 261–84.

Eckstein, Susan. 1975. "How Economically Consequential are Revolutions? A Comparison of Mexico and Bolivia." *Studies in Comparative International Development* 10(3): 48–62.

Eckstein, Susan. 1982. "The Impact of Revolution on Social Welfare in Latin America." *Theory and Society* 11(1): 43–94.

Eckstein, Susan. 1985. "Revolutions and the Restructuring of National Economies: The Latin American Experience." *Comparative Politics* 17(4): 473–94.

Ehrlich, Paul R., and Liu, Jianguo. 2002. "Some Roots of Terrorism." *Population and Environment* 24(2): 183–92.

Einwohner, Rachel L. 2002. "Bringing the Outsiders in: Opponents' Claims and the Construction of Animal Rights Activists' Identity." *Mobilization: An International Quarterly* 7(3): 253–68.

Eisenstadt, S. N. 1999. *Fundamentalism, Sectarianism, and Revolution: The Jacobin Dimension of Modernity.* Cambridge: Cambridge University Press.

Eisinger, Peter K. 1973. "The Conditions of Protest Behavior in American Cities." *American Political Science Review* 67(1): 11–28.

Enders, Walter, and Jindapon, Paan. 2010. "Network Externalities and the Structure of Terror Networks." *Journal of Conflict Resolution* 54(2): 262–80.

Enders, Walter, and Sandler, Todd. 1993. "The Effectiveness of Antiterrorism Policies: A Vector-Autoregression-Intervention Analysis." *American Political Science Review* 87(4): 829–44.

Enders, Walter, and Sandler, Todd. 2000. "Is Transnational Terrorism Becoming More Threatening? A Time-Series Investigation." *Journal of Conflict Resolution* 44(3): 307–32.

Enders, Walter, and Sandler, Todd. 2005. "Transnational Terrorism 1968–2000: Thresholds, Persistence, and Forecasts." *Southern Economic Journal* 71(3): 467–82.

Enders, Walter, Sandler, Todd, and Gaibulloev, Khusrav. 2011. "Domestic versus Transnational Terrorism: Data, Decomposition, and Dynamics." *Journal of Peace Research* 48(3): 319–37.

Ermakoff, Ivan. 2009. "Groups at the Crossroads: Turning Points and Contingency in Revolutionary Conjunctures." Paper presented at the annual meeting of the American Sociological Association, San Francisco. Accessed July 15, 2013 (http://citation.allacademic.com/meta/p_mla_apa_research_citation/3/0/8/9/8/p308980_index.html).

Eyal, Gil. 2010. *The Autism Matrix.* Cambridge: Polity.

Fair, C. Christine, and Shepherd, Bryan. 2006. "Who Supports Terrorism? Evidence from Fourteen Muslim Countries." *Studies in Conflict and Terrorism* 29(1): 51–74.

References

Farhi, Farideh. 1988. "State Disintegration and Urban-Based Revolutionary Crisis." *Comparative Political Studies* 21(2): 231–56.

Farhi, Farideh. 1990. *States and Urban-Based Revolutions: Iran and Nicaragua.* Champain-Urbana, IL: University of Illinois Press.

Fearon, James D., and Laitin, David D. 2003. "Ethnicity, Insurgency, and Civil War." *American Political Science Review* 97(1): 75–90.

Feinstein, Yuval. 2012. "Rallying around the Flag: Nationalist Emotions in American Mass Politics." Dissertation, University of California, Los Angeles, Los Angeles, CA.

Fielding, David, and Shortland, Anja. 2010. "'An Eye for an Eye, a Tooth for a Tooth': Political Violence and Counter-Insurgency in Egypt." *Journal of Peace Research* 47(4): 433–48.

Findley, Michael G., and Young, Joseph K. 2011. "Terrorism, Democracy, and Credible Commitments." *International Studies Quarterly* 55: 1–22.

Fitzgerald, Kathleen J., and Rodgers, Diane M. 2000. "Radical Social Movement Organizations: A Theoretical Model." *Sociological Quarterly* 41(4): 573–92.

Foran, John. 1993. "Theories of Revolution Revisited: Toward a Fourth Generation?" *Sociological Theory* 11(1): 1–20.

Foran, John. 2005. *Taking Power: On the Origins of Third World Revolutions.* New York: Cambridge University Press.

Foran, John, and Goodwin, Jeff. 1993. "Revolutionary Outcomes in Iran and Nicaragua: Coalition Fragmentation, War, and the Limits of Social Transformation." *Theory and Society* 22(2): 209–47.

Foran, John, Klouzal, Linda, and Rivera, Jean Pierre. 1997. "Who Makes Revolutions? Class, Gender, and Race in the Mexican, Cuban, and Nicaraguan Revolutions." *Research in Social Movements, Conflict, and Change* 20: 1–60.

Foreman, Dave. 1991. *Confessions of an Eco-Warrior.* New York: Harmony Books.

Gage, Beverly. 2008. *The Day Wall Street Exploded: A Story of America in Its First Age of Terror.* New York: Oxford University Press.

Gambetta, Diego, and Hertog, Steffen. 2009. "Why are there So Many Engineers among Islamic Radicals?" *European Journal of Sociology* 50(2): 201–30.

Gamson, William A. 1975. *The Strategy of Social Protest.* Belmont, CA: Dorsey Press.

Gamson, William A. 1992. *Talking Politics.* New York: Cambridge University Press.

Ganz, Marshall. 2000. "Resources and Resourcefulness: Strategic Capacity in the Unionization of California Agriculture, 1959–1966." *American Journal of Sociology* 105(4): 1003–62.

Gest, Justin. 2010. *Apart: Alienated and Engaged Muslims in the West.* London: Hurst & Co.

Gibbs, Jack P. 1989. "Conceptualization of Terrorism." *American Sociological Review* 54(3): 329–40.

References

Githens-Mazer, Jonathan. 2008. "Islamic Radicalisation among North Africans in Britain." *British Journal of Politics & International Relations* 10(4): 550–70.

Gitlin, Todd. 1980. *The Whole World is Watching: Mass Media in the Making and Unmaking of the New Left.* Berkeley, CA: University of California Press.

Giugni, Marco G. 1995. "The Cross-National Diffusion of Protest," in Hanspeter Kriesi, Ruud Koopmans, and Jan W. Duyvendak (eds), *New Social Movements in Western Europe: A Comparative Analysis.* Minneapolis, MN: University of Minnesota Press, pp. 181–206.

Giugni, Marco G. 1998. "The Other Side of the Coin: Explaining Crossnational Similarities between Social Movements." *Mobilization: An International Quarterly* 3(1): 89–105.

Godechot, Jacques L. 1965. *France and the Atlantic Revolution of the Eighteenth Century, 1770–1799.* New York: Free Press.

Goffman, Erving. 1974. *Frame Analysis: An Essay on the Organization of Experience.* Boston, MA: Harvard University Press.

Goldfrank, Walter L. 1979. "Theories of Revolution and Revolution Without Theory: The Case of Mexico." *Theory and Society* 7(1/2): 135–65.

Goldstein, Joshua S. 1988. *Long Cycles: Prosperity and War in the Modern Age.* New Haven, CT: Yale University Press.

Goldstone, Jack A. 1982. "The Comparative and Historical Study of Revolutions." *Annual Review of Sociology* 8(1): 187–207.

Goldstone, Jack A. 1991a. "Ideology, Cultural Frameworks, and the Process of Revolution." *Theory and Society* 20(4): 405–53.

Goldstone, Jack A. 1991b. *Revolution and Rebellion in the Early Modern World.* Berkeley, CA: University of California Press.

Goldstone, Jack A. 1998. *The Encyclopedia of Political Revolutions.* Chicago, IL: Fitzroy Dearborn.

Goldstone, Jack A. 2001. "Toward a Fourth Generation of Revolutionary Theory." *Annual Review of Political Science* 4(1): 139–87.

Goldstone, Jack A. 2002. "The *Longue Durée* and Cycles of Revolt in European History," in John A. Marino (ed.), *Early Modern History and the Social Sciences.* Kirksville, MO: Truman State University Press, pp. 169–87.

Goldstone, Jack A. 2004. "More Social Movements or Fewer? Beyond Political Opportunity Structures to Relational Fields." *Theory and Society* 33(3/4): 333–65.

Goldstone, Jack A. 2011. "Understanding the Revolutions of 2011: Weakness and Resilience in Middle Eastern Autocracies." *Foreign Affairs* 90(3): 8–16.

Goldstone, Jack A. 2013. *Bringing Regimes Back In – Explaining Success and Failure in the Middle East Revolts of 2011.* Rochester, NY: Social Science Research Network. Accessed August 21, 2013 (http://papers.ssrn.com/abstract=2283655).

Goldstone, Jack A. et al. 2010. "A Global Model for Forecasting Political Instability." *American Journal of Political Science* 54(1): 190–208.

References

Goodwin, Jeff. 2001. *No Other Way Out: States and Revolutionary Movements, 1945–1991*. New York: Cambridge University Press.

Goodwin, Jeff. 2006. "A Theory of Categorical Terrorism." *Social Forces* 84(4): 2027–46.

Goodwin, Jeff, and Jasper, James M. 1999. "Caught in a Winding, Snarling Vine: The Structural Bias of Political Process Theory." *Sociological Forum* 14(1): 27–54.

Goodwin, Jeff, and Skocpol, Theda. 1989. "Explaining Revolutions in the Contemporary Third World." *Politics & Society* 17(4): 489–509.

Gorski, Philip S. 2003. *The Disciplinary Revolution: Calvinism and the Rise of the State in Early Modern Europe*. Chicago, IL: University of Chicago Press.

Gould, Roger V. 1991. "Multiple Networks and Mobilization in the Paris Commune, 1871." *American Sociological Review* 56(6): 716–29.

Gould, Roger V. 1995. *Insurgent Identities: Class, Community, and Protest in Paris from 1848 to the Commune*. Chicago, IL: University of Chicago Press.

Gould, Roger V. 1996. "Patron-Client Ties, State Centralization, and the Whiskey Rebellion." *American Journal of Sociology* 102(2): 400–29.

Gramsci, Antonio. 1971. *Selections from the Prison Notebooks of Antonio Gramsci*. New York: International.

Granovetter, Mark. 1974. *Getting a Job: A Study of Contacts and Careers*. Chicago, IL: University of Chicago Press.

Gurr, Ted Robert. 1970. *Why Men Rebel*. Princeton, NJ: Princeton University Press.

Hadden, Jennifer, and Tarrow, Sidney. 2007. "Spillover or Spillout? The Global Justice Movement in the United States after 9/11." *Mobilization: An International Journal* 12(4): 359–76.

Hafner-Burton, Emilie M., and Tsutsui, Kiyoteru. 2005. "Human Rights in a Globalizing World: The Paradox of Empty Promises." *American Journal of Sociology* 110(5): 1373–1411.

Haines, Herbert H. 1984. "Black Radicalization and the Funding of Civil Rights: 1957–1970." *Social Problems* 32(1): 31–43.

Haines, Herbert H. 1995. *Black Radicals and the Civil Rights Mainstream, 1954–1970*. Knoxville, TN: University of Tennessee Press.

Hale, Henry E. 2013. "Regime Change Cascades: What We Have Learned from the 1848 Revolutions to the 2011 Arab Uprisings." *Annual Review of Political Science* 16(1): 331–53.

Hall, John R. 2003. "Religion and Violence," in Michelle Dillon (ed.), *Handbook of the Sociology of Religion*. New York: Cambridge University Press, pp. 359–84.

Halliday, Fred. 1999. *Revolution and World Politics: The Rise and Fall of the Sixth Great Power*. Durham, NC: Duke University Press.

Hamilton, Malcolm B. 1987. "The Elements of the Concept of Ideology." *Political Studies* 35(1): 18–38.

References

Han, Shin-Kap. 2009. "The Other Ride of Paul Revere: The Brokerage Role in the Making of the American Revolution." *Mobilization: An International Quarterly* 14(2): 143–62.

Harris, Kevan. 2010. "Lineages of the Iranian Welfare State: Dual Institutionalism and Social Policy in the Islamic Republic of Iran." *Social Policy & Administration* 44(6): 727–45.

Harris, Kevan. 2012. "The Brokered Exuberance of the Middle Class: An Ethnographic Analysis of Iran's 2009 Green Movement." *Mobilization: An International Quarterly* 17(4): 435–55.

Hechter, Michael. 1995. "Introduction: Reflections on Historical Prophecy in the Social Sciences." *American Journal of Sociology* 100(6): 1520–7.

Hedström, Peter, Sandell, Rickard, and Stern, Charlotta. 2000. "Mesolevel Networks and the Diffusion of Social Movements: The Case of the Swedish Social Democratic Party." *American Journal of Sociology* 106(1): 145–72.

Hellmich, Christina. 2005. "Al-Qaeda – Terrorists, Hypocrites, Fundamentalists? The View from Within." *Third World Quarterly* 26(1): 39–54.

Hellmich, Christina. 2014. "How Islamic is Al-Qaeda? The Politics of Pan-Islam and the Challenge of Modernisation." *Critical Studies on Terrorism* 7(2): 241–56.

Herb, Michael. 1999. *All in the Family*. Albany, NY: State University of New York Press.

Hillmann, Henning. 2008. "Mediation in Multiple Networks: Elite Mobilization before the English Civil War." *American Sociological Review* 73(3): 426–54.

Hironaka, Ann. 2005. *Neverending Wars: The International Community, Weak States, and the Perpetuation of Civil War*. Cambridge, MA: Harvard University Press.

Hoffer, Eric. 1951. *The True Believer: Thoughts on the Nature of Mass Movements*. New York: Harper & Row.

Hoffman, Bruce. 1998. *Inside Terrorism*. New York: Columbia University Press.

Hoffman, Bruce. 2008. "The Myth of Grass-Roots Terrorism – Why Osama Bin Laden Still Matters." *Foreign Affairs* 87(3): 133–8.

Hopkins, Terence K., and Wallerstein, Immanuel. 1979. "Cyclical Rhythms and Secular Trends of the Capitalist World-Economy: Some Premises, Hypotheses, and Questions." *Review* 2(4): 483–500.

Hung, Ho-Fung. 2009. "Cultural Strategies and the Political Economy of Protest in Mid-Qing China, 1740–1839." *Social Science History* 33(1): 75–115.

Hung, Ho-Fung. 2011. *Protest with Chinese Characteristics: Demonstrations, Riots, and Petitions in the Mid-Qing Dynasty*. New York: Columbia University Press.

Huntington, Samuel P. 1993. "The Clash of Civilizations?" *Foreign Affairs* 72(3): 22–49.

Huntington, Samuel P. 1996. *The Clash of Civilizations and the Remaking of World Order*. Chicago, IL: University of Chicago Press.

References

Isaac, Larry, McDonald, Steve, and Lukasik, Greg. 2006. "Takin' It from the Streets: How the Sixties Mass Movement Revitalized Unionization." *American Journal of Sociology* 112(1): 46–96.

Jackson, Richard. 2005. *Writing the War on Terrorism: Language, Politics and Counter-Terrorism*. Manchester: Manchester University Press.

Jansen, Robert S. 2007. "Resurrection and Appropriation: Reputational Trajectories, Memory Work, and the Political Use of Historical Figures." *American Journal of Sociology* 112(4): 953–1007.

Jasper, James M. 1997. *The Art of Moral Protest: Culture, Biography, and Creativity in Social Movements*. Chicago, IL: University of Chicago Press.

Jasper, James M. 2011. "Emotions and Social Movements: Twenty Years of Theory and Research." *Annual Review of Sociology* 37(1): 285–303.

Jenkins, J. Craig, and Eckert, Craig M. 1986. "Channeling Black Insurgency: Elite Patronage and Professional Social Movement Organizations in the Development of the Black Movement." *American Sociological Review* 51(6): 812–29.

Jenkins, J. Craig, and Perrow, Charles. 1977. "Insurgency of the Powerless: Farm Worker Movements (1946–1972)." *American Sociological Review* 42(2): 249–68.

Johnson, Chalmers. 1966. *Revolutionary Change*. New York: Little, Brown and Company.

Johnson, Chalmers. 2001. *Blowback: The Costs and Consequences of American Empire*. New York: Macmillan.

Johnson, Larry C. 2001. "The Future of Terrorism." *American Behavioral Scientist* 44(6): 894–913.

Johnston, Hank. 2008. "Ritual, Strategy, and Deep Culture in the Chechen National Movement." *Critical Studies on Terrorism* 1(3): 321–42.

Johnston, Hank. 2014. *What is a Social Movement?* Cambridge: Polity.

Johnston, Hank, and Alimi, Eitan Y. 2013. "A Methodology Analyzing for Frame Dynamics: The Grammar of Keying Battles in Palestinian Nationalism." *Mobilization: An International Quarterly* 18(4): 453–74.

Joll, James. 1964. *The Anarchists*. London: Eyre and Spottiswoode.

Jones, Seth G., and Libicki, Martin C. 2008. *How Terrorist Groups End: Lessons for Countering Al Qa'ida*. Santa Monica, CA: RAND Corporation.

Juergensmeyer, Mark. 1994. *The New Cold War? Religious Nationalism Confronts the Secular State*. Berkeley, CA: University of California Press.

Juergensmeyer, Mark. 2001. *Terror in the Mind of God: The Global Rise of Religious Violence*. Berkeley, CA: University of California Press.

Kadivar, Mohammad Ali. 2013. "Alliances and Perception Profiles in the Iranian Reform Movement, 1997 to 2005." *American Sociological Review* 78(6): 1063–86.

Kandil, Hazem. 2012. *Soldiers, Spies, and Statesmen: Egypt's Road to Revolt*. London: Verso.

References

Katz, Mark. 1997. *Revolutions and Revolutionary Waves*. New York: Palgrave Macmillan.

Kavanagh, Jennifer. 2010. "Selection, Availability, and Opportunity: The Conditional Effect of Poverty on Terrorist Group Participation." *Journal of Conflict Resolution* 55(1): 106–32.

Keddie, Nikki R. 1995. *Debating Revolutions*. New York: New York University Press.

Kern, Holger Lutz. 2011. "Foreign Media and Protest Diffusion in Authoritarian Regimes: The Case of the 1989 East German Revolution." *Comparative Political Studies* 44(9): 1179–1205.

Khawaja, Marwan. 1994. "Resource Mobilization, Hardship, and Popular Collective Action in the West Bank." *Social Forces* 73(1): 191–220.

Kibris, Arzu. 2010. "Funerals and Elections: The Effects of Terrorism on Voting Behavior in Turkey." *Journal of Conflict Resolution* 55(2): 220–47.

King, Michael, and Taylor, Donald M. 2011. "The Radicalization of Homegrown Jihadists: A Review of Theoretical Models and Social Psychological Evidence." *Terrorism and Political Violence* 23(4): 602–22.

Kittikhoun, Anoulak. 2009. "Small State, Big Revolution: Geography and the Revolution in Laos." *Theory and Society* 38(1): 25–55.

Koopmans, Ruud. 1993. "The Dynamics of Protest Waves: West Germany, 1965 to 1989." *American Sociological Review* 58(5): 637–58.

Koopmans, Ruud. 2004. "Protest in Time and Space: The Evolution of Waves of Contention," in David A. Snow, Sarah A. Soule, and Hanspeter Kriesi (eds), *The Blackwell Companion to Social Movements*. Oxford: Blackwell, pp. 19–46.

Koopmans, Ruud, and Olzak, Susan. 2004. "Discursive Opportunities and the Evolution of Right-Wing Violence in Germany." *American Journal of Sociology* 110(1): 198–230.

Kornhauser, William. 1959. *The Politics of Mass Society*. Glencoe, IL: Free Press.

Kowalewski, David. 1991. "Core Intervention and Periphery Revolution, 1821–1985." *American Journal of Sociology* 97(1): 70–95.

Krause, Peter. 2013. "The Political Effectiveness of Non-State Violence: A Two-Level Framework to Transform a Deceptive Debate." *Security Studies* 22(2): 259–94.

Kriesi, Hanspeter, Koopmans, Ruud, Duyvendak, Jan Willem, and Giugni, Marco G. 1992. "New Social Movements and Political Opportunities in Western Europe." *European Journal of Political Research* 22(2): 219–44.

Krueger, Alan B., and Maleckova, Jitka. 2003. "Education, Poverty and Terrorism: Is There a Causal Connection?" *Journal of Economic Perspectives* 17(4): 119–44.

Kuran, Timur. 1995. "The Inevitability of Future Revolutionary Surprises." *American Journal of Sociology* 100(6): 1528–51.

Kurzman, Charles. 1996. "Structural Opportunity and Perceived Opportunity in Social-Movement Theory: The Iranian Revolution of 1979." *American Sociological Review* 61(1): 153–70.

Kurzman, Charles. 2004a. "Can Understanding Undermine Explanation? The Confused Experience of Revolution." *Philosophy of the Social Sciences* 34(3): 328–51.

Kurzman, Charles. 2004b. *The Unthinkable Revolution in Iran.* Cambridge, MA: Harvard University Press.

Kurzman, Charles. 2008. *Democracy Denied, 1905–1915: Intellectuals and the Fate of Democracy.* Cambridge, MA: Harvard University Press.

Kurzman, Charles. 2011. *The Missing Martyrs: Why There Are So Few Muslim Terrorists.* New York: Oxford University Press.

Kurzman, Charles, and Hasnain, Aseem. 2014. "When Forecasts Fail: Unpredictability in Israeli–Palestinian Interaction." *Sociological Science* 1: 239–59.

Kurzman, Charles, and Naqvi, Ijlal. 2010a. "Do Muslims Vote Islamic?" *Journal of Democracy* 21(2): 50–63.

Kurzman, Charles, and Naqvi, Ijlal. 2010b. "Who Are the Islamists?" in Carl W. Ernst and Richard C. Martin, *Rethinking Islamic Studies: From Orientalism to Cosmopolitanism.* Columbia, SC: University of South Carolina Press, pp. 133–58.

Kuzio, Taras. 2006. "Civil Society, Youth and Societal Mobilization in Democratic Revolutions." *Communist and Post-Communist Studies* 39(3): 365–86.

Lachmann, Richard. 2013. *What is Historical Sociology?* Cambridge: Polity.

LaFree, Gary, Morris, Nancy A., and Dugan, Laura. 2010. "Cross-National Patterns of Terrorism Comparing Trajectories for Total, Attributed and Fatal Attacks, 1970–2006." *British Journal of Criminology* 50(4): 622–49.

LaFree, Gary, Yang, Sue-Ming, and Crenshaw, Martha. 2009. "Trajectories of Terrorism." *Criminology & Public Policy* 8(3): 445–73.

Larson, Jeff A., and Lizardo, Omar. 2007. "Generations, Identities, and the Collective Memory of Che Guevara." *Sociological Forum* 22(4): 425–51.

Lawson, George. 2005. *Negotiated Revolutions: The Czech Republic, South Africa and Chile.* Aldershot: Ashgate.

Le Bon, Gustave. 1896. *The Crowd: A Study of the Popular Mind.* New York: Macmillan.

Le Bon, Gustave. 1913. *The Psychology of Revolution.* London: T. Fisher Unwin.

Lee, Alexander. 2011. "Who Becomes a Terrorist?: Poverty, Education, and the Origins of Political Violence." *World Politics* 63(02): 203–45.

Lee, Chia-yi. 2013. "Democracy, Civil Liberties, and Hostage-Taking Terrorism." *Journal of Peace Research* 50(2): 235–48.

Leenders, Reinoud. 2012. "Collective Action and Mobilization in Dar'a: An

References

Anatomy of the Onset of Syria's Popular Uprising." *Mobilization: An International Quarterly* 17(4): 419–34.

Lewis, Bernard. 2002. *What Went Wrong?: The Clash Between Islam and Modernity in the Middle East*. New York: Perennial.

Lewis, Bernard. 2003. *The Crisis of Islam: Holy War and Unholy Terror*. New York: Random House.

Li, Quan. 2005. "Does Democracy Promote or Reduce Transnational Terrorist Incidents?" *Journal of Conflict Resolution* 49(2): 278–97.

Li, Rebecca S. K. 2002. "Alternative Routes to State Breakdown: Toward an Integrated Model of Territorial Disintegration." *Sociological Theory* 20(1): 1–23.

Lichbach, Mark Irving. 1987. "Deterrence or Escalation? The Puzzle of Aggregate Studies of Repression and Dissent." *Journal of Conflict Resolution* 31(2): 266–97.

Lichbach, Mark Irving, and Gurr, Ted Robert. 1981. "The Conflict Process: A Formal Model." *Journal of Conflict Resolution* 25(1): 3–29.

Lincoln, Bruce. 2003. *Holy Terrors: Thinking About Religion After September 11*. Chicago, IL: University of Chicago Press.

Lipset, Seymour Martin. 1959a. "Democracy and Working-Class Authoritarianism." *American Sociological Review* 24(4): 482–501.

Lipset, Seymour M. 1959b. "Social Stratification and 'Right-Wing Extremism.'" *British Journal of Sociology* 10(4): 46–82.

Lipset, Seymour Martin. 1983. "Radicalism or Reformism: The Sources of Working-Class Politics." *American Political Science Review* 77(1): 1–18.

Lipset, Seymour Martin, and Marks, Gary Wolfe. 2001. *It Didn't Happen Here: Why Socialism Failed in the United States*. New York: W. W. Norton & Company.

Lizardo, Omar. 2008. "Defining and Theorizing Terrorism: A Global Actor-Centered Approach." *Journal of World-Systems Research* 14(2): 91–118.

Loadenthal, Michael. 2013. "Deconstructing 'Eco-Terrorism': Rhetoric, Framing and Statecraft as Seen through the Insight Approach." *Critical Studies on Terrorism* 6(1): 92–117.

Loadenthal, Michael. 2014. "Eco-Terrorism? Countering Dominant Narratives of Securitisation: A Critical, Quantitative History of the Earth Liberation Front (1996–2009)." *Perspectives on Terrorism* 8(3): 16–50.

Lynch, Marc. 2013. *The Arab Uprising: The Unfinished Revolutions of the New Middle East*. New York: PublicAffairs.

Magnus Theisen, Ole. 2008. "Blood and Soil? Resource Scarcity and Internal Armed Conflict Revisited." *Journal of Peace Research* 45(6): 801–18.

Mampilly, Zachariah Cherian. 2011. *Rebel Rulers: Insurgent Governance and Civilian Life during War*. Ithaca, NY: Cornell University Press.

Maney, Gregory M. 2001. "Transnational Structures and Protest: Linking

References

Theories and Assessing Evidence." *Mobilization: An International Quarterly* 6(1): 83–100.

Mann, Michael. 2004. *Fascists*. Cambridge: Cambridge University Press.

Mann, Michael. 2005. *Incoherent Empire*. London: Verso.

Mann, Michael. 2012. *The Sources of Social Power: Volume 3, Global Empires and Revolution, 1890–1945*. New York: Cambridge University Press.

Mann, Michael. 2013. *The Sources of Social Power: Volume 4, Globalizations, 1945–2011*. Cambridge: Cambridge University Press.

Mao, Tse-tung. 1937. *On Guerrilla Warfare. Marxists Internet Archive*. Accessed December 1, 2014 (http://www.marxists.org/reference/archive/mao/works/1937/guerrilla-warfare/).

Markoff, John. 1988. "Allies and Opponents: Nobility and Third Estate in the Spring of 1789." *American Sociological Review* 53(4): 477–96.

Markoff, John. 1996. *Waves of Democracy: Social Movements and Political Change*. Thousand Oaks, CA: Pine Forge Press.

Marx, Karl, and Engels, Friedrich. 1848. *Manifesto of the Communist Party. Marxists Internet Archive*. Accessed December 1, 2014 (https://www.marxists.org/archive/marx/works/1848/communist-manifesto/).

Mayntz, Renate. 2004. *Organizational Forms of Terrorism: Hierarchy, Network, or a Type Sui Generis?* MPIfG Discussion Paper.

McAdam, Doug. 1982. *Political Process and the Development of Black Insurgency: 1930–1970*. Chicago, IL: University of Chicago Press.

McAdam, Doug. 1983. "Tactical Innovation and the Pace of Insurgency." *American Sociological Review* 48(6): 735–54.

McAdam, Doug. 1988. *Freedom Summer*. New York: Oxford University Press.

McAdam, Doug. 1995. "'Initiator' and 'Spin-Off' Movements: Diffusion Processes in Protest Cycles," in Mark Traugott (ed.), *Repertoires and Cycles of Collective Action*. Durham, NC: Duke University Press, pp. 217–39.

McAdam, Doug, and Paulsen, Ronnelle. 1993. "Specifying the Relationship between Social Ties and Activism." *American Journal of Sociology* 99(3): 640–67.

McAdam, Doug, and Rucht, Dieter. 1993. "The Cross-National Diffusion of Movement Ideas." *Annals of the American Academy of Political and Social Science* 528(1): 56–74.

McAdam, Doug, Tarrow, Sidney, and Tilly, Charles. 2001. *Dynamics of Contention*. New York: Cambridge University Press.

McCarthy, John D., and Zald, Mayer N. 1973. *The Trend of Social Movements in America: Professionalization and Resource Mobilization*. Morristown, NJ: General Learning Press.

McCarthy, John D., and Zald, Mayer N. 1977. "Resource Mobilization and Social Movements: A Partial Theory." *American Journal of Sociology* 82(6): 1212–41.

References

McDermott, Terry. 2009. *Perfect Soldiers*. New York: HarperCollins.

McFaul, Michael. 2005. "Transitions from Postcommunism." *Journal of Democracy* 16(3): 5–19.

McFaul, Michael. 2007. "Ukraine Imports Democracy: External Influences on the Orange Revolution." *International Security* 32(2): 45–83.

Melucci, Alberto. 1980. "The New Social Movements: A Theoretical Approach." *Social Science Information* 19(2): 199–226.

Merriman, Roger Bigelow. 1938. *Six Contemporaneous Revolutions*. New York: Jackson, Son and Company.

Meyer, David S. 2004. "Protest and Political Opportunities." *Annual Review of Sociology* 30(1): 125–45.

Meyer, David S., and Minkoff, Debra C. 2004. "Conceptualizing Political Opportunity." *Social Forces* 82(4): 1457–92.

Meyer, David S., and Whittier, Nancy. 1994. "Social Movement Spillover." *Social Problems* 277–98.

Meyer, John W. 2010. "World Society, Institutional Theories, and the Actor." *Annual Review of Sociology* 36: 1–20.

Meyer, John W., and Jepperson, Ronald L. 2000. "The 'Actors' of Modern Society: The Cultural Construction of Social Agency." *Sociological Theory* 18(1): 100–20.

Meyer, John W., Boli, John, Thomas, George M., and Ramirez, Francisco O. 1997. "World Society and the Nation-State." *American Journal of Sociology* 103(1): 144–81.

Meyer, John W., Frank, David John, Hironaka, Ann, Schofer, Evan and Tuma, Nancy Brandon. 1997. "The Structuring of a World Environmental Regime, 1870–1990." *International Organization* 51(04): 623–51.

Mishal, Shaul, and Rosenthal, Maoz. 2005. "Al Qaeda as a Dune Organization: Toward a Typology of Islamic Terrorist Organizations." *Studies in Conflict and Terrorism* 28(4): 275–93.

Moaddel, Mansoor. 1992. "Ideology as Episodic Discourse: The Case of the Iranian Revolution." *American Sociological Review* 57(3): 353–79.

Moaddel, Mansoor. 2002. *Jordanian Exceptionalism: A Comparative Analysis of State-Religion Relationships in Egypt, Iran, Jordan, and Syria*. New York: Palgrave Macmillan.

Moaddel, Mansoor, and Karabenick, Stuart A. 2008. "Religious Fundamentalism among Young Muslims in Egypt and Saudi Arabia." *Social Forces* 86(4): 1675–1710.

Modelski, George. 1987. *Long Cycles in World Politics*. Seattle, WA: University of Washington Press.

Modelski, George, and Thompson, William R. 1988. *Seapower in Global Politics, 1494–1993*. Seattle, WA: University of Washington Press.

Moghadam, Valerie M. 1995. "Gender and Revolutionary Transformation: Iran 1979 and East Central Europe 1989." *Gender & Society* 9(3): 328–58.

References

Moghaddam, Fathali M. 2008. *How Globalization Spurs Terrorism: The Lopsided Benefits of "One World" and Why That Fuels Violence*. Westport, CT: Praeger Security International.

Moore, Barrington. 1969. *Social Origins of Dictatorship and Democracy*. New York: Penguin Books.

Moskalenko, Sophia, and McCauley, Clark. 2009. "Measuring Political Mobilization: The Distinction Between Activism and Radicalism." *Terrorism and Political Violence* 21(2): 239–60.

Munson, Ziad W. 2010. *The Making of Pro-Life Activists: How Social Movement Mobilization Works*. Chicago, IL: University of Chicago Press.

Myers, Daniel J. 2000. "The Diffusion of Collective Violence: Infectiousness, Susceptibility, and Mass Media Networks." *American Journal of Sociology* 106(1): 173–208.

Myers, Daniel J., and Oliver, Pamela E. 2008. "The Opposing Forces Diffusion Model: The Initiation and Repression of Collective Violence." *Dynamics of Asymmetric Conflict* 1(2): 164–89.

Najeeb Shafiq, M., and Sinno, Abdulkader H. 2010. "Education, Income, and Support for Suicide Bombings: Evidence from Six Muslim Countries." *Journal of Conflict Resolution* 54(1): 146–78.

Nepstad, Sharon Erickson, and Bob, Clifford. 2006. "When Do Leaders Matter? Hypotheses on Leadership Dynamics in Social Movements." *Mobilization: An International Journal* 11(1): 1–22.

Norris, Pippa, and Inglehart, Ronald. 2002. "Islamic Culture and Democracy: Testing the 'Clash of Civilizations' Thesis." *Comparative Sociology* 1(3/4): 235–63.

Oliver, Pamela E. 1989. "Bringing the Crowd Back In: The Nonorganizational Elements of Social Movements." *Research in Social Movements, Conflict and Change* 11: 1–30.

Oliver, Pamela E., and Johnston, Hank. 2000. "What a Good Idea! Ideologies and Frames in Social Movement Research." *Mobilization: An International Quarterly* 5(1): 37–54.

Oliverio, Annamarie. 1998. *The State of Terror*. Albany, NY: State University of New York Press.

Olzak, Susan. 1994. *The Dynamics of Ethnic Competition and Conflict*. Stanford, CA: Stanford University Press.

Oots, Kent Layne. 1989. "Organizational Perspectives on the Formation and Disintegration of Terrorist Groups." *Terrorism* 12(3): 139–52.

Ortiz, David G. 2007. "Confronting Oppression with Violence: Inequality, Military Infrastructure and Dissident Repression." *Mobilization: An International Journal* 12(3): 219–38.

Osa, Maryjane. 2003. *Solidarity and Contention: Networks of Polish Opposition*. Minneapolis, MN: University of Minnesota Press.

Paige, Jeffery M. 1975. *Agrarian Revolution*. New York: Free Press.

References

Paige, Jeffery M. 1997. *Coffee and Power: Revolution and the Rise of Democracy in Central America*. Cambridge, MA: Harvard University Press.

Paige, Jeffery M. 2003. "Finding the Revolutionary in the Revolution: Social Science Concepts and the Future of Revolution," in John Foran (ed.), *The Future of Revolutions: Rethinking Radical Change in the Age of Globalization*. London: Zed Books, pp. 19–29.

Palmer, R. R. 1954. "The World Revolution of the West: 1763–1801." *Political Science Quarterly* 69(1): 1–14.

Palmer, R. R. 1959. *The Age of Democratic Revolution: The Challenge*. Princeton, NJ: Princeton University Press.

Pape, Robert A. 2003. "The Strategic Logic of Suicide Terrorism." *American Political Science Review* 97(3): 343–61.

Pape, Robert A. 2005. *Dying to Win: The Strategic Logic of Suicide Terrorism*. New York: Random House.

Pape, Robert A., and Feldman, James K. 2010. *Cutting the Fuse: The Explosion of Global Suicide Terrorism and How to Stop It*. Chicago, IL: University of Chicago Press.

Parsa, Misagh. 2000. *States, Ideologies, and Social Revolutions: A Comparative Analysis of Iran, Nicaragua, and the Philippines*. New York: Cambridge University Press.

Pedahzur, Ami, and Perliger, Arie. 2006. "The Changing Nature of Suicide Attacks: A Social Network Perspective." *Social Forces* 84(4): 1987–2008.

Pedahzur, Ami, Perliger, Arie, and Weinberg, Leonard. 2003. "Altruism and Fatalism: The Characteristics of Palestinian Suicide Terrorists." *Deviant Behavior* 24(4): 405–23.

Perry, Nicholas J. 2003. "The Numerous Federal Legal Definitions of Terrorism: The Problem of Too Many Grails." *Journal of Legislation* 30: 249–74.

Pettee, George Sawyer. 1938. *The Process of Revolution*. New York: Harper & Brothers.

Piazza, James A. 2006. "Rooted in Poverty? Terrorism, Poor Economic Development, and Social Cleavages." *Terrorism and Political Violence* 18(1): 159–77.

Piven, Frances Fox, and Cloward, Richard A. 1977. *Poor People's Movements: Why They Succeed, How They Fail*. New York: Pantheon Books.

Polletta, Francesca. 1998. "'It Was like a Fever . . .': Narrative and Identity in Social Protest." *Social Problems* 45(2): 137–59.

Polletta, Francesca. 1999. "'Free Spaces' in Collective Action." *Theory and Society* 28(1): 1–38.

Powell, Walter W., and DiMaggio, Paul J. 1991. *The New Institutionalism in Organizational Analysis*. Chicago, IL: University of Chicago Press.

Putnam, Robert D. 2001. *Bowling Alone: The Collapse and Revival of American Community*. New York: Simon & Schuster.

References

Ragin, Charles C. 2008. *Redesigning Social Inquiry: Fuzzy Sets and Beyond*. Chicago, IL: University of Chicago Press.

Rapoport, David C. 1984. "Fear and Trembling: Terrorism in Three Religious Traditions." *American Political Science Review* 78(3): 658–77.

Rapoport, David C. 2004. "The Four Waves of Modern Terrorism," in Audrey Kurth Cronin and James M. Ludes, *Attacking Terrorism: Elements of a Grand Strategy*. Washington, DC: Georgetown University Press, pp. 46–73.

Rasler, Karen A. 1996. "Concessions, Repression, and Political Protest in the Iranian Revolution." *American Sociological Review* 61(1): 132–52.

Reed, Jean-Pierre, and Foran, John. 2002. "Political Cultures of Opposition: Exploring Idioms, Ideologies, and Revolutionary Agency in the Case of Nicaragua." *Critical Sociology* 28(3): 335–70.

Reese, Ellen et al. 2008. "Research Note: Surveys of World Social Forum Participants Show Influence of Place and Base in the Global Public Sphere." *Mobilization: An International Quarterly* 13(4): 431–45.

Riley, Dylan. 2010. *The Civic Foundations of Fascism in Europe: Italy, Spain, and Romania, 1870–1945*. Baltimore, MD: Johns Hopkins University Press.

Robison, Kristopher K., Crenshaw, Edward M., and Jenkins, J. Craig. 2006. "Ideologies of Violence: The Social Origins of Islamist and Leftist Transnational Terrorism." *Social Forces* 84(4): 2009–26.

Rogers, Everett M. 1962. *Diffusion of Innovations*. New York: Simon and Schuster.

Rosebraugh, Craig. 2004. *Burning Rage of a Dying Planet: Speaking for the Earth Liberation Front*. New York: Lantern Books.

Ross, Jeffrey Ian, and Gurr, Ted Robert. 1989. "Why Terrorism Subsides: A Comparative Study of Canada and the United States." *Comparative Politics* 21(4): 405–26.

Roy, Olivier. 2004. *Globalized Islam: The Search for a New Ummah*. New York: Columbia University Press.

Rudd, Mark. 2009. *Underground: My Life with SDS and the Weathermen*. New York: HarperCollins.

Rudé, George. 1964. *The Crowd in History: A Study of Popular Disturbances in France and England, 1730–1848*. New York: Wiley & Sons.

Russell, Charles A., and Miller, Bowman H. 1977. "Profile of a Terrorist." *Terrorism* 1(1): 17–34.

Rydgren, Jens. 2007. "The Sociology of the Radical Right." *Annual Review of Sociology* 33(1): 241–62.

Sageman, Marc. 2004. *Understanding Terror Networks*. Philadelphia, PA: University of Pennsylvania Press.

Sageman, Marc. 2008. *Leaderless Jihad: Terror Networks in the Twenty-First Century*. Philadelphia, PA: University of Pennsylvania Press.

Savun, Burcu, and Phillips, Brian J. 2009. "Democracy, Foreign Policy, and Terrorism." *Journal of Conflict Resolution* 53(6): 878–904.

References

Schmid, Alex Peter, and Jongman, Albert J. 1988. *Political Terrorism: A New Guide to Actors, Authors, Concepts, Data Bases, Theories and Literature.* Amsterdam: North-Holland.

Schofer, Evan, Hironaka, Ann, Frank, David John, and Longhofer, Wesley. 2012. "Sociological Institutionalism and World Society," in Edwin Amenta, Kate Nash, and Alan Scott (eds), *The Wiley-Blackwell Companion to Political Sociology*, vol. 33. London: Wiley-Blackwell, pp. 57–68.

Schwedler, Jillian. 2006. *Faith in Moderation: Islamist Parties in Jordan and Yemen.* New York: Cambridge University Press.

Schwedler, Jillian. 2011. "Can Islamists Become Moderates? Rethinking the Inclusion-Moderation Hypothesis." *World Politics* 63(02): 347–76.

Selbin, Eric. 1993. *Modern Latin American Revolutions.* Boulder, CO: Westview Press.

Selbin, Eric. 2010. *Revolution, Rebellion, Resistance: The Power of Story.* London: Zed Books.

Sewell, William H. 1985. "Ideologies and Social Revolutions: Reflections on the French Case." *Journal of Modern History* 57(1): 7–85.

Sewell, William H. 1992. "A Theory of Structure: Duality, Agency, and Transformation." *American Journal of Sociology* 98(1): 1–29.

Sewell, William H. 1996. "Historical Events as Transformations of Structures: Inventing Revolution at the Bastille." *Theory and Society* 25(6): 841–81.

Sharman, J. C. 2003. "Culture, Strategy, and State-Centered Explanations of Revolution, 1789 and 1989." *Social Science History* 27(1): 1–24.

Sharp, Gene. 2010. *From Dictatorship to Democracy: A Conceptual Framework for Liberation.* Boston, MA: Albert Einstein Institution.

Shepherd, Nicole. 2002. "Anarcho-Environmentalists: Ascetics of Late Modernity." *Journal of Contemporary Ethnography* 31(2): 135–57.

Shor, Eran. 2008. "Conflict, Terrorism, and the Socialization of Human Rights Norms: The Spiral Model Revisited." *Social Problems* 55(1): 117–38.

Shor, Eran. 2011. "Constructing a Global Counterterrorist Legislation Database: Dilemmas, Procedures, and Preliminary Analyses." *Journal of Terrorism Research* 2(3): 49–77.

Shor, Eran, Charmichael, Jason, Munoz, Jose Ignacio Nazif, Shandra, John, and Schwartz, Michael. 2014. "Terrorism and State Repression of Human Rights: A Cross-National Time-Series Analysis." *International Journal of Comparative Sociology* 55(4): 294–317. Accessed October 1, 2014 (http://cos.sagepub.com. ccl.idm.oclc.org/content/early/2014/09/19/0020715214552460).

Simi, Pete, and Futrell, Robert. 2009. "Negotiating White Power Activist Stigma." *Social Problems* 56(1): 89–110.

Siqueira, Kevin. 2005. "Political and Militant Wings within Dissident Movements and Organizations." *Journal of Conflict Resolution* 49(2): 218–36.

Skocpol, Theda. 1973. "A Critical Review of Barrington Moore's Social Origins of Dictatorship and Democracy." *Politics & Society* 4(1): 1–34.

References

Skocpol, Theda. 1979. *States and Social Revolutions*. New York: Cambridge University Press.

Skocpol, Theda. 1982. "Rentier State and Shi'a Islam in the Iranian Revolution." *Theory and Society* 11(3): 265–83.

Skocpol, Theda. 1985. "Cultural Idioms and Political Ideologies in the Revolutionary Reconstruction of State Power: A Rejoinder to Sewell." *Journal of Modern History* 57(1): 86–96.

Slater, Dan. 2010. *Ordering Power: Contentious Politics and Authoritarian Leviathans in Southeast Asia*. New York: Cambridge University Press.

Smelser, Neil J. 1962. *Theory of Collective Behavior*. New York: Routledge & Kegan Paul.

Smith, Jackie. 2004. "The World Social Forum and the Challenges of Global Democracy." *Global Networks* 4(4): 413–21.

Smith, Jackie, and Wiest, Dawn. 2012. *Social Movements in the World-System: The Politics of Crisis and Transformation*. New York: Russell Sage Foundation.

Smith, Jackie, Reese, Ellen, Byrd, Scott C., and Smythe, Elizabeth (eds) 2012. *Handbook on World Social Forum Activism*. New York: Paradigm Publishers.

Smith, Rebecca K. 2008. "Ecoterrorism: A Critical Analysis of the Vilification of Radical Environmental Activists as Terrorists." *Environmental Law* 38: 537–76.

Snow, David A., and Benford, Robert D. 1988. "Ideology, Frame Resonance, and Participant Mobilization." *International Social Movement Research* 1(1): 197–217.

Snow, David A., and Benford, Robert D. 1999. "Alternative Types of Cross-National Diffusion in the Social Movement Arena," in Hanspeter Kriesi, Donatella Della Porta, and Dieter Rucht (eds), *Social Movements in a Globalizing World*. New York: St Martin's Press, pp. 23–39.

Snow, David A., and Byrd, Scott C. 2007. "Ideology, Framing Processes, and Islamic Terrorist Movements." *Mobilization: An International Journal* 12(2): 119–36.

Snow, David, and Cross, Remy. 2011. "Radicalism within the Context of Social Movements: Processes and Types." *Journal of Strategic Security* 4(4): 115–30.

Snow, David A., Burke Rochford E., Jr, Worden, Steven K., and Benford, Robert D. 1986. "Frame Alignment Processes, Micromobilization, and Movement Participation." *American Sociological Review* 51(4): 464–81.

Sohrabi, Nader. 1995. "Historicizing Revolutions: Constitutional Revolutions in the Ottoman Empire, Iran, and Russia, 1905–1908." *American Journal of Sociology* 100(6): 1383–1447.

Sohrabi, Nader. 2011. *Revolution and Constitutionalism in the Ottoman Empire and Iran*. New York: Cambridge University Press.

Sorenson, John. 2009. "Constructing Terrorists: Propaganda About Animal Rights." *Critical Studies on Terrorism* 2(2): 237–56.

References

Soule, Sarah A. 1997. "The Student Divestment Movement in the United States and Tactical Diffusion: The Shantytown Protest." *Social Forces* 75(3): 855–82.

Soule, Sarah A. 1999. "The Diffusion of an Unsuccessful Innovation." *Annals of the American Academy of Political and Social Science* 566(1): 120–31.

Soule, Sarah A. 2004. "Diffusion Processes Within and Across Movements," in David A. Snow, Sarah A. Soule, and Hanspeter Kriesi (eds), *The Blackwell Companion to Social Movements*. Malden, MA: Blackwell, pp. 294–310.

Spilerman, Seymour, and Stecklov, Guy. 2009. "Societal Responses to Terrorist Attacks." *Annual Review of Sociology* 35(1): 167–89.

Staggenborg, Suzanne. 1988. "The Consequences of Professionalization and Formalization in the Pro-Choice Movement." *American Sociological Review* 53(4): 585–605.

Stampnitzky, Lisa. 2010. "Disciplining an Unruly Field: Terrorism Experts and Theories of Scientific/Intellectual Production." *Qualitative Sociology* 34(1): 1–19.

Stanton, Jessica A. 2013. "Terrorism in the Context of Civil War." *Journal of Politics* 75(4): 1009–22.

Stecklov, Guy, and Goldstein, Joshua R. 2010. "Societal Responses to Endemic Terror: Evidence from Driving Behavior in Israel." *Social Forces* 88(4): 1859–84.

Stepan, Alfred C., and Robertson, Graeme B. 2004. "Arab, Not Muslim, Exceptionalism." *Journal of Democracy* 15(4): 140–6.

Stephan, Maria J., and Chenoweth, Erica. 2008. "Why Civil Resistance Works: The Strategic Logic of Nonviolent Conflict." *International Security* 33(1): 7–44.

Stern, Jessica. 2003. *Terror in the Name of God: Why Religious Militants Kill.* New York: HarperCollins.

Stinchcombe, Arthur L. 1999. "Ending Revolutions and Building New Governments." *Annual Review of Political Science* 2(1): 49–73.

Strang, David, and Meyer, John W. 1993. "Institutional Conditions for Diffusion." *Theory and Society* 22(4): 487–511.

Strang, David, and Soule, Sarah A. 1998. "Diffusion in Organizations and Social Movements: From Hybrid Corn to Poison Pills." *Annual Review of Sociology* 24: 265–90.

Strentz, Thomas. 1988. "A Terrorist Psychosocial Profile: Past and Present." *FBI Law Enforcement Bulletin* 57(4): 13–18.

Sutton, Philip W., and Vertigans, Stephen. 2006. "Islamic 'New Social Movements'? Radical Islam, Al-Qa'ida, and Social Movement Theory." *Mobilization: An International Quarterly* 11(1): 101–15.

Swidler, Ann. 1986. "Culture in Action: Symbols and Strategies." *American Sociological Review* 51(2): 273–86.

Tarde, Gabriel. 1903. *The Laws of Imitation.* New York: Henry Holt and Company.

References

Tarrow, Sidney G. 1989. *Democracy and Disorder: Protest and Politics in Italy, 1965–1975*. New York: Oxford University Press.

Tarrow, Sidney. 1993a. "Cycles of Collective Action: Between Moments of Madness and the Repertoire of Contention." *Social Science History* 17(2): 281–307.

Tarrow, Sidney. 1993b. "Modular Collective Action and the Rise of the Social Movement: Why the French Revolution Was Not Enough." *Politics & Society* 21(1): 69–90.

Tarrow, Sidney. 1998. *Power in Movement: Social Movements and Contentious Politics*. New York: Cambridge University Press.

Tarrow, Sidney. 2005. *The New Transnational Activism*. New York: Cambridge University Press.

Taylor, Bron. 1998. "Religion, Violence and Radical Environmentalism: From Earth First! to the Unabomber to the Earth Liberation Front." *Terrorism and Political Violence* 10(4): 1–42.

Taylor, Verta. 1989. "Social Movement Continuity: The Women's Movement in Abeyance." *American Sociological Review* 54(5): 761–75.

Tejerina, Benjamín. 2001. "Protest Cycle, Political Violence and Social Movements in the Basque Country." *Nations & Nationalism* 7(1): 39–57.

Tetlock, Philip E. 2005. *Expert Political Judgment: How Good Is It? How Can We Know?* Princeton, NJ: Princeton University Press.

Tezcur, Gunes Murat. 2010. "When Democratization Radicalizes: The Kurdish Nationalist Movement in Turkey." *Journal of Peace Research* 47(6): 775–89.

Tilly, Charles. 1977. "Getting It Together in Burgundy, 1675–1975." *Theory and Society* 4(4): 479–504.

Tilly, Charles. 1978. *From Mobilization to Revolution*. New York: McGraw-Hill.

Tilly, Charles. 1986. *The Contentious French*. Cambridge, MA: Belknap Press of Harvard University Press.

Tilly, Charles. 1993a. "Contentious Repertoires in Great Britain, 1758–1834." *Social Science History* 17(20): 253–80.

Tilly, Charles. 1993b. *European Revolutions, 1492–1992*. Oxford: Blackwell.

Tilly, Charles. 1995. "To Explain Political Processes." *American Journal of Sociology* 100(6): 1594–1610.

Tilly, Charles. 2004. "Terror, Terrorism, Terrorists." *Sociological Theory* 22(1): 5–13.

Tilly, Charles. 2008. *Contentious Performances*. New York: Cambridge University Press.

Tocqueville, Alexis de. 1835. *Democracy in America*. London: Saunder and Otley.

Tocqueville, Alexis de. 1856. *The Old Regime and the Revolution*. New York: Harper & Brothers.

References

Traugott, Mark. 2010. *The Insurgent Barricade*. Berkeley, CA: University of California Press.

Trevizo, Dolores. 2006. "Between Zapata and Che." *Social Science History* 30(2): 197–229.

Trotsky, Leon. 1932. *History of the Russian Revolution*. Ann Arbor, MI: University of Michigan Press.

Tsintsadze-Maass, Eteri, and Maass, Richard W. 2014. "Groupthink and Terrorist Radicalization." *Terrorism and Political Violence* 26(5): 735–58. Accessed February 25, 2014 (http://www.tandfonline.com/doi/abs/10.1080/0 9546553.2013.805094).

Tsutsui, Kiyoteru, and Wotipka, Christine Min. 2004. "Global Civil Society and the International Human Rights Movement: Citizen Participation in Human Rights International Nongovernmental Organizations." *Social Forces* 83(2): 587–620.

Ulfelder, Jay, and Lustik, Michael. 2007. "Modelling Transitions to and from Democracy." *Democratization* 14(3): 351–87.

United States National Commission on Terrorist Attacks upon the United States. 2004. *The 9/11 Commission Report: Final Report of the National Commission on Terrorist Attacks Upon the United States*. Washington, DC: Government Printing Office.

Urdal, Henrik. 2006. "A Clash of Generations? Youth Bulges and Political Violence." *International Studies Quarterly* 50(3): 607–29.

Van Dyke, Nella, and Soule, Sarah A. 2002. "Structural Social Change and the Mobilizing Effect of Threat: Explaining Levels of Patriot and Militia Organizing in the United States." *Social Problems* 49(4): 497–520.

Varon, Jeremy. 2004. *Bringing the War Home: The Weather Underground, the Red Army Faction, and Revolutionary Violence in the Sixties and Seventies*. Berkeley, CA: University of California Press.

Victoroff, Jeff. 2005. "The Mind of the Terrorist: A Review and Critique of Psychological Approaches." *Journal of Conflict Resolution* 49(1): 3–42.

Viterna, Jocelyn S. 2006. "Pulled, Pushed, and Persuaded: Explaining Women's Mobilization into the Salvadoran Guerrilla Army." *American Journal of Sociology* 112(1): 1–45.

Wallerstein, Immanuel. 1974. "The Rise and Future Demise of the World Capitalist System: Concepts for Comparative Analysis." *Comparative Studies in Society and History* 16(4): 387–415.

Wallerstein, Immanuel. 1980. *The Modern World-System II: Mercantilism and the Consolidation of the European World-Economy, 1600–1750*. New York: Academic Press.

Wallerstein, Immanuel. 1983. "The Three Instances of Hegemony in the History of the Capitalist World-Economy." *International Journal of Comparative Sociology* 24(1–2): 100–8.

Wallerstein, Immanuel. 2000. "Globalization or the Age of Transition? A Long-

Term View of the Trajectory of the World-System." *International Sociology* 15(2): 249–65.

Wallerstein, Immanuel. 2003. *The Decline of American Power: The US in a Chaotic World.* New York: New Press.

Walt, Stephen M. 1996. *Revolution and War.* Ithaca, NY: Cornell University Press.

Walton, John. 1984. *Reluctant Rebels: Comparative Studies of Revolution and Underdevelopment.* New York: Columbia University Press.

Wang, Dan J., and Soule, Sarah A. 2012. "Social Movement Organizational Collaboration: Networks of Learning and the Diffusion of Protest Tactics, 1960–1995." *American Journal of Sociology* 117(6): 1674–1722.

Weinberg, Leonard. 1991. "Turning to Terror: The Conditions under Which Political Parties Turn to Terrorist Activities." *Comparative Politics* 23(4): 423–38.

Weinberg, Leonard, Pedahzur, Ami, and Hirsch-Hoefler, Sivan. 2004. "The Challenges of Conceptualizing Terrorism." *Terrorism and Political Violence* 16(4): 777–94.

Weyland, Kurt. 2009. "The Diffusion of Revolution: '1848' in Europe and Latin America." *International Organization* 63(3): 391–423.

Weyland, Kurt. 2014. *Making Waves: Democratic Contention in Europe and Latin America since the Revolutions of 1848.* New York: Cambridge University Press.

White, Jonathan R. 2001. "Political Eschatology: A Theology of Antigovernment Extremism." *American Behavioral Scientist* 44(6): 937–56.

Wickham-Crowley, Timothy P. 1992. *Guerrillas and Revolution in Latin America: A Comparative Study of Insurgents and Regimes Since 1956.* Princeton, NJ: Princeton University Press.

Wiktorowicz, Quintan. 2005. *Radical Islam Rising: Muslim Extremism in the West.* Lanham, MD: Rowman & Littlefield.

Wolf, Eric R. 1969. *Peasant Wars of the Twentieth Century.* New York: Harper & Row.

Wright, Lawrence. 2006. *The Looming Tower: Al-Qaeda and the Road to 9/11.* New York: Alfred A. Knopf.

Wuthnow, Robert. 1989. *Communities of Discourse: Ideology and Social Structure in the Reformation, the Enlightenment, and European Socialism.* Cambridge, MA: Harvard University Press.

Xu, Xiaohong. 2013. "Belonging Before Believing Group Ethos and Bloc Recruitment in the Making of Chinese Communism." *American Sociological Review* 78(5): 773–96.

Yang, Guobin. 2000. "The Liminal Effects of Social Movements: Red Guards and the Transformation of Identity." *Sociological Forum* 15(3): 379–406.

Young, Joseph K., and Dugan, Laura. 2014. "Survival of the Fittest:

References

Why Terrorist Groups Endure." *Perspectives on Terrorism* 8(2): 1–23.

Zald, Mayer N. 2000. "Ideologically Structured Action: An Enlarged Agenda for Social Movement Research." *Mobilization: An International Quarterly* 5(1): 1–16.

Zunes, Stephen. 1994. "Unarmed Insurrections against Authoritarian Governments in the Third World: A New Kind of Revolution." *Third World Quarterly* 15(3): 403–26.

Index

Index

narratives 38
nationalism 63–4, 92, 94, 103
natural historians of revolution 5,
    111, 125, 153
networks 49–52, 56, 80, 135–8
    see also diffusion; organizations
New Left 4, 6, 29, 59, 79, 118, 141,
    146, 155
Nicaraguan Revolution 4, 39, 104–7,
    123, 144, 155
nonviolence 17–18, 52, 59, 97, 118,
    129, 138, 146, 149

occupation, foreign 40, 67, 74, 82,
    125, 127
Occupy Wall Street 19
oil 48, 68, 73, 156–7
organizations 6, 17–8, 43–4, 58–61,
    110–12, 116, 121–2
    types of 44–52
outcomes 163–6
    of revolution 15, 69, 73–4, 105,
    122–30
    of terrorism 120–2

Palestine Liberation Organization 7,
    47, 117, 157
Paris Commune 131, 136, 143, 153
patrimonialism 72, 124, 156
Patriot militias 70, 84
peasantry 26, 33, 54, 66, 69, 71, 90,
    117
performance 78, 93, 96–99, 102
Philippines 72, 104, 158, 162
PKK 47, 90, 117, 122, 155
Poland 55, 124, 126, 158
political exclusion 54, 72–6, 145,
    149, 166
political opportunity 6, 64–5, 68, 77,
    82, 85, 147, 149–50
    discursive 78
    negative 75
post-revolutionary states 20, 37,
    122–4, 147, 161
    see also outcomes
prediction 161–7
    see also forecasting

protest cycle 110–19, 130, 142–3,
    166
psychology 5, 23–5, 30, 40
    crowd 5, 93, 132

radical environmentalism 39, 103
    see also Animal Liberation Front;
    Earth Liberation Front
radical flank 58–9, 62
radicalism 9, 17–20, 159–60
radicalization 25, 29, 35, 37, 47, 60,
    77, 79, 102, 110, 112, 115
Red Army Faction 37, 53, 141,
    155
Red Brigades 53, 83, 155
regimes 15–16, 71–6, 124–5
    personalist 72–3, 83, 149
religious fundamentalism 8, 31,
    98–103
repertoire(s) of contention 112–19,
    130, 133, 137, 144
repression 28, 34, 36, 46, 51, 54–7,
    61, 72–4, 102, 115–21
repression–protest paradox 118–19
resource mobilization 6, 43, 55, 61,
    111
revolution 14–17
    from above 14, 71, 73
    negotiated 56, 127
    political 15
    social 14–15, 17, 53, 66, 69, 83,
    105–6, 122
revolutionary situation 16–17, 73,
    104, 123, 165
revolutionary waves 83, 132, 138,
    144–9, 163
Revolutions of 1848 39, 89, 131, 142,
    153
Revolutions of 1989 55, 56, 73, 126,
    139, 158, 162
    see also Poland; Russia
Right Sector 70, 158
roles, social 34–5
Russia 3, 6, 42, 56, 59, 63–4, 66,
    89–90, 93, 109–10, 123–4,
    131–2, 139, 141, 153–4, 156–8,
    161, 162